LINE IN THE
SAND

Alistair Forrest

SAPERE
BOOKS

LINE IN THE SAND

Published by Sapere Books.

24 Trafalgar Road, Ilkley, LS29 8HH

saperebooks.com

ISBN: 978-0-85495-567-1

LOCATION OF THE STRUGGLES BETWEEN THE KINGDOM OF JUDAH
AND THE PHILISTINES, CIRCA 1000 BC

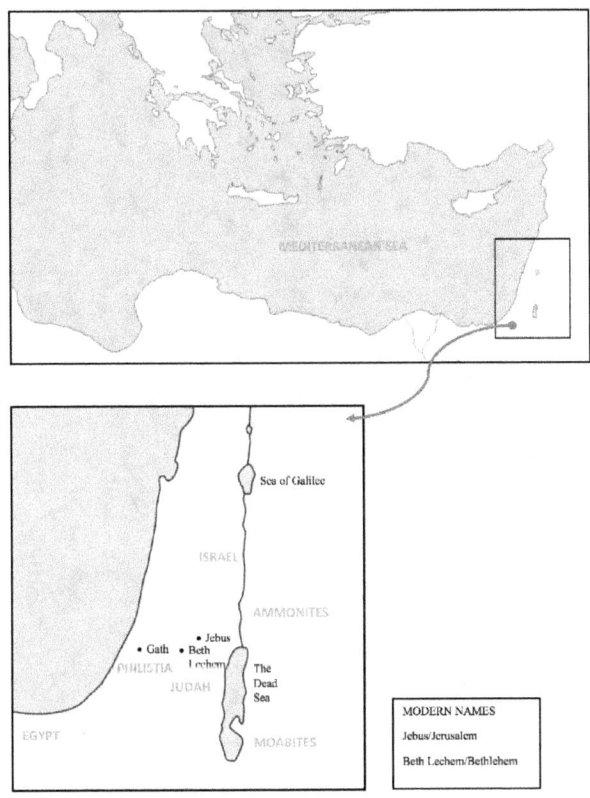

PART ONE: BETH LECHEM

CHAPTER ONE

Israelite tribal territory of Judah, Early Iron Age, around 1000 BC

The woman's eyes searched for help as she was led, forcibly, by two powerful youths outside the gates where judgement was made. The crowd was ruthless, and almost entirely women. Insults were hurled in her direction. Two priests waited, beards twitching with menace, their shawls pushed back, revealing cruel eyes yearning for bloodshed.

'What is going on?' the woman asked.

'It's nothing,' said the taller man with a false smile. 'They just want to ask you a few questions, that's all.'

'About what? Why are all these women here? And why outside the gates?'

The woman took a step back, but the other youth grabbed her wrist. She felt the strength of his large farmer's hand and tried to pull away. 'Let go of me,' she hissed, but he pulled her towards the priests, the other pushing her onwards. Her headscarf slipped with the sudden movement, revealing greying shoulder-length hair. She struggled but the men were too strong.

'Why do you not treat me with the respect due to your mother?' She fought back tears.

The women in the crowd fell silent and turned to watch the peculiar sight of two of the headman's sons dragging their reviled mother towards the priests, then voiced a rising swell of scorn and curses. The woman felt a hopeless shame wash over her. Her knees gave way so that she was dragged, stumbling, before the priests. How had she allowed this to happen after so many years of keeping herself away from these ignorant people? She muttered a prayer to Yahweh, the distant god who demanded secrecy and silence in the face of bitter accusations.

She fell to her knees as her wrists were released. She groped for her head covering and pulled it loosely over her hair to try to cover her shame. Her tears fell freely now, splattering in the dust before the sandalled feet of the priests. She noticed the black dirt under their jagged toenails.

The taller youth crouched beside her and spoke calmly, his mouth close to her ear. 'Everything will be all right if you just tell the priests where your little bastard is.'

She looked up at the priests. The older one was hunched and round-shouldered, his skin cracked like sun-baked earth. Small, bloodshot eyes looked vacantly and without pity at her, his brittle, yellowing beard a testament to his long years of neither caring for himself nor the people of Beth Lechem. The other priest was younger, but he had the same scornful stare.

'Where is the boy?' It was the younger priest who spoke, his tone accusing.

'I do not know,' she replied.

'And where is the silver he gave you?'

'What? What are you talking about?' She turned to look at her sons and tried to rise, but the hand on her shoulder kept her firmly in place. She felt a surge of panic. 'What is this? I don't know what you mean.'

'So you refuse to tell us where the bastard is?' The priest spoke loudly enough for the onlookers to hear.

'Please tell me what this is about,' she sobbed.

The younger priest stepped forward, motioning the youths to release the woman, and gently touched her shoulder to invite her to stand. She looked around nervously. She was afraid of these corrupt men and had always avoided them. Now, as she stood, one of them was so close that she could smell his stale sweat. His thin lips were drawn back, revealing three black teeth, giving her the impression that he was leering at her. She pulled her threadbare robe tighter around herself.

'I'll tell you what this is all about,' said the priest in a voice laden with intimidation. 'What we want to know, and what these good citizens here want to know, is quite simple. Where is the boy and where is the silver he has stolen?'

She closed her eyes. The despair was overwhelming. They would not believe her protests of innocence. The priests acted out of greed because they wanted to get their hands on the non-existent silver, and the onlookers saw her as a loose woman and a temptation to their men.

'You have been misinformed,' she said, fighting to control her quivering lip.

'Then tell us who the father is, so we may question him.' The older priest said this softly, then took a step back, looked at the watching crowd and then pointed at the woman. He raised his voice, so that everyone could hear. 'I charge you before God the All-Seeing to tell us now the name of the man you seduced.'

In the silence that followed, she understood. She would be lucky to leave this place alive. Her long years of seclusion and secrecy were over, and now her only hope was to break her vow of silence, her promise to the seer, her oath to Yahweh. Even her own sons despised her, and now she could feel the hostility of the crowd building like water brought to the boil. She opened her eyes and looked directly at the priest who had challenged her.

'If your God is all-seeing, why don't you ask him?'

The priest blinked rapidly, unused to being spoken to in such a commanding tone, and by a mere woman. He seemed lost for words, so she found the strength to continue.

'You dare to accuse me of sins against the Almighty and the people of Beth Lechem? You should look to yourselves. You call yourselves priests and yet you do not hear the voice of God, much less do anything for these people save rob them of what little they have so that you can sacrifice a hen or a goat on their behalf. You know nothing, you see nothing but gold and silver, and you do nothing except that which makes you fat and lazy!'

A murmur of protest came from the crowd, which had been swelled by several more inquisitive women.

The older priest had heard enough. 'Silence, woman!' he yelled at her. 'You blaspheme!'

The younger priest had regained his composure and opened his mouth to speak, but the woman was fuelled by indignation and rage.

'Believe me when I tell you that I will be freed from my oath of silence only when God tells me it is time —' at this, both priests put their hands over their ears to block out the woman's blasphemies — 'and only then will I reveal what God has said to me about my son.'

The crowd's murmurs turned to cries of anger and protest.

'She's a filthy whore!' a shrill voice shouted.

'She bewitches our men,' said another, picking up a stone, 'and now she blasphemes.'

The woman glared at the priests, daring them to challenge her words, but they stepped backwards into the shadow of the town wall. All around her the noise of protest was mounting but, focused on the cruel faces of her religious adversaries who blocked their ears, she didn't hear it.

She felt a blow on her arm. At first, she couldn't think what it was and continued staring at the priests. Then she felt another, this time on her shoulder blade, the pain sharp. As she turned to the crowd, a rock crashed into her face, breaking her nose, and her head rang. She crumpled to the ground. Sharp rocks ripped at her brittle skin, pounded her frail bones and tore at her dignity. Her screams seemed to come from a great distance. When she tried to lift herself from the ground to implore them to stop, pain shot through her shoulders and blurred her vision so that the maddened faces seemed to spin around her.

She didn't see her accusers slip away unnoticed, nor the priests as they left the crowd to its righteous duty. Neither did she feel the pounding lessen as fewer rocks were thrown and the crowd began to turn away in silent shame.

Nitzevet, once the pearl of Beth Lechem's women, lay broken and bleeding in the dust.

CHAPTER TWO

Shemu'el, prophet and judge of the tribes of Israel, stood tall in the ornate cart. His silver hair was tied at the nape of his neck with a regal purple scarf decorated with tiny silver pomegranates and bells. His beard, coloured with henna and luxuriously oiled, had been carefully shaped to square his jaw and enhance the aura of power that had been bestowed on him by his god. His heavy robe hung loose over his blue tunic of fine Egyptian linen and in his hand he held the Staff of Moshe.

He needed no weapon to emphasise his authority — that was provided by the ten youths who rode beside the ox-drawn cart. The people of Beth Lechem had never seen such fine mounts, and neither had Shemu'el when he had demanded them as a tithe after a brutal skirmish with Aramean raiders. He had selected the strongest youths from his School of the Prophets, armed them, given them the horses and told them that from now on the sword carried as much persuasion as the Word of Yahweh.

'You are no longer children,' he told them. 'You are my anointed warriors and the people are stubborn mules. You will help them to hear the Truth of El Shaddai.' What he meant, and what the young men understood perfectly, was that nobody, especially not their warlike king, Saul, should ever think twice about obeying their prophet in these changing times when a new god was making his mark among the older gods of Canaan. At first the young riders called themselves The Fist of El Shaddai, but this was soon shortened to The Fist.

As the driver coaxed the two oxen up the snaking track towards Beth Lechem, Shemu'el surveyed the small crowd that was gathering at the gates to greet him. He hoped the elders would have observed that this was no trading mission and that refreshments befitting his importance would be provided: it had been a tiring journey from Gibeon, and he craved the delicate wine from Beth Lechem's famed vineyards. As he neared, he observed how poorly dressed the townsfolk were, the men sullen and suspicious, the women ululating their praise, the children wildly enthused by the rarity of armed horsemen and such a large chariot bearing a colourful dignitary.

He also observed the bloodstains amid the rocks and stones, the dark patches crusting at the gate's pillars, and marvelled at how zealous this town's priests must be to express the judgement of Yahweh in such brutal ways.

Shemu'el held up his hand to halt the procession and the riders of The Fist eased their horses to stand in line facing the gathering crowd, five either side of their master's cart. The women fell silent and at last the children stood still, expectant. One of the oxen defecated noisily, prompting giggles from some of the children who were instantly hushed by their parents.

'Send forth Jesse.' Shemu'el's deep, resonant voice called for the only Beth Lechemite he had heard of, the farmer and landowner who had provided three well-provisioned sons for King Saul's last campaign to halt a Philistine advance.

'I am Jesse.' A rotund, red-faced man pushed through the crowd and stood looking at Shemu'el.

'You are an elder of this town?'

'Yes.'

Shemu'el raised a bushy eyebrow. 'I think you meant to say, "Yes, lord," did you not?'

'Yes, lord,' said Jesse meekly, and bowed, looking around at the quizzical faces of those nearest him. He turned back to Shemu'el. 'I … we…' he stammered. 'We can all see that you are a great man…'

'But you don't know who I am, is that it?' Shemu'el permitted himself a half smile as Jesse nodded. He turned to nearest rider and addressed him in a weary tone. 'Nathan, announce me to these people.'

The youth grinned. His dark hair was cut short in defiance of the accepted custom and his chin showed the first wisps of manhood. But he sat easily in the saddle, suggesting experience of horsemanship beyond his years.

'Men of Beth Lechem,' he began in a scratchy voice, then coughed and deliberately deepened his speech, 'the Prophet of the Most High has come among you, Shemu'el the Seer, the Mouth of Elohim, the Voice of El Shaddai, the great…'

'Enough, enough,' said Shemu'el, loudly enough for his modesty to be heard by the townsfolk. 'I think they understand now.'

Jesse knelt and put his nose to the dusty ground, the hem of his embroidered robe dragging in the dirt. The nearest men copied him. Those further behind who had not heard Nathan's rhetoric just looked puzzled.

Raising his head just enough to be heard, Jesse spoke to the prophet. 'Lord Shemu'el, we are honoured that you have come among us. We beg you to call down God's mercy upon us and grant us peace and prosperity…'

'Yes, yes,' cut in Shemu'el impatiently. 'I am sure He will smile upon you. It is, after all, the Feast of Shavuoth, and I am sure you and I will celebrate in the customary way.'

Jesse kept his head bowed as he confirmed the people's enthusiasm for the last day of the spring harvest celebration. 'Indeed, the people rejoice in the fat of the land.'

'Good,' beamed Shemu'el. 'But do you always keep your visitors standing in the sun?'

Jesse leapt to his feet. 'Our humblest apologies, lord. I would be honoured if you would stay at my house for as long as you grace us with your presence. Your men, too, can rest in the servant halls.'

Shemu'el nodded his assent and immediately laughter and chatter filled the air as it began to dawn on the people of Beth Lechem that the man of God might have come in peace and friendship rather than judgement. Relieved, Jesse called for his servants and sent them running to prepare his house for guests, and a calf for a sacrifice to Yahweh.

Jesse ducked into the large tent where his family and guests were feasting and saw Shemu'el laughing with his three eldest sons, Eliab, Abinadab and Shimea. A skin was being passed between them, each taking it in turns to hold it high and, with practised skill, send a looping stream of dark wine into their open mouths. Jesse's younger sons watched with undisguised adoration. He forced a smile and went to play the genial host.

'Jesse!' Shemu'el slapped the headman on the back. 'Your table is everything I had expected and more. And this wine … wonderful!'

Jesse inclined his head in acknowledgement of the compliment — the prophet's approval could lead to improved trade with neighbouring cities. 'I'm honoured, lord. You are most welcome among my people.'

Shemu'el tossed an almond into his mouth and moved closer to Jesse, crunching noisily. He put a powerful arm around his host's shoulders. 'I have heard good reports of your sons,' he said conspiratorially, even though they could all hear. 'They have acquitted themselves well in battle and many men follow them gladly. Saul has noticed this —'

A look of surprise and concern crossed Jesse's face. It was well known that Israel's first king was prone to fits of insane jealousy. He had been chosen by popular acclaim mainly because he was a tall, powerful brute. If Jesse's sons shone too brightly, their light could be suddenly and cruelly extinguished, and they wouldn't be the first.

'The world is changing and we have need of such men,' Shemu'el was saying, too drunk to notice Jesse's alarm. 'There are plenty of opportunities for men such as these.' He gave Jesse's shoulder a squeeze and added, 'Who knows how far they might go, eh?'

Suddenly Jesse saw the possibilities. 'What do you mean?'

'Well, my friend, I do not think that even I know what I mean,' Shemu'el laughed, but Jesse noticed that the prophet's audience had suddenly gone quiet, expectant. 'These are difficult times and we need leaders, not just men of power and strength, but men who think faster than our enemies.'

Jesse followed Shemu'el's gaze as the prophet looked at his eldest son, Eliab. 'And you are already looking for alternatives?'

Shemu'el frowned. 'Absolutely not. I anointed Saul as king, and I will not tear down a building that doesn't yet have a roof on it!' He paused and winked at Jesse. 'But who knows what God will do about it…?'

Jesse laughed nervously. 'Well,' he said, trying to show a confidence that he did not feel, 'perhaps we can give God a little help. I have seven sons you might like to introduce to Him…'

CHAPTER THREE

The youth they called Leper considered the town's stables to be his home. The building was the biggest in Beth Lechem, as if the elders had decided the stabling of mules, horses and donkeys for visiting dignitaries was more important than housing for its humble residents. It had enough dark corners and convenient haylofts for a ratboy like Leper to make himself scarce and avoid the brutal attentions of his half-brothers, especially the bully Raddai and sly Elihu. At the same time, he could keep watch on comings and goings in the filthy streets outside.

He had sneaked unnoticed to his usual hayloft and deposited a purse of silver among his favoured belongings, which included his shepherd's pipes for personal entertainment and his trusty sling. Many a rat had died suddenly, the target of one of the pebbles stockpiled nearby for this purpose.

The silver was for his mother. Technically, it belonged to Jesse because it had been handed over for the headman's flock in Jebus some days earlier, but now it was in his possession and should be distributed to those in need. He was clear in his mind about that, and his mother deserved it after she had been so cruelly treated by Jesse. But he hadn't been able to find her. She was not at her hovel in the slum district, and a search of the market and the town's meeting places had been fruitless.

And now the streets outside were a hive of activity, with folk dashing to and fro as though something momentous was going on. An attack by Moabites or Ammonites? It could even be Philistines, though their warriors had not yet been seen in Judah's hill country, thank the gods. Important visitors, perhaps? Or his brothers and Jesse's ruffians looking for the stolen silver?

He decided to lie low until sleepy normality returned.

The hermit picked his way through a crowded market alive with news of the prophet's visit. He was not an old man like the frenzied seers of Naioth, though many mistook his ragged clothes and wild greying hair as the uniform of either a holy one or a madman. But he saw every nuance of nature and listened to every whisper of the spirits, so he knew where to find the errant youth. He stole a fig from a trader who would have given it to him anyway.

Elhanan smelled the stables before he turned into the courtyard. He disliked buildings. His home was a cave outside the town where the boy they called Leper would visit, a good place to keep watch over the goats while he sat at the hermit's feet to hear tales of ancient heroes — Moshe, Yoshua, Samson. And now the new king, Saul, chosen and anointed by the prophet Shemu'el, peace be upon him.

But the boy was in danger. He knew it not just from old women's gossip but from tension in the air and the strange rippling in the firmament. Of course the boy was a thief; how else could he live and moreover provide for his mother, so cruelly set aside by the headman Jesse after the meddling priests had questioned her ancestry? The truth was, Jesse had preferred his handmaiden.

The boy must leave Beth Lechem, thought Elhanan. *It is time he began the journey for which he was born; he is old enough and strong enough. But he must not know what they have done to his mother; his impetuosity would simply get him killed. He must leave.*

Elhanan covered his nose as he entered the stables, waiting for his eyes to adjust from the bright sunlight to the cooler gloom. 'Boy?' he called, and moved between nervous animals to the recesses beyond, ignored by stable hands and grooms who tended The Fist's horses. 'Boy, I know you are here.' One of the stable hands, dung-shovel in hand, indicated with a nod and a glance that the hermit should look in the east wing.

He found the boy asleep on a makeshift bed of straw, clutching his shepherd's bag. Elhanan studied the long, unkempt hair and the scar that ran past the corner of his right eye, blemishing a handsome face. He had a wiry and athletic frame, an asset that had saved the boy from trouble on numerous occasions. He nudged him with his foot so that Leper instantly recoiled, fear in his eyes.

'Peace, child. It's me.'

'Barak?' A term of devotion. The boy always called him that out of respect, though Elhanan chided him for overdoing it.

Elhanan handed him the fig and sat beside him, studying the ruddy youth's face. Leper looked away, so Elhanan playfully ruffled his hair. 'I know why you're hiding,' he said, 'but you can explain it to me, and then we will decide what to do.'

Leper ate the fig greedily. 'They call me names and they beat me,' he said as he swallowed.

'Who calls you names?'

'Raddai and Elihu. All of them except Eliab.'

'What do they call you?'

'Goat-turd. Worm. Leper.'

Elhanan smiled. 'But everyone calls you Leper — even you name yourself thus, so why should you care what your half-brothers call you?' Leper shrugged and said nothing, so the sage continued, 'Like it or not, you are a man now. You are, what, seventeen? And you are wasting your life with every minute you stay here.'

'What would you have me do?' asked Leper. 'I can't leave my mother. She needs me, and that's why I steal, to care for her, because no one else will. She is scorned by my brothers and just about everyone in Beth Lechem, so she hides herself away. She never speaks of what happened, not even to me. And now I can't find her.'

'Do you know why she is reviled?' Elhanan's tone was compassionate.

'If the gossip is true, she took a lover and then I was born. But she had been set aside, so I cannot understand why she is hated so.'

'And your brothers treat you harshly too? That's not uncommon.'

'Yes,' Leper said quietly. 'But it's when they are cruel to her that I become angry.'

'What are you thinking when you are angry?'

He thought for a moment, then admitted, 'I think I would like very much to kill them.'

'And...?'

'What can I do? They beat me and they spit at my mother.' His eyes misted.

With a sigh, Elhanan swatted at a pestering fly. 'What else do you think?'

'That I should do as you say and leave Beth Lechem with its spiteful people — then I won't be beaten by my brothers and given the worst jobs that even slaves won't do.'

Elhanan nodded slowly, as if at last the boy was beginning to see his destiny. 'Why don't you?' he asked.

Leper shrugged. He had often thought of running away. There was nothing to keep him in Beth Lechem, save one person. 'My mother needs me,' he said.

'There are others who will care for your mother,' said Elhanan. He hoped the boy wouldn't ever find out what had happened to Nitzevet. He had found her outside the gates and carried her limp and bloodied body to his cave, where he had bathed her and bound her wounds as best he could, begging his god to let her live long enough to see what would become of her youngest son.

'Where must I go?' Leper studied his hands, calloused from his outdoor life. He had no rings like the ones his brothers wore, no gifts from a wealthy father, no bracelets and no oil for his hair. He picked absently at the dirt under his fingernails and wrestled with the burden now placed upon him. Would it be so bad to start again, to leave Beth Lechem and discover the freedom that had always been denied him?

'For now, go nowhere,' Elhanan was saying. 'I will bring you food and water. You will know when it is time to leave.'

'How will I know?'

'The prophet will tell you.'

Leper laughed. 'Why would a prophet talk to me?'

'Just have faith,' said Elhanan.

Leper rummaged in his shepherd's bag and handed a purse to Elhanan. 'For the poor,' he said, 'especially my mother.'

Elhanan loosened the pouch and peered inside. 'Now where did you get this, I wonder? Did you steal it?'

'I saved it from some marauders. It's better that you have it.'

Elhanan, who held the opinion that Yahweh would always provide, pocketed it. 'There's one more thing,' he said. 'When the prophet asks your name, what will you tell him?'

'My name? Leper, of course.'

'No, your real name.'

The youth studied his nails again, then looked up. 'Dawid, then.'

CHAPTER FOUR

After two days of hiding, Leper's skin was raw from his scratching at a thousand insect bites and the irritation caused by the dusty mixture of hay and straw. His eyes streamed and he found it hard not to cough. His muscles felt cramped and his body yearned for sunlight. He had climbed a rickety ladder to a more comfortable and better-concealed hayloft, but he would have to move soon.

The horses and the young strangers who groomed them intrigued Leper. He had been bold enough to walk among the fine animals when all was quiet, running his hands down their muscular flanks to calm their skittishness at his presence, and blowing gently into the nostrils of a grey that looked at him with wild eyes. These were horses of rare quality, especially as they stamped and whinnied next to petulant mules and docile donkeys. Horses were rare in Israel and Judah; those he had seen before, and only from a distance, were ridden by the mysterious traders from the north who occasionally camped near Beth Lechem on their journey to Egypt. But they were skin and bone, lethargic creatures compared to the ten fine animals with which he now shared a temporary living space.

Their owners were all young and energetic, laughing and teasing each other. It was obvious that some of them had enjoyed a measure of success with Beth Lechem's young maidens and one, a youth they called Nathan, had been lucky to escape a beating after he had been discovered in a fumbling embrace by the girl's older brother.

Once, the grooms had saddled their horses and led them from the stables. When they returned them, the horses were steaming with sweat on their flanks, their mouths and necks flecked with white saliva. The riders had removed the simple goatskin saddles and silver-ringed bridles, then each had drenched their mount with buckets of well water before taking stiff-bristled brushes to them. Then they paid attention to their weapons, sharpening daggers and bronze-tipped thrusting spears, oiling leather jerkins and polishing buckles. These things Leper had watched his soldier brothers do, but never before had he seen the strange rope contraptions — three round wooden balls connected by cords — that he guessed could be thrown to tangle the legs of an enemy or his mount to disable them.

Though young, the youths seemed disciplined. Leper found himself envying their exuberance and sense of brotherhood; he had been tempted to come out from the hayloft to beg them to let him join their group, whoever they were, but he could not take the risk. Perhaps they had endeared themselves to his brothers and would hand him over to the injustices of Raddai and Elihu, and the wrath of Jesse.

He decided to wait for nightfall. Then he would leave Beth Lechem. Perhaps he might even meet these riders on his journey, wherever that might take him. He slept and dreamt of riding into war.

'You can come out now!' the prophet boomed.

Leper froze, suppressing a strong urge to sneeze. How had he been discovered? Who was this man with the commanding voice?

'He's usually up there, hiding in the straw.' He recognised the voice of one of the young grooms.

'We know you're hiding here,' said Shemu'el, a little softer this time. 'Don't worry, it's safe to come out. I just want to talk.'

Thoughts raced through Leper's mind. He could not trust anyone, least of all complete strangers. He considered making a dash for freedom, but there was only one way out and the voice came from the direction of the stable doors.

He heard the creaking of the crude ladder bearing someone's weight; very soon his hiding place would be revealed. He edged deeper into the scratching straw. He saw hands on the top of the ladder, then the face of a youth looking straight at him. The youth smiled at him.

'Come on out, wild boy,' he said in a coaxing tone, as if he were offering a scrap to befriend a nervous dog. Leper didn't move.

'Is he there?' Shemu'el asked.

Without taking his eyes off Leper, the youth spoke. 'Yes, he's here, but I don't think he trusts us.'

No, thought Leper, *I don't trust you, whoever you are, and I don't trust anyone in this town.* He braced himself to spring at the fresh-faced youth who was now heaving himself onto the hayloft, one more spiteful enemy among the many who hated him. Leper against the world, with nobody to trust, nobody to talk to, no laughter like that shared by these young foreigners with their wonderful horses…

'Nitzevet,' said the prophet, and Leper hesitated. 'Your mother is Nitzevet?'

So they know who I am, he thought. *That makes it worse still.* He sprang at the youth, intending to push him aside as he jumped, but instead the two of them fell heavily to the earth floor of the stables, the commotion causing the nearby horses to whinny in alarm and strain against their tethers. Leper fell on top of the youth, who grunted as the wind was forced from his lungs. He rolled sideways, trying to get to his feet, not noticing the blood that flowed from a gash on the side of his head. He felt weak and dizzy, but still he tried to stand up. Strong hands picked him up and held him, and he found his arms pinned by the large, bearded man with the loud voice.

'Now then,' said Shemu'el with a hint of amusement, 'are we going to fight or talk?'

The youth was sitting on the floor now, trying to catch his breath. Leper looked at his captor, taking in his fierce eyes and groomed beard. He felt the power of Shemu'el's grip on his shoulders and was aware of the warm trickle of blood on his neck.

'Look, I know you are sought by Jesse and his sons, but I'm not going to hand you over to them. Do you understand?'

Sweat stung Leper's open wound.

'I know a lot more about you than you realise, and I'm going to help you get away from here, but first I need you to swear that you will listen to me and not carry on trying to fight me or young Nathan here.'

'I swear it,' said Leper through clenched teeth.

Shemu'el released him, and he sat heavily on the ground next to Nathan. They eyed each other warily.

'Bring water and a cloth,' Shemu'el ordered Nathan. 'Let's get that wound cleaned while we talk.' Nathan heaved himself to his feet and went to find one of the stable pails. While he was gone, Leper studied the large, finely dressed stranger.

'Who are you, and why do you speak of my mother?' he asked with a boldness that surprised him.

'I am Shemu'el,' said the prophet. 'In answer to your second question, a friend sent word to me that you were in danger, and I'm here to help you.'

'Was it Barak … I mean, Elhanan?'

'The seer? Yes. He knows I'm looking for young men like you to serve in my household, such as it is. I trust this seer, despite his wild appearance. Maybe you have a greater purpose away from Beth Lechem.'

Leper blinked when he heard these words and an unfamiliar sense of hope flickered in a corner of his mind. Nathan returned with water and dabbed at his wound, while Shemu'el fumbled in a leather bag that hung from his belt and brought out a stoppered clay bottle. He carefully removed the wooden plug and poured oil directly onto the wound.

'It will speed the healing,' he muttered as Nathan watched him, wide-eyed. 'And of course it's holy oil, same as I used to anoint your king.'

Leper jerked his head to look at the stranger, a few drops of the precious oil falling to the hard mud floor. 'You made Saul king?'

'Yes, now keep still.'

'You must be the one they call the prophet. I've heard about you.'

'Well, yes. I've tried my best.'

'You talk to God?'

'We all do, or should…'

'No, I mean…' stammered Leper, blushing.

'You mean, does God speak to me?'

'Yes. Does He?'

'Between you and me, it gets harder and harder to hear God's voice the older you get.' Shemu'el looked at the young shepherd, remembering his own youthful days as a firebrand preacher before fine clothes, good food and home comforts meant more to him, and he wondered whether the lad could see through his deception. He thought of his wives in Ramah and the several children whose noise and energy drowned out the voice in his head.

Leper had heard only what he wanted to hear and was talking excitedly about the joys of being alone in the hills with his goats. Shemu'el stilled him with a gesture. Nathan dabbed again at the blood that was now mingled with thick olive oil.

'The point is,' continued Shemu'el, 'if you want to get away from here, and you clearly do, there is a way.'

'You don't know my brothers. They'll still be looking for me.'

'Oh, but I do know your brothers. Five of them are coming with me to join Saul's army, along with at least fifty other young men from Beth Lechem and several wagons of supplies…'

Dismayed, Leper interrupted. 'They'll see me and send me straight to Jesse for punishment. I can't come with you.'

'I didn't say you could come with me,' said Shemu'el, sternly. 'I'm sending Nathan here with half of the riders to scout the land of the Philistines and report back to me with the next waning moon. By then I'll be with Saul at Gibeah. And your brothers will be too busy in the ranks of Saul's host to notice a scruffy desert scout who rides with The Fist.'

'You mean I can ride with Nathan?' Leper looked from Nathan to the horses. 'I can ride one of those?'

'Well, can you?' Nathan seemed unconvinced.

Leper thought how easily the young grooms had mounted their horses and the total control they had exerted over them as they rode out for their daily exercise. He had always enjoyed an affinity with most animals.

'I can try.' He stood and went to the nearest horse, running his hand along its flank.

Shemu'el smiled. 'Tell me your name.'

'Lep... Dawid,' he replied.

'Be ready at dawn tomorrow, young Dawid,' said the prophet, returning the oil phial to his bag and turning to leave. 'You won't see me again until Gibeah.'

But Dawid didn't hear him. He was lost in wonder as he walked among The Fist's horses.

CHAPTER FIVE

Dawid couldn't sleep. Several times his eyes became heavy and his mind slowed, but the insects resumed their invasion and rats were scavenging noisily. When the five youths of The Fist came at dawn, he had already doused himself with the brackish water left for the horses and several times had repositioned his waist pouch containing his meagre possessions, chiefly a shepherd's sling and reed pipes, and belted his outdoor mantle tight.

Nathan burst in through the stable doors and looked him up and down. He put down several waterskins and a basket of dates without taking his eyes off the new recruit.

'You can take that off straight away,' he snorted, pointing at Dawid's mantle. 'You can't ride in that.'

Dawid gave him his fiercest glare. Behind Nathan were four other youths, one of them tall and aloof, one of them short and chubby, the other two the same height and build as Nathan. All except the chubby one wore black robes, and each had a black *pe'er* headcloth sewn to a conical top piece with loose tails that Dawid guessed would be tied across the face for riding in dusty terrain. The robes, too, could easily be tied between the legs and around the waist for riding, unlike his heavy, clumsy mantle.

The chubby youth was carrying an identical robe and headwear, which he thrust at Dawid. 'Put these on. I won't be needing them,' he grumbled.

Dawid muttered his thanks and took off the mantle.

'This is Ari,' said Nathan while Dawid put on his riding clothes. 'You're to take his place. Shemu'el has ordered him to ride in his chariot to Gibeah instead.'

The robe was too big for Dawid. The tall youth, who seemed older than the others, stepped forward to make adjustments so that it was hitched around his waist, and the tailpiece was tugged between his legs to tuck into the folds.

'Thank you,' said Dawid, thinking how unusual the garment was. He could see that it would free his legs to ride and give essential padding to his rump.

'I'm Oren,' said the tall youth. 'Useful if you need someone to look over a high wall.'

'Dookhi,' said another, who bobbed his head as he said his name. He was skinny and energetic, with a long nose and hair that looked like the crest of a hoopoe. Dawid couldn't help smiling as he saw the connection — he had watched the striped *dukhifat* birds grubbing under rocks and thought the nickname highly appropriate. Dookhi even had small, round eyes that blinked rapidly, and Dawid wondered what moniker he would earn if he stayed with The Fist. He was about to comment when the fifth youth stepped forward and punched him playfully on the shoulder.

'Rimon,' he said with a smile. 'By name and nature.' With paler skin than the others, his rosy cheeks looked like a pair of ripe pomegranates.

'Do we all get a nickname?' asked Dawid.

'Well, you smell like a goat…' laughed Rimon.

'Enough,' said Nathan, who was clearly the leader of the small group. 'We have a long way to go, but first we need to show Dawid the basics of riding and get him away from here without him being spotted.'

'A fugitive from justice, are you?' quipped Oren as he picked one of the light saddles from its wooden peg. 'Or have you defiled a maiden?'

Dawid blushed and was about to answer when he realised that the others had briskly gone about their business of readying the horses. Ari beckoned to Dawid and pointed to the dappled grey, the mare with which he had felt a natural bond during his two days of hiding in the stables. He showed him how to place the saddle and bridle. The mare pricked up its ears and blew heavily in anticipation.

Nathan shared the dates and waterskins among the five riders while Dookhi explained the principles of riding. The others placed the food in their pouches, but Dawid ate his hungrily. He copied the others when they looped the skins around their necks and under one arm to carry them on their chests, positioned to easily take a draught while riding in the heat of the day.

'Ready?' asked Nathan. They all nodded and mounted. Ari gave Dawid a leg up and he felt the power of the mare beneath him.

'She wants you to talk to her through her flanks,' said Ari. 'Squeeze with your knees, let your body move with her, and keep speaking to her. She'll follow the others.'

'What's her name?' asked Dawid nervously.

'Morning Star,' said Ari proudly as he tied a leading rope to one of the silver rings on the mare's bridle and handed the free end to Oren. 'I can tell she likes you.'

Raddai, red-haired and the most aggressive of Jesse's sons, was loading grain onto one of his father's carts when the five black-robed horsemen clattered through Beth Lechem's gates, wheeling away west on the Socoh track. Each had his *pe'er* bound tight around his mouth and nose to protect against dust and flies. Raddai wiped the sweat from his eyes and watched them canter towards the hills in a yellow cloud kicked up by flying hooves. He had never before seen such fine creatures as these, nor seen such skill as rider and beast moved as one. He was so awed he didn't notice that one of the horsemen seemed a little unsteady, crouching low over the neck of his pale horse, nor did he see the leading cord attached to the grey's bridle. He spat in the dust and returned to his work.

The Fist had been riding at a gentle canter for no more than a hundred heartbeats when Dawid chose his moment. He tugged, not too hard, on the bridle rope and squeezed with his knees, twisting slightly to his right. Morning Star began to wheel. He reached down and grasped the leading cord and pulled sharply. Oren barely noticed it slip through his grasp.

Dawid bent low over the mare's neck and squeezed yet tighter with his knees and nudged her with both heels, the message clear. He felt a surge of exhilaration as the wind tugged at his hair and Morning Star galloped back towards Beth Lechem.

Raddai looked up as the young rider came toward him at a full gallop, a dust cloud billowing behind. The horse's nostrils flared. She made a grunting sound, her powerful body barely rising and falling as the rider crouched low at her neck. Raddai dropped a sack of barley and moved swiftly behind the cart, seeking refuge from the charging beast.

Dawid waited until the last moment, then pulled sharply downwards on Morning Star's bridle. She came to a halt in a swirl of angry grit and stone. He looked down on his half-brother and pulled his *pe'er* aside.

'Look on this face, brother,' he croaked, trying to sound manly despite the choking dust in his throat. 'You are a liar and a bully, and you have not seen the last of me.'

Raddai flapped at the dust that enveloped him. He saw the wild eyes of Morning Star and the dark rider upon her, barely recognising Leper. He wanted to shout at him, leap upon him and pull him from the panting horse, but he couldn't speak. He took a few steps toward him. He reached for where his knife should have been but clutched at air.

Dawid squeezed Morning Star again. She bounded forward, and as she passed his half-brother, he eased his foot out of the stirrup and kicked. His heel caught Raddai on the chin. He flew backwards, landing heavily on the stony ground.

'Remember me!' he barked at Raddai. 'Remember me when I return.' Morning Star wheeled full circle, and Raddai scrabbled in the dirt to push himself away from her. Dawid twisted in the saddle and yelled over his shoulder, 'I piss on the sons of Jesse!'

And he squeezed again, leaning into the long curve back towards his new friends. The horses were still as their riders watched, aghast.

When Dawid returned to The Fist, he did not allow Oren to pick up the leading rein. The youths looked at him with respect as Morning Star trotted beside them, her chest heaving with effort and pride.

They rode away from Dawid's seventeen years of misery.

CHAPTER SIX

Jesse sat on his favourite cedarwood chair and clasped plump hands together in his lap. His wife Kerith stood beside him, the hood of her blue *addereth* covering her hair, the loose folds of the robe's embroidered linen giving her an aura of wealth and dignity. In comparison, Jesse seemed to be crumpled, dishevelled.

Before them stood two of Jesse's sons — Raddai, looking flushed and agitated, and behind him his furtive younger brother Elihu. Both knew they should wait until they were bidden to speak, but the headman was unhurried, flicking away a fly, sighing at the interruption to his game of thirty squares with Kerith. It had been a pleasant way to start the day after the painful business of agreeing with Shemu'el his share of the supplies for Saul's troops — mostly grain, olives and preserved figs. And many of his farm tools for use as weapons. Life seemed so much more expensive now that Israel had a king to keep in the business of warfare.

'Well, what is it, boy?' He fixed Raddai with a glare to emphasise his displeasure.

Raddai, tall and well built, did not like being called 'boy', but he disliked the brat Leper too much to let the barb fluster him. There was a way to make him suffer far more than by a simple accusation over some stolen silver. He rubbed the welt on his chin where Leper had kicked him and took a deep breath. He would destroy the bastard, just as he had taken care of the woman he no longer considered worthy of being his mother.

'You sent us to Jebus to sell one of your flocks, Father.'

'I did,' said Jesse wearily. 'How did you fare?'

'We sold them for twenty shekels of silver.'

'Good. So where is it?'

Raddai looked at the floor. 'Stolen, Father.'

'*What*?' Nothing roused Jesse's ire more than the theft of his wealth. Raddai took a step back, like a reed bending in the wind, regretting that he had not immediately laid the blame at Leper's feet. 'I see no wounds on you, so you have not been attacked and robbed. Are you telling me you lost the silver by your own stupidity?'

'As I say, Father, it was stolen. By Nitzevet's brat.' Neither son noticed Kerith bridle at the tone of disrespect. 'We gave him the silver to hide while we laid a false trail for a band of Ammonites. They chased us but let us go when they saw we had nothing of value. We searched for the boy but could not find him, nor the silver.'

'Then gather men from the servant halls and find him. Start with the house of Nitzevet.'

At this, Kerith stepped forward and bowed before her husband. 'My lord, have you not heard? The lady Nitzevet has been sorely treated by your sons and the people who threw stones at her —' she turned and gave both Raddai and Elihu a scornful glare — 'and she is not to be found. I fear she may be dead.'

Raddai stared at Kerith, open-mouthed, his face flushing with anger. He struggled to control himself. He wanted to confront her, scream at her for daring to interfere, but he knew that approach would only alienate his father.

'What am I hearing?' said Jesse. 'First you lose my silver and then you drag a poor old woman before the mob? You will find the boy, you will bring the silver to me, and then you will prostrate yourself before me and explain what you have done.'

While Raddai looked flustered, Elihu, the more cunning of the two, spoke quietly. 'The boy was seen this very day.'

'Then where is he?' Jesse demanded. 'Bring him to me!'

Raddai summoned his courage. 'He has fled Beth Lechem. This morning, early. On horseback. And not before trying to kill me.'

Next to him, Elihu kept his voice steady. 'Give us men and horses and we will bring the boy to justice.'

Raddai couldn't resist further interjection. 'The crime is the boy's, but Nitzevet conspired with him. She was not to be trusted.'

'Enough!' roared Jesse. 'Raddai, Elihu, you are confined to the servant's quarters while I think on what I have heard. And I remind you that Nitzevet is your mother, and though she is no longer my wife, she is under my protection.'

The brothers looked at each other, knowing full well that they might have cost Nitzevet her life. Their intention had been to make the boy a fugitive, giving them the right to hunt him down, and now their embellishments had drawn the woman who had shamed their family into their trap. Raddai was slow-witted and had embraced the conspiracy without once questioning his cunning brother, or the consequences.

Kerith stepped towards Raddai, her eyes flashing. 'It is you who is not to be trusted, you who have borne false witness against two innocent people, and you who should be punished...'

'Kerith!' Jesse interrupted fiercely. 'If you have any facts to back up your claims on Dawid's and Nitzevet's behalf, I want to hear them. In private.' He turned back to Raddai and Elihu. 'And as for you two, I hope what you are telling me isn't true. But you are my sons, and I want to believe you.'

'You know you can trust us,' said Elihu, his voice like honey. Kerith snorted, earning another glare from Jesse.

'It's my wish that the wisdom of God be brought into this matter. I will talk with the priests. I cannot judge this matter. I need to know the mind of God.'

Raddai and Elihu bowed to their father. 'May Yahweh bring you peace and prosperity,' said Elihu.

But he knew he and his brother had been outwitted by a youth they had only ever viewed as a victim. Until now.

The five youths rode hard, fearing that Dawid's foolhardy display of aggression might bring pursuers out of Beth Lechem, but as the sun rose higher they slowed, realising that no one followed. They rested in the leafy shade of the terebinths that clothed the Elah valley's hillsides, letting the horses loose to drink from a meagre stream, and allowing Dawid an opportunity to question his new friends about their destination.

Nathan pointed along the valley, where clusters of cane marked the course of the drying brook, snaking west towards the lands of the Philistines that bordered the Great Sea. 'That way is Socoh,' he said, 'but before we reach the city we will head south, into those hills there.' A series of rocky ridges was framed by darker slopes beyond.

'Looks like a desolate place to me,' said Dawid, tossing a small, flat stone in his hand before dropping it into his shepherd's pouch. 'Nothing much living up there by the look of it.'

'Oh, you'd be amazed,' Nathan smiled. 'It looks like an unfriendly wilderness, which is why not many people go there. But you'll be pleasantly surprised by what's hidden in those hills.'

They left the valley long before the approach to the walls of Socoh, taking a track that narrowed to a gorge through which the riders could only pass in single file. Sheer cliffs rose on either side with barely a foothold for shrubs, the still air cooler in the shadows. No birds sang in the dim pass, home only to lizards and crawling insects. Awed, Dawid put away his pipes, feeling as though the towering rock would crush him if the gorge could breathe.

Nathan, leading the column, put his fingers to his mouth and gave three warbling whistles, which echoed in the eerie gorge. He was answered with a similar call from somewhere up ahead. They picked up their pace, the only sound the thudding of hooves on the barren ground, sloping downwards now as though they were being drawn into the bowels of mother earth.

CHAPTER SEVEN

Nathan's mount whinnied and quickened towards a shaft of bright sunlight that marked the end of the gorge, and one by one the riders emerged into a valley concealed amid the baked, rocky uplands that marked Judah's western borders. The valley floor was adorned with tamarisks in bloom, providing shade for an abundance of herbs and shrubs that gave the warm air a heady fragrance. Several large aloes fanned their pointed spikes outwards. A spring splashed noisily into a pool that hinted at cool depths below. Beside the pool stood a patriarchal olive tree, its girth thick and gnarled. It stood sentry at the mouth of a cave shaded by its silvery leaves, its roots snaking into the ancient rock. Before the tree was a large, flat-topped boulder that, Dawid thought, could easily serve as an altar to whichever god was worshipped here. A six-pointed star was carved on the surface of the rock, two triangles superimposed on each other.

There was no one to be seen.

Dawid gave a low, appreciative whistle and Nathan turned to him, smiling. 'Welcome to the Caves of Adullam,' he said, 'home of the dispossessed, the outcast and the dispirited.'

'But where are all these sorry people? And the caves? I can only see one...'

'Follow me. You haven't seen anything yet.'

As they passed the cave entrance, Dawid had the distinct impression that eyes were watching from within, a feeling that would have unnerved him had he been alone, but he sensed no fear in the horses or their riders. He reined in Morning Star, allowing Nathan, Oren, Dookhi and Rimon to continue, and peered into the depths of the cave. For a few heartbeats he could see and hear nothing and was beginning to think that his senses were playing tricks on him when he saw movement.

Two figures emerged from the gloom. There was a tall, dark-haired girl of about his own age, and beside her a child, clutching her hand. They walked into the light and he was immediately struck by the girl's large black eyes, deep and mysterious like the pool outside her cave. Her oiled hair fell extravagantly around her sun-bronzed shoulders and over a simple, deep red tunic tied at the waist. Dawid held her gaze, but the moment was broken when the child at her side grinned widely at him. She had the same long, dark hair as the older girl but was missing her front teeth, giving her an impish look. He smiled at them both and nudged Morning Star to catch up with his friends. He looked back once, but the pair had vanished like woodland spirits.

A series of ledges rising towards a deep blue sky hosted dozens of cave openings. Before these were cooking fires attended by chattering women and children playing happily. Men worked below, tending a strip of dark earth where onions, leeks, barley and lentils were growing in abundance. Near this was a dam made from stone lined with branches and clay, and fed from a mountain spring, where women scrubbed clothing and blankets.

As the five riders of The Fist approached, men and women waved and called; a throng of noisy children ran to welcome them. The riders dismounted, handing reins to the older children to lead their horses to the pool. Oren and Nathan swept squealing children into their arms. Dookhi bobbed his head in greeting, ruffling the hair of an untidy boy with a beaming, grubby face. Dawid stood apart, uncertain at this show of affection, until he, too, was mobbed.

Nathan led them to a large cave near the base of the slope where a woman stood, her arms folded across her prominent bosom. Following behind, Dawid's first impression was that, for the second time since their arrival, he had set eyes upon a powerful woman. Was this hidden place full of such people? Did they rule here? He could tell from the strength in her thighs and the jauntiness of her pose that she was a woman whose word was law and whose opinion was not to be challenged. A long plait of greying hair dangling over one shoulder confirmed that she had wisdom to go with her mettle.

'Where in the name of Ashtoreth have you been?' She fixed Nathan with a fiery glare, but there was humour in her eyes.

He laughed and ran to her. 'Greetings, Mother. I've missed you too.' Mother and son embraced, Nathan gasping for air in her powerful grip. She kissed him until he pushed her away, embarrassed.

'I expect you're going to tell me you've been about Yahweh's work,' she said in a voice loud enough for all to hear, 'and that these fine young men are about the god's business too?'

'Absolutely not,' said Nathan with a wink, turning to his fellow travellers. 'These are just wasteful no-goods I happened across in a tavern. They're hungry and thirsty.'

The woman cast an eye over the five dusty youths and beamed a matronly smile at them all. 'Then it's a good thing I have some roots for the pot and plenty of last year's wine.' Suddenly her eyes narrowed as she noticed the wound on Dawid's head. She moved towards him. 'That looks nasty,' she clucked. 'I've got a good remedy for that.'

Nathan stopped her with a hand on her arm. 'There's no need,' he said. 'He's already been anointed with holy oil. He'll live.'

The woman shrugged, turned and strode into the cave, her low-slung skirts sashaying comically from side to side as she went. Nathan cast a warning look at his friends. 'That's my mother. If any of you dare laugh at her, or me...' His companions shook their heads in feigned innocence, choking back their amusement. 'If she's in a good mood, you can call her Mother, like I do. But most of the time you can call her Martha.'

'Shemu'el can't decide whether he likes this place or not,' said Nathan, wiping his mouth then taking a draught of wine. 'He thinks his loyal Hebrews should be either farmers or in the ranks of Saul's army, or both. But he still sends tilling tools and supplies of barley from his fields at Ramah.'

'Can't see much wrong with it,' Dawid muttered, chewing appreciatively on a mouthful of bread while reaching eagerly into the pot with a crust for more of the rich stew.

'He's uneasy because the place is full of criminals, I think.' Nathan's use of the word "criminals" caught his companions' attention. 'And because the goddess is revered here.'

'Goddess?' In his harsh world of male brutality, Dawid had never before considered the possibility of a female god.

'Yes, the Lady of the Moon. Ashtoreth,' replied Nathan. 'She is worshipped at night when the other gods are asleep.'

Dawid basked in the welcome he felt among these adventurous youths, copying them as they wiped crusts of bread around the edge of the fast-emptying pot. He yawned. 'Where do we sleep?' he asked hopefully.

'There'll be plenty of time for sleeping when you've been stuck by a Philistine spear,' said Nathan.

Dookhi looked up, alarmed. 'Philistines?'

'Yes, Philistines. Gath is barely more than a day's ride from here, and we begin tomorrow.'

'Begin what?' asked Dawid, naively.

Nathan sighed. 'I'll tell you tomorrow, before we ride out. Right now we've got other duties to attend to, like finishing this wine.' He stood, straightening his tunic. 'But first, we can all wash in the cleansing pool. Last one in is a Philistine pig herder.'

They needed no further encouragement, dashing towards the pool. Nathan pulled off his clothes as he ran. Dawid followed more cautiously, thinking about the Philistines. He had never seen one, only heard tales of huge stone cities, their iron tools and weapons, their fearsome war chariots and their strange gods whose thirst for blood was legendary.

CHAPTER EIGHT

Dawid was woken by the sound of animated discussion outside the cave. He found his four friends hunched over what he took to be a map scratched into the earth. They barely acknowledged him. Nathan used a stick to point to five rocks that seemed to be randomly dotted close to a line in the ground.

'Gaza, Ashkelon, Ashdod.' Nathan pointed to the three rocks nearest the line. 'These are the three Philistine cities of the coast.'

Dawid peered between Rimon and Oren, realising that the line must represent the shore of the Great Sea, a sight he had never seen. He thought better of asking what the sea was like as Nathan continued.

'Inland, but much further north, near Timnah —' he pointed to another rock set further apart from the others — 'is Ekron.'

'That looks like a long way from here,' interrupted Dookhi.

'It is,' said Nathan solemnly. 'But Gath isn't.' He pointed to the fifth stone with his stick, then moved it barely a hand's breadth and scratched a cross in the ground. 'We are here, a day's ride from Gath, the biggest and the most threatening of the Philistine cities. That's where Shemu'el believes their push will come from, though he wants us to keep a watch on Ekron too.'

All five youths stared in silence, as if by looking at Nathan's untidy map they could influence the outcome of a war between the Israelites and Philistines. The tone of Nathan's voice had roused mixed feelings in Dawid, who had not only never seen the sea, but had also never seen these mysterious warriors.

They were said to have sailed across the ocean to settle on the borders of the very land to which the Hebrew tribes laid claim, building impregnable cities of stone and great temples to their invincible gods of war. Time and again their raiding parties had taken slaves from innocent nomadic tribes, taxing their passage to the lush coastal pastures and forcing them to drive their flocks inland, where they could pitch their tents in relative safety.

Oren broke the spell. 'What do we already know about them?'

'Actually, quite a bit,' replied Nathan. 'They're a wealthy people because they trade with lands across the sea. And they trade with us.'

'With us?' exclaimed Dookhi. 'I thought we were their enemies.'

'Think about it. You can take an enemy's life, or you can take his wealth.' Nathan watched understanding dawn on the faces of his men. 'The Philistines have the dark metal, which is stronger and more plentiful than ours, but they won't tell us how to make it. So our farmers have to go to them for ploughs and tilling tools, and the Philistines can charge what they like for them. In most cases, our Hebrew farmers seem to think it's worth it.'

'What about swords and spears?' asked Rimon. 'If this metal is so good, can't our merchants buy weapons too?'

'No, they won't let any Israelite buy iron weapons. They think Dookhi here with a bronze sword is bad enough!' All laughed, including Dookhi, who bowed at the reference to his prowess.

Nervously, Dawid made his first contribution to the debate. 'Couldn't we steal them?' The others looked at him, weighing up his courage.

'Well, yes,' said Nathan deliberately, 'but that's not what Shemu'el has asked us to do. We can take their weapons when we defeat them in battle. In the meantime, we should stay out of sight and out of trouble so we can find out as much information about the Philistines as we can.'

'How?' asked Dawid. 'What can we find out just by hiding and watching?'

Nathan sighed and pointed to the five rocks marking the Philistine cities. 'Each of these has its own warlord and an army of several thousand men. If they are going to march on Israel, there will be considerable movement of soldiers, chariots and supplies towards Gath, where they will muster under the banner of their king, Akish. And they will step up their iron foundries to make weapons, not farm tools. The next market when Israelite traders are allowed to barter begins the day after the Feast of the Moon, three days from today. We've got until then to decide who looks most like a farmer and can go into the viper's nest.'

Dawid swore to himself that he would be chosen for the task. After all, he was a farmhand and knew the feel of a mattock in his hands. He was about to suggest this when Nathan glanced up at the sun and then clapped his hands to stir The Fist to action.

'Oren, Dookhi — you ride to Ekron,' he said firmly. 'Rimon, you'll come with me to watch the approaches to Gath. We'll all four ride the first part together.'

Dawid was crestfallen. 'Nathan...?'

Nathan put an arm around Dawid's shoulders and led him to one side while the others ran to where the horses were hobbled. He tried to humour him by talking about the lively girls of the community, and he emphasised the dangers of riding into enemy territory where capture would mean death or slavery, but Dawid was inconsolable.

'Look,' said Nathan at last, 'you have to prove yourself before you can come on a mission like this. I promise you we will have need of you. But not yet. Stay here, look after Morning Star, exercise her well and feed her.' Dawid nodded. 'Stay within this place. And go to see the priestess; she will tell you all you need to know about the Philistines.'

'The priestess?'

'Yes, the priestess. Her name is Rachael. You'll find her at the place where we entered the caves yesterday.'

Dawid remembered the dark-eyed girl and the child who had smiled at him.

Nathan embraced him and whispered in his ear. 'If she tells you everything she knows about them, you might be glad you stayed behind.'

Dawid let Morning Star nuzzle his back as he stared at the spot where he had last seen his friends riding away from the caves. He wondered why he couldn't be trusted to go with them.

He looked around his new community. The men were already working in the fields, the sounds of women and children about their chores mingling with the symphonies of cicadas and the chattering of birds. Somewhere a lone voice struck up an unfamiliar song and soon others joined in with a pure joy that he didn't share. He was a stranger among these peculiar people, he thought, and he didn't belong here.

He made up his mind.

He left Morning Star hobbled where she stood, attaching a good length to a tree where she sought shade, allowing her the freedom to graze on scratchy grass. He ran back to the cave where he had slept, gathered up his sling and shepherd's pouch, then filled his waterskin from the spring. He ran to Martha's cave, where he thought the saddles and weapons had been stored.

He almost collided with Nathan's mother as he dashed into the gloomy cave.

'Hold steady, boy,' she said firmly as she leaned on her straw broom. 'What's all this about? In a bit of a hurry, are you?'

Panting, he eyed the powerful woman and tried to think of an excuse. It came easily.

'Nathan told me to exercise my horse, and I couldn't find the bridle.' He looked around the cave and saw what he had come for.

Martha narrowed her eyes. 'Why haven't you gone with them? Nathan told me you were riding on a mission for the prophet today.'

'Nathan doesn't think I'm ready,' he said truthfully, studying his feet. Then he looked at her, and she saw defiance in his eyes.

'You are anguished,' she said. 'There are demons fighting inside you.'

'There's nothing wrong with me,' he replied indignantly.

'Oh, there's nothing wrong with you physically. But there is something amiss.' Martha resumed sweeping the rock floor with such enthusiasm that clouds of dust swirled around her feet. 'Yes, definitely something amiss,' she muttered.

Confused, he watched her for several moments, then said, 'I'd better see to Morning Star.' He picked up the saddle and bridle, pleased to see that his hunting knife was still with the bundle. He slipped it into his belt and turned to leave.

'Wait,' said Martha. Dawid stopped but didn't turn around, so she spoke to his back. 'Don't ride too far. Nathan says there are reports of bandits near the Socoh road, so be careful.'

He nodded his assent without looking back and stepped into the bright sunlight. *Bandits don't have horses*, he thought. *They'd never catch Morning Star.*

CHAPTER NINE

Dawid was reluctant to push Morning Star too hard until he had safely negotiated the gorge and the precarious track that wound into the valley. He had been plagued by children again as he left the caves, darting dangerously close to Morning Star's steady hooves. They laughed all the more when he scowled at them, lightening his spirit with their innocent joy.

There had been no sign of the priestess, Rachael, as he passed her cave, though there was evidence of her care around the great rock, where fresh blooms covered the smooth surface and, in the old olive tree, spirit totems tinkled with Ashtoreth's music. He clung to the memory of her, but it faded as he approached the trading route snaking through the valley below, hidden mostly by the riverbed's tenacious cane forest and proud copses of palms, almonds and terebinths. He was certain that was the road The Fist would have taken to ride towards Socoh, where they would divide into pairs, Dookhi and Oren heading north towards Ekron, Nathan and Rimon riding towards Gath. The sun was at its zenith now, and though the others would not be travelling with any great haste, Dawid realised he would still need to ride hard to catch them up. Once he was on the track, he peered at the ground, looking for signs that the four riders had chosen the Socoh direction. He decided that the pile of fresh, fly-infested dung was evidence enough.

The wind snatched at his hair as Morning Star broke into a canter. He laughed aloud at the freedom, bending low over her neck and sensing her strength and agility. He was still laughing when he rounded an outcrop clothed with thick gorse and saw the riders. He reined Morning Star to a halt too firmly; she protested in a cloud of swirling dust. A flock of small birds took flight from the nearby cane beds, twittering at the intrusion.

Something was wrong.

Dawid studied the riders. Yes, there were four of them, but even at this distance he could see these were not The Fist. They were riding mules, not horses. His friends wore black; these were more colourful, with strange blue headwear, possibly some kind of helmet. And they were armed; he could make out what could be bows or swords strapped to their backs, and two of them carried spears. The Fist preferred more easily concealed weapons. Worse still, they were riding towards him, not in the direction of Socoh, and they quickened their pace when they spotted him. He was easy prey for an enemy.

Dawid was about to wheel Morning Star to flee when he heard a warbling bird call — definitely not the sound of any creature he had encountered around Beth Lechem, but one he knew he had heard before. Then he remembered. It was the call Nathan had made as they approached the caves yesterday, and it seemed to come from deep within the cane forest, where the fronds grew thickest. He searched for signs of his friends; at first he could not detect their presence, but then he heard a soft whinny and saw movement. The Fist must have seen the riders and hidden behind the tall, leafy canes to remain unseen while the strangers passed.

The approaching men were much closer now, riding with purpose towards Dawid. *What should I do?* he thought. *Flee or face them?* Perhaps Nathan needs to know if they are friends or foes? Now he could see that each wore the same kind of helmet, a band of copper-coloured metal with blue bristles thrusting upright like bizarre artificial hair, strapped with studded leather beneath their chins. This did not seem like the apparel of Hebrew soldiers. Dawid realised that if he stood his ground he would meet Israel's enemies for the first time in his life. With the knowledge that four colleagues of The Fist lay concealed a stone's throw from the road, he made up his mind.

He eased the sling from his belt and without taking his eyes off the riders, felt in his pouch for four of the flat stones he always kept there. He promised himself he would make each one count — here was larger prey than a wolf or a lynx. He placed one of the stones in the sling's leather pocket and clutched the remaining three in his left hand. He took a deep breath to calm his pounding heart.

The riders stopped as one, about a spear's throw from where Dawid waited. The only sound was the rustling of the cane in the gentle breeze. Dawid studied them, noting the thick beards and muscular arms of seasoned warriors, their dark, menacing eyes watching him calmly. They appeared to be discussing him in guttural, rumbling voices. He fought the urge to turn and flee and, summoning all the courage of his years in the hostile wilderness, he challenged them.

'Who are you, strangers in the land of Judah?' He hoped his voice sounded older than it did to him. The men looked at each other and one of them laughed.

'A child!' the laughing warrior exclaimed and nudged his mule forward a few paces.

'Hold there until you have stated your business!' Dawid surprised himself with the commanding tone of his voice and took courage from it.

The leading soldier scowled. 'We might ask the same of you,' he shouted, 'though you are clearly a thief who has stolen that mount!' As if acknowledging their admiration, Morning Star shook her head with a contemptuous-sounding snort.

Dawid ignored the insult. 'In the name of El Shaddai, the almighty Lord of Hosts, state your business!'

'And if we do not…?' At their leader's challenge, two of the men behind eased their small bows from their strapping and each pulled an arrow from quivers that hung at the mules' flanks, while the other two levelled their spears. Dawid noticed their metal points were clearly not bronze, and at the back of his mind he thought this must be proof that these men were Philistine warriors. He had a chance to strike a blow for Judah and Yahweh.

'If you do not, you will surely die,' he replied firmly.

This time, all four warriors laughed. 'Your El Shaddai god must be very powerful,' chuckled the leader, and looking around, he added, 'but we cannot see him. Where is he? How is he going to protect a boy like you, without a weapon, against the four of us? When we have fed your guts to the birds, we will have that fine animal you stole.'

Without a word of command all four moved forward, the mules gathering pace as they trotted, each larger than Morning Star but without the strength and agility to gallop like a well-kept horse. Dawid swung his sling, waiting for them to come closer so he could be sure of finding the most vulnerable target.

The first arrows flashed past him. He sensed the warriors' aim would be poor from such an unsteady riding position, but he was wary that they could still hit him with a lucky shot. Morning Star was still and solid. He whirled his sling faster, fixing his eye on the leader's forehead, in his mind seeing the missile fly true at a spot just below the helmet's rim. He loosed his first stone with the powerful thrust of a practised arm and watched it spin exactly where he had willed it. It took the warrior's eye with a fleshy thud, jerking his head back, dislodging him from his mount and sending him sprawling in the dust, his spear clattering beside him.

The others rode past him, one readying his spear as he neared, the other two nocking deadly arrows. Dawid's second stone flew at one of the archers just as The Fist attacked, distracting him. From the corner of his eye he sensed rather than saw three spinning objects, heavy olive wood balls joined by ropes, fly from the cane thickets. As the first bola wrapped viciously around the forelegs of a mule, bringing it crashing to the ground, a second and third followed. Another mule fell, but somehow the second spearman came on.

Dawid watched his stone flash towards the screaming rider, striking him between the eyes at the same moment he loosed his spear. The rider crashed to the ground just as Dawid felt a searing pain in his side; he tried to ignore it as he watched his four friends hurl themselves on the fallen riders. Their knives worked swiftly, and all were bloodied except Nathan's; he crouched over the enemy leader who lay where he had fallen, groaning in agony as he clutched the mangled mess that had been his eye.

Dawid peered at the wound in his side. The spear had slashed through his thin tunic and torn yielding flesh as it had passed. His head swam and he slumped over Morning Star's neck, clinging to her mane, determined not to fall like his victims, hoping he had proved himself to Nathan and The Fist by bringing down two warriors.

Perhaps now, at last, he was more than a simple shepherd boy.

The screaming kept Dawid conscious.

By the time Nathan's blade relieved the one-eyed warrior of his last breath, he had told The Fist much of what they wanted to know. The four men were Philistine scouts looking for suitable ground to bring their war chariots into Judah and Israel, but it was hard-won information that left Nathan sullen and filled with self-loathing. While his knife had worked in the vacant eye socket, he had hinted at a slower removal of the other eye, along with other body parts.

The warrior was brave and had tried not to scream or give this vicious youth any information, but Nathan's skill had broken him. When the Philistine had revealed his mission, after confessing that Gath had allies throughout Canaan, he knew that Nathan would take his life swiftly. He had therefore gathered the strength to curse his torturers in the name of his god, Dagon.

'Nobody can stand against mighty Dagon,' he had spat through bloody lips and broken teeth. 'He has given us the Invincibles. You will see, and when they come all of Israel will quake with fear and your bones will turn to wax. You will all flee before the Great Ones, whose spears are like a weaver's beam and whose breath is fire…'

Nathan had silenced him, as much to stop his terrifying curses as to keep his word.

Oren and Rimon began the task of dispatching the two incapacitated mules and dragging the Philistines' bodies away from the track to cover them with stones, while Dookhi washed Dawid's wound and cut a strip from his spare robe to bind it. When this was done, Dookhi gathered up the spears and other weapons, together with any valuables the Philistines had been carrying.

Nathan sat apart on a rock and brooded. No one spoke. When their work was done and Dawid began to hope for some praise for his part in the fight, Oren and Rimon went to sit in silence with Nathan. It seemed to Dawid to be some kind of ritual, sitting and saying nothing, when they should be celebrating. They had defeated Yahweh's enemy. He was about to speak when Dookhi silenced him with a curt shake of his head. Eventually, Nathan spoke.

'I had to do it.'

When he lifted his head to look into the eyes of first Oren and then Rimon, as if seeking absolution, both youths put an arm around him. They remained in that position for some time, ignoring the cries of sand partridges foraging in the cane thickets and the restlessness of the horses. Then, suddenly and without warning, Nathan leapt to his feet.

'Come, we've been delayed, so we'll try to reach Socoh by nightfall and pair off early tomorrow,' he said, then appeared to notice Dawid for the first time. 'You, return to the caves, and say nothing of this to my mother.'

'I ... I thought...' Dawid stammered, but Nathan glared at him.

'You didn't think. That's the problem. I told you to stay and you chose to follow us. You disobeyed an order.'

'But if I hadn't...'

Again Nathan cut him short. 'If you hadn't what? If you hadn't been so foolish we would have let those men go and two of us would have followed them. To find out what they were up to.'

'But you did find out what they were doing.' Dawid was indignant that his fighting skills had been ignored.

'You don't really think that poor heathen told us everything, do you? For all we know, they were meeting up with spies in our own lands. We're not the only ones playing this game, can't you see that? But now we'll never know, will we?' Dawid's mouth worked, but no words came. 'You'd be a liability, so go back now and get that wound seen to.' Nathan mounted his horse with an easy leap.

Dookhi tried to defend their newest companion. 'He was very good with that sling, though.'

Nathan snorted, giving Dawid an angry glare. 'We'll discuss that when we return. Now do as I say for once and get back to Adullam. And take the spears and those mules with you. If we're caught with iron weapons, we'll be exposed. We'll keep the bows, though — they will be useful.' He nudged his stallion forward, towards Socoh. The others mounted and followed, Dookhi looking back over his shoulder at the forlorn youth standing next to his mare.

Dawid went to the compliant mules, gathering their leading reins. With a grunt of pain, he eased himself onto Morning Star, the effort tearing at his wound as Dookhi's dressing loosened. He removed his belt, pulled the tunic over his head and tried to adjust the makeshift bandage. He swatted at a large horsefly, intent on settling on the gash, preferring fresh blood to the rotten goat carcass it had been feasting on.

When more came, he gave up, barely noticing their attentions.

CHAPTER TEN

Dawid opened his eyes and looked into the face of an angel. Rachael smiled at his confusion.

'What…? Where…?' Dawid looked weakly around as Rachael shushed him. He saw the totems dangling in the old olive tree, the ancient altar stone and the lush plants of the valley. He lay on a bed of loose cloths, beside him a pail of clean spring water. He tried to prop himself up, but his arm was weak and unresponsive, so he sank back onto his makeshift outdoor bed. Rachael slid an arm under his neck and shoulder and gently lifted, reaching for a ladle with her other hand and bringing the water to his cracked, swollen lips.

'You've been in a fever for two days,' she said. 'Your horse brought you here. She's a beautiful animal, very clever. You slid from her back right here outside our cave. Sparrow found you.'

'Sparrow?'

'My little sister. She's gone to fetch food.' Dawid remembered the grinning child at her side when The Fist had arrived, and he thought the name appropriate for the little girl. 'We could tell you were about to wake, with the way you were thrashing around, probably still fighting whoever did that to you.'

She lifted the covering that lay across his waist and suddenly Dawid realised he was naked apart from the binding around his midriff, stained a murky yellow where it covered the wound. He snatched at the bed cloth to keep it in place, the effort bringing a dizzying wave of nausea, but Rachael smiled again and gently moved his hand away, leaving his modesty covered.

She probed the edge of the bandage where the skin was inflamed, but Dawid felt no pain.

'You're healing well,' she said as a lock of her thick, dark hair brushed against his chest. He fought against his arousal, hoping Rachael wouldn't notice the cover stirring as it betrayed him. She turned to him, amusement playing at the corners of her mouth. 'Yes, you're definitely healing.'

'You're the priestess, aren't you?' said Dawid, desperately trying to distract her.

'Yes.'

'And a healer too?'

'I have a little knowledge. I used honey and thyme to salve your wound. I've seen it work before.'

'Did you say I've been asleep for two days?' he asked. 'I don't remember anything about the journey after the fight.'

'Your wound was covered with flies, and we thought that was how the fever had come to you. Your whole body was hot to the touch. We thought you were going to die, but somehow Sparrow got you to drink some hyssop for the fever. Most of all we asked Ashtoreth to help you, and she did.'

Dawid murmured his thanks. He was happy to listen to her lilting voice and watch her smooth, pale lips and her lively dark eyes.

'Were they bandits?' Rachael asked gently. 'The men who attacked you, I mean.'

Dawid realised he was staring at her dumbly. 'Bandits? No. They were soldiers.'

'And you defeated them all by yourself?'

He shook his head, finding it hard to speak. 'Nathan, the others…'

A look of alarm crossed her face. 'Are they…?'

'Oh, they're unharmed. We killed them all.'

'Why? Did they attack you?'

'Yes. They were Philistine ruffians.'

Rachael frowned at his abrupt reasoning and was about to ask him more when Sparrow called her name. Both looked up. Sparrow was tugging energetically at the arm of Nathan's mother, Martha, who carried a basket that Dawid hoped contained something to abate his ravenous hunger. Sparrow saw that the patient was awake and half ran, half skipped between the aloe quills, squealing with delight, then stood before him and stared. Following at a more sedate pace, Martha handed the basket to Rachael and fixed Dawid with a glare.

'It seems to me that you didn't heed my advice,' she said. 'I warned you there was danger on the Socoh road, and you didn't listen, did you?'

Dawid felt his face redden and thought better of attempting an explanation. Guiltily, he eyed the food basket and Martha softened.

'You'd better eat and get your strength up. Then you can convince us you're not a troublemaker.'

Dawid made the best of his days as an invalid, cared for by Rachael and Sparrow. On the day that Nathan and Rimon returned from their mission, disgusted that the Beth Lechem shepherd luxuriated in female attention and grew fat on Martha's cooking, Rachael revealed how she had encountered Philistine cruelty and the horror of their warriors. She seemed to be warning him not to get involved in Nathan's dangerous missions.

'My family lived not far from here, beyond Socoh, towards Gath,' she said. 'We were poor but happy. We had a few goats for milk and hides, some sheep and two asses. We lived in tents but we didn't move them, because the land was good and the well never dried up. Others came with their tents to share in Ashtoreth's bounty, and we traded our cheeses and new lambs with the people of Gath, bringing home pots and farming tools, and seeds for new crops. We didn't look on them as foreigners, just as city-dwellers with fine clothes and pretty bracelets. My father was even planning to offer me in marriage to a young merchant, and probably Sparrow too when she became a woman. He often spoke enviously of Philistine ways.' She was thoughtful for a moment, remembering the good times.

'But then it turned unpleasant,' Dawid speculated into the silence, and immediately wished he had kept quiet as a tear formed in Rachael's eye and rolled down her cheek. She wiped angrily at it with the back of her hand.

'Yes,' she whispered, 'things happened. First my brothers came home with barely anything to show for their goods, so my father went to Gath to remonstrate with the Philistines. I'll never forget the sight of him when he came home, all bruised and broken, the joy driven out of him. He wouldn't talk about it, not in front of me anyway, but I overheard my mother begging him to leave and find somewhere else to pitch our tents, somewhere safer. I heard her shouting at him, saying the Philistines would stop at nothing to take our goods and property, but he was proud and refused to give up what he said belonged to the families who lived near the well.

'Then one day men came to our settlement, some of them soldiers, but there was a young man dressed in a fine embroidered robe with a gold band around his head, which we took to mean he was quite important in Gath. He told my father and the elders from the families that we were on Philistine land and we must pay taxes or leave. When my father questioned them about the taxes, it seemed that they wanted everything we had and would give us nothing in return. There was a lot of arguing and shouting.' She sighed and took a deep breath. 'But my father…'

She paused to wipe away more tears. Then her words came out in a rush.

'My father stood up to them. He said Gath should find some other people to pick on, as the land where our tents were pitched belonged to Judah, and the God of Judah was mightier than all of the gods of Philistia, and if the king of Gath knew what was good for him he would keep his nose out of Judah's business. The young Philistine was so angry. He shouted curses at my father and told him it would be worse for us now because he would return with more men to take what we owed, and also take our children as slaves and —' Dawid looked away as she sobbed — 'sacrifice them to their gods.'

For a moment, Rachael couldn't speak. Her lip quivered and her cheeks were wet with tears. Then she told how the young tax collector returned, this time with two huge warriors more terrifying than any Philistine they had seen before, riding in enormous chariots. 'Just the sight of them was enough for the men of our settlement to throw down their sickles and pitchforks,' she said. 'I had never seen such giants, and I never want to see them again. They were twice the height of any of us, even Oren, and he's tall enough. But it wasn't just their height, or the size of their legs and arms, it was their faces. When they rode into our camp, their heads were covered. While our men cowered, they unwrapped their headcloths…'

Her story was interrupted by Martha, who yelled from the mouth of the cave that there was food for them, but Rachael kept her gaze on Dawid.

'What was it?' he asked. 'What about their faces?'

'It's hard to put into words,' said Rachael, 'but the first thing that struck me was that they had no beards. All the men of Gath, and all the men of the hill country around us, believe it is shameful to cut off one's beard. But these giants had no hair on their heads at all. Not even a few strands. I had the impression these giants were *old*, ancients even, with skin like leather. But it wasn't just their hairless faces, it was their eyes. They seemed to flash like lightning. I've never seen anything like it. Our men who had defied the Philistines cowered before them like old women — even my father was face down on the ground. It was so easy for the Philistine soldiers to just walk among the men of our settlement and kill them.' Rachael lowered her eyes and her shoulders slumped. 'I saw my father run through by a Philistine spear. They even slaughtered the old women. There was screaming and blood everywhere. I managed to grab Sparrow — I don't think she understood what was happening — and we ran to the well. That was where she used to hide in our games with the other children, in a crevice between the huge stones that our forebears had used to keep the sands back, and I told her not to come out until I came for her. The Philistines were rounding up all the children and killing everyone else — except the young women...'

She let the meaning hang between them, her eyes defiant. Dawid couldn't speak, though he wanted to know how she had escaped, what had happened to her family, especially little Sparrow. Darkness boiled inside him as he realised that the enmity of his rancorous half-brothers was nothing compared to the cruelty inflicted by these barbaric Philistines.

'If you don't come soon, there'll be nothing left!' Martha yelled again.

'Go, eat,' Rachael insisted. 'You must be hungry.'

Dawid continued to study her face. She returned his gaze and a flicker of a smile lit her eyes. With a sigh, she gathered herself and moved closer to him, brushing her lips against his.

'You'd be wise to leave the Philistines well alone,' she said.

CHAPTER ELEVEN

'I'm leaving tomorrow to find Shemu'el at Gibeah.'

Nathan had said little since his return, his eyes steely and his look grim for all but Rachael.

'Just you?' asked Dawid. He didn't want to leave, not yet, unless it was to inflict more damage on the Philistines. He was still recovering from his fever and hoped for more attention from Rachael.

'With Rimon, as soon as Oren and Dookhi return from Ekron. Oren will come with us too.'

'What about me? And Dookhi?'

Nathan's fierce eyes bored into Dawid's. 'Can I trust you?' he asked.

'Of course.'

Nathan smiled at last. 'Well, you're well qualified for what I have in mind for you. It's just that you must do everything that Dookhi tells you, without question. No tearing off with that sling of yours, attacking Philistines on your own. Remember, you're a spy. Spies don't pick fights with the enemy; they find things out by stealth!'

Dawid nodded enthusiastically, happy to be chosen.

'You're a shepherd, a farmer. Just the person to be buying farm tools for his village, right?'

Dawid thought he could see where this was leading.

'You're going to Gath,' said Nathan. 'Dressed like a farmer, behaving like a farmer, quibbling and bartering like a farmer…'

'For iron tools?'

'Yes. And while you're there, ask a few questions to find out what stockpiles of weapons the Philistines have.'

Dawid felt exhilarated, trusted at last, but Nathan had one more thing to add.

'And while you're asking about weapons, see what you can find out about these giants.'

Dookhi rode into Adullam like an all-conquering hero, reining in his mare in a swirl of dust before her hooves could harm any of the children who swarmed around him, Oren riding more circumspectly behind. Across Dookhi's knees was a great sword, its blade brown with rust, the binding of its hilt frayed. He held it point down with both hands and thrust it into the red earth as the children gasped and drew back, terrified of the enormous weapon. It swayed before falling slowly to the hard ground with a dull thud.

Dookhi laughed and yelled for Nathan. Oren watched with a bemused look on his face.

Nathan and Dawid had already heard the commotion and came running. Nathan stooped to pick up the heavy sword.

'Don't tell me you won this in a game of dice, Dookhi?'

'Aha. Not in a game,' said Dookhi, with a twinkle in his eye. 'Full blooded, man-to-man warfare, of course…'

Nathan chortled. He knew that was not Dookhi's way — the lad was not cut out for fighting, usually preferring to wear down an opponent with witty chatter. 'Tell me, Dookhi,' he said, 'exactly how did you come to find a Philistine sword? Thrown out with their other waste, was it?'

'Well, in a manner of speaking it was,' replied Dookhi. 'Its owner was an old warrior who wandered away from his friends to void his bowels. Stank, it did, with all the pig meat those Philistines eat!' He held his nose to emphasise the point. 'He was farting and heaving, making so much noise that he didn't notice me. I tossed a scorpion into his undergarments. I'm afraid he forgot his sword belt as he ran away.'

This sent the gathered children into fits of giggles, Nathan and Dawid finding it hard not to join in.

Oren just watched impassively. 'He's so brave when his enemy is unclothed,' he said with a wry smile. 'You could say it was a messy encounter.'

Dookhi noticed how gaunt Dawid looked. 'What's up with you? Suffering after your first taste of battle? No stomach for a fair fight — one on four!'

Dawid was uncertain whether he meant it. 'I was sick. I...'

'Never mind. You'll toughen up. Now, what about this trophy?' He laughed, pointing to the sword that Nathan held. 'That's Philistine iron, that is, forged at Ekron and lost for the sake of a shit!'

Nathan was resting the point of the blade on the ground. 'It's a good find,' he said after a moment's contemplation. 'Seems heavy, though. Come on, let's see how good it is.'

The old bronze helmet had been bought from a Kenite tradesman from Khadem, a smelting town in the copper-rich desert wastes that bordered Egypt. It had last seen action when its owner, Shemu'el, was young and fit enough to call himself a warrior-prophet and had paid a shekel of silver for the uncomfortable-looking headgear with a jaunty horsehair plume, polished cheek guards and camel-hide neck flap. Back then it had been the symbol of the prophet's authority in battle, mainly because Shemu'el was the one and only warrior to possess such a rare thing as a metal helmet. Every one of Israel's foot soldiers, hastily assembled in times of crisis, had to make do with their peasant clothes and farm tools.

The Kenite had also rummaged in his store of tools and trinkets to come up with a rare sword that looked more like a sickle than a weapon of war, but which nonetheless served Shemu'el well when reaping the wicked souls of invaders. That both had been left to tarnish in the darker recesses of Martha's cave owed as much to her insistence that the prophet adopt a more peaceful mission as to his own silent admission that his ageing body could no longer cope with the rigours of leading bloodthirsty Hebrews into battle against better equipped enemies. Though his battered sword had slashed at the limbs of Moabites, Edomites and Amalekites and his helmet had turned many a nomad blade as his god delivered him victory after victory, Shemu'el had been ill-equipped to resist the strength of Martha, Ashtoreth's young priestess of the time. She had stood before him with her hands on her hips and ordered him to find a younger man to lead Yahweh's people into battle and start behaving like a real man of god by teaching them the law. Especially the part that said, "You shall not kill."

This was why the old Kenite helmet and sword had come to be discarded in Martha's cave until now when, some eighteen years later, Nathan brought them into the sunlight to face the might of Philistine iron.

'Brothers,' he announced to the four other members of The Fist and the intrigued crowd of children who watched, 'this is just like the bronze helmets that Saul and the captains of our army wear. Some of them have swords like this one —' he held up the chipped sickle sword, now dulled with age and tinged with green — 'but none of them have iron weapons.'

Clutching the helmet, he handed the bronze sword to Dawid and looked around for somewhere to test the relative strengths of old and new metal. The stump of a long-dead almond tree served his purpose. He placed the helmet on it.

'Dawid, imagine you're the enemy and that's King Saul under that helmet.' The children crowded closer, fascinated and unusually silent.

Dawid held the sword in two hands, feeling its balance and trying to sense the heat of battle it had seen, the lives it had claimed. It was the first time he had touched such a weapon. He eyed his target and took careful aim, lifting the sickle sword above his head then sweeping it downwards. The blade glanced off the helmet's curved dome with a bright ringing sound, throwing him off balance as it carved into the ground, showering the watching children with grit and small stones.

The almondwood king lived.

'Now the Philistine sword,' said Nathan, passing the iron weapon to Rimon. He grinned, grasping the hilt in two hands and feeling the weight of it. Though pitted and blunt through lack of care, it *looked* more formidable than the sickle sword. And so it proved when Rimon's powerful shoulders brought the heavy blade crashing down onto the helmet, crushing it easily. The children gasped and backed away nervously.

'More like a club than a sword,' observed Nathan, putting the side of his hand into the savage dent. 'This poor soldier wouldn't have stood a chance.'

Rimon passed the sword to Nathan. 'Imagine if it was sharp as well as heavy,' he said. 'It would've split that helmet in two and probably the skull beneath it.'

Several of the bolder children crowded around the damaged helmet, chattering excitedly about the strange weapons.

Nathan looked worried. He turned to Dookhi. 'How many weapons like this did you see at Ekron?'

Dookhi shrugged. 'Not that many,' he replied, 'but from a distance it's hard to distinguish whether a sword is iron or bronze, least of all a spearhead. But we did notice something about the chariots.'

'What?'

'The noise they made when they moved. And their speed. The Philistines are using horses like ours, probably raising them on the coastal plains.'

Nathan's eyes narrowed. 'Were there many chariots?'

'We could only guess. We only saw two, but who's to say the Philistines aren't hiding them?' For the first time since Dawid had met The Fist back in the Beth Lechem stables, Dookhi was grim-faced. 'My guess is they've been producing weapons and new chariots and training the men to use them.'

'It was the same at Gath, wasn't it, Rimon?' said Nathan. 'Lots of clues but no hard evidence.'

Rimon nodded. 'We thought that if they have an abundance of iron, they'll be using it to strengthen the chariot wheels.'

'That's why the ones we observed sounded different, isn't it?' said Dookhi, with sudden understanding. 'With metal rims, they can go over rougher ground at speed. But they also squeak like rats.'

'Squeak?' Nathan looked confused. Some of the children helped him out by making rat noises.

Dookhi's head was bobbing furiously now. 'Yes. We were watching from a distance, but they were definitely squeaking.'

'Of course,' said Rimon. 'Metal rubbing against metal. They're not just making iron rims, they're making iron wheels, with stronger axles. That's why they squeak.'

'And if they're stronger, they'll be bigger too,' observed Nathan. 'Big enough to carry more archers and spearmen with their weapons or drive them straight through our unprotected ranks.'

Dawid tried to imagine what it must be like to face a large number of horse-drawn chariots, each spitting arrows and spears, crashing into the lines of terrified farmers. Carnage. Screaming. Broken, mutilated bodies. He thought about his misguided half-brothers eagerly joining King Saul's so-called army and allowed himself to hope they would be placed right at the front of the Hebrew ranks to face this Philistine terror. Everything he was learning since leaving Beth Lechem was bad — first giants, then iron weapons, now war chariots. He swore to himself that he would never ever be so stupid as to allow himself to become a Hebrew foot soldier, standing in the heat of day with the massed ranks of farmers and shepherds, waiting to be scythed down by giants riding in huge chariots.

'Dawid?'

He realised Nathan had been talking to him. 'I'm sorry, I…'

'I know. We've all been afraid at some time.' Dawid was about to defend himself, but Nathan continued, 'You'll just have to leave sooner than we planned. Don't worry, Dookhi here will look after you.'

Dawid nodded. He was ready, even excited about seeing Gath and its warmongering people. 'And then…?'

'And then you both find me in Gibeah. Dookhi knows the way. Remember, do what he says and keep out of trouble. Just observe. Saul and Shemu'el will need to know how many warriors and chariots they have and how well armed they are.'

Dawid looked at Dookhi, his companion for the journey to Gath's market. But Dookhi was looking intently at the Philistine sword that Nathan held.

'These farmers,' he said, as if an idea had dawned on him, 'they take their ploughshares and sickles to the Philistines for sharpening, don't they?'

'Yes, why?' said Nathan.

'Well, we could take that sword for sharpening…'

Nathan shook his head. 'Might as well confess that it's stolen and ask them to chop your head off with it!'

'But if we convince them we're Philistine sympathisers…?'

'Hmmm.' Nathan seemed to be considering the idea. 'Risky…'

'There must be many folk farming near the Philistine borders who give their allegiance to the people with the most powerful army. Why not Hebrew farmers protected by Gath? We could convince them we need more weapons for our tribe, and even tell them we will bring more men if the smiths of Gath could arm them.'

Nathan looked hard at Dookhi, weighing up his plan. 'I suppose that might give us some meaningful information to take to Shemu'el,' he said. 'He'll want to know much more than we've found out so far.'

'If we can gain their confidence,' said Dookhi, warming to his theme, 'we might also be able to find out how many chariots they'll be able to send against us.'

'And,' said Nathan, handing the sword to Dookhi, 'they will believe you. No Hebrew farmer would be so stupid as to pull out an iron sword in the presence of a Philistine smith — unless he had a legitimate reason for having it in the first place.' He pointed to the weapon that Dookhi now clutched. 'Wrap it in rags and conceal it on the provisions donkey.'

'Donkey?' Dookhi exclaimed. 'That'll slow down the horses.'

'Only as far as Socoh. You'll be stabling the horses there and going on to Gath on donkeys or asses, just like all the other farmers do. Riding to the market on a pair of fine horses would be your undoing, don't you think?'

All laughed at the obvious point they might otherwise have overlooked, and the children joined in too, sensing that the serious business had been concluded.

Nathan heaved the crushed helmet from its tree stump and handed it to the nearest child, a freckle-faced boy in a grubby tunic. His eyes lit up, and suddenly the other children surrounded him as if he was the new king of Adullam. He clutched it to his chest, revelling in the attention, then pushed his way past them and skipped away. His friends ran after him, shouting and laughing.

CHAPTER TWELVE

Nathan, Oren and Rimon left for Gibeah that day, dressed in their customary riding clothes, over-provisioned by Martha and her friends, and abundantly blessed by the priestess.

Two days later Rachael decreed that Dawid was strong enough to make the journey to Gath. He had revelled in her attentions and had come to know her carefree ways, the musical lilt of her voice and the endearing way she rolled her dark eyes when he spoke of his dismal life in Beth Lechem. She made him laugh, drawing him gradually out of his self-loathing with chirpy observations as she dressed his wound, declaring him fit for action after discovering that he was hopelessly ticklish. It was in the moments after her teasing fingers stopped their wicked probing, when they looked into each other's eyes, that the demon that lurked within Dawid's soul began to release its malignant grip. She sensed his struggle and saw the flicker of light, sensitivity flowering within this boorish shepherd, like benign Ashtoreth contending with mighty Yahweh.

The roughness of his kiss violated the moment, and the demon tightened its grip as Rachael recoiled. She saw the pain in his eyes and moved closer, gently placing her hands on his cheeks and feeling the heat of his shame.

She could foresee the battles that lay ahead for this wounded youth — battles that she, too, had fought since that dreadful day when the Philistines had laid waste to her soul, which was why she now wanted Dawid to turn his back on Nathan's missions and keep away from the Philistines. She told him there was no need to go, no need to discover what Nathan already knew, that the Philistines were preparing for war and they would be remorseless and cruel.

'I must go,' he mumbled. 'It's not just that Nathan asked me to. I have to go. There's something pulling me. I can't explain it.'

'Your destiny?'

'I think so.'

Rachael pulled a thong from around her neck, revealing a small leather bag that had been concealed beneath her tunic. She loosened its drawstring and shook out a deep blue gemstone into the palm of her hand. Dawid gasped. It was exquisitely smooth and flecked with gold, more precious than anything he had ever seen in Beth Lechem.

'Beautiful, isn't it?' she sighed. 'Martha said it's called *sappir* and probably came from Egypt or across the sea.' She handed it to Dawid, who took it gingerly, then held it up as if it could drink in the sunlight. Rachael noticed the desire in his eyes. 'It's yours,' she said.

At first Dawid didn't hear her, then reluctantly he dragged his eyes from the gem and looked at her with questioning eyes.

'Nathan said you would be taking a few shekels of silver,' she said, 'but we don't have much to give. This might be useful. You may need to barter with it.'

'I couldn't...' said Dawid, still fingering the gem. 'Where did you get it?'

She looked away as if the memory was painful, then took a deep breath. 'It was when I was biting, kicking and scratching that loathsome Philistine tax collector. I must have grabbed it when we fought. He had called over one of those giants to subdue me, but when it was over I had this little bag in my hand. The leather thong had snapped. I must have held on to it. Perhaps I was trying to strangle him with it, I don't know. He didn't notice I had it in my hand when he walked away.'

'And the giant?' he asked.

'He was told to kill me.'

Dawid looked into Rachael's eyes and saw blazing defiance there. He waited for her to explain.

'I closed my eyes and waited for the deathblow, but it never came. I think I was calling out to Ashtoreth. When I looked up, I saw those strange eyes, but they weren't terrifying at all. They were… He was … sorrowful. I lay there, clutching this pouch, battered and bleeding, expecting to die. Then the warrior spoke. His voice was as strange as his eyes, as if it was inside my head. It sounded like thunder.'

'What did he say?'

'He said, "No kill girl. Golyat no kill."'

'Golyat?'

'Golyat.'

PART TWO: GATH

CHAPTER THIRTEEN

Most of Socoh lay outside crumbling mudbrick walls that would offer scant protection against an invader. This was why the town's elders welcomed all strangers and adapted their politics accordingly, and why inside its walls Socoh was a thriving community of inns and trinket shops but outside was a muddle of hovels and frayed goatskin tents. Visitors entering through the permanently open gates were usually aloof Egyptians, sometimes Phoenician traders from the north and occasionally Philistines, most of whom parted with rare bracelets and precious stones for the services of the sacred prostitutes. The priests and elders were well versed in the customs of each of these peoples and their various deities, duly impressing all visitors with their devotion to the appropriate gods. They diverted a steady stream of wealth into Yahweh's storerooms or, more usually, into the accommodating pockets of their fine robes.

The two travellers who picked their way through the filth towards the gates, mouths and noses covered in a vain attempt to keep out the stench, would not normally have attracted attention. There had been many farmers passing through Socoh to the market at Gath in recent days. But these rode horses, and the donkey that trotted behind was heavily laden with supplies and a bundle that could contain various weapons.

Dookhi and Dawid urged their mounts into a quicker pace to shake off the attentions of Socoh's beggars, unaware that they were being watched from the roof of one of the town's larger houses. Naboth ben Ezra often kept an eye on the approaches to Socoh, weighing up potential custom for his well-kept courtyard inn, and now as he took in the rare sight of horses coming towards the gates, he called for his eldest son.

'Obed! Get your lazy backside up here.'

Obed came running. Tall and muscular for his sixteen years, he wasn't lazy at all and took the stone stairs on the outside of the house two at a time. Obed was as honest and hardworking as his father was crooked and idle.

'Go to those men and bring them to me before someone else sees them,' ordered Naboth, pointing over the parapet towards the two horsemen. Obed turned to obey. 'And tell your mother to prepare food. And have your sisters fetch fresh straw for the stable.'

Obed thought about asking which he should do first but he knew better. Naboth was not a violent man — that required too much effort — but his verbal rage was a force to be reckoned with. Obed ran back down the stairs, yelling to the women inside as he sprinted towards Socoh's gates.

He was easily first to greet the travellers. He chased away a number of pestering children and beggars, took the reins of the horses in each hand, and smiled up at the riders.

'Shalom, brothers.'

'Shalom,' replied Dookhi with a bird-like twitch of his head.

Dawid just grunted, but he liked the look of this youth and managed a smile.

'You're going to take us to your master's inn, aren't you?' said Dookhi knowingly. Obed just beamed. 'Lead on, then, but remember we're just poor farmers.'

Obed looked at the majestic animals and saw the workmanship in their bridles but thought better of saying anything. His father had his own way of doing business with poor farmers.

In the event, Naboth couldn't disguise his greed when he saw the half shekel of silver that Dookhi placed before him. He reached for it without hesitation, then loosened the cord of his money pouch.

'Food, fresh straw for bedding, and you look after our horses until we return,' said Dookhi firmly. Slowly, reluctantly, Naboth returned the piece of silver to the table and seemed to study it. He had assumed these youths would only want some food and somewhere to sleep.

'Hay and fodder for such fine animals is hard to come by, my friends,' said Naboth, wringing his hands.

Dookhi ignored the hint. 'And two asses, or donkeys, to take us to Gath. We'll return them within two days.' The silver was more than enough to cover this.

But it was not enough for Naboth. He rolled his eyes at the ceiling as if appealing to his god for help in explaining the finer points of commerce to these youths who perhaps had more silver to part with.

'And how am I to pay for two such beasts?'

'Come now,' said Dookhi with an easy smile, 'you have several in your stable, do you not?' No one could have mistaken the noisy braying when Obed had led the horses into Naboth's courtyard.

Naboth sniffed and looked from Dookhi to Dawid. He wanted to ask why they did not use their own mounts for the remainder of the journey, but it was not the place of an innkeeper to pry. He waited for Dookhi to increase his offer.

Dookhi obliged. He reached into the pouch at his belt and produced a second half-shekel, holding it before Naboth's piggy eyes. 'This will be yours when we return. You have our horses as surety.'

Naboth reached for the silver, but Dookhi swiftly dropped it back into his pouch, then placed his hands on the table. 'Well?' he asked. 'Are we agreed?'

Naboth decided not to press the youths further; a shekel of silver was far more than he could have hoped for. He nodded curtly and called for his wife, a round woman with rosy cheeks who revelled in feeding hungry travellers.

'Feed them well,' commanded Naboth. 'And tell that sluggard Obed to bring fresh straw to the stables for these young men to sleep on.'

The night air was heavy and oppressive, laying a film of sweat on Naboth's brow as he picked his way through familiar streets, small dogs and rodents scurrying away from the bulky figure with the rolling gait. The only sounds were his wheezing and the slapping of his sandals on the hard ground. Socoh slept, its oil lamps long doused.

Naboth stopped beside a small house built into the town's wall, leaned on the crumbling mudbrick to catch his breath, and looked furtively around, even though he knew he was unobserved. There was no door, just an opening covered by a ragged curtain. He whispered a name and looked around again before repeating it a little more loudly. There was a grunt and a shuffling sound, then the curtain was pulled aside. Naboth whispered a few words to the shadowy occupant and held out a hand for payment. He pocketed his small fee and hurried away, pleased that there was more than one way to make money out of travellers this close to Philistia's border.

Socoh burst into life with the dawn. Dawid tried to block out the sounds of cockerels and children who showed scant respect for Judah's weary travellers, pulling the threadbare blanket over his head, but it was Obed's tuneless singing that was the more intrusive. He was milking a goat, the *splish splish* sound in the pail providing the rhythm for his ditty.

Dookhi stirred him with a playful kick to the rump. 'Up, farmer boy. We've got a long journey ahead on those bone-jarring donkeys.'

Dawid groaned. 'Tell that bard to be quiet. Or is it the goat singing?'

Obed giggled and resumed his song, louder still.

Dawid looked at his clothes and pulled a face. Neither he nor Dookhi had changed since leaving Adullam.

'Any water?' he shouted over the din.

Obed abruptly stopped singing and pointed to a barrel that stood in the corner of the courtyard nearest the shaded wall, where the horses and donkeys were tethered. Next to it was a large wooden ladle. 'Should be fresh,' he said. 'I filled it yesterday.'

Dawid took the ladle and peered inside. The water was green and teeming with insect larvae. 'That's fresh?' he grimaced.

'Well, it might have been the day before when I filled it,' muttered Obed, 'or the day before that...'

'Who cares?' said Dawid and ladled the foul water over his head, then refilled the ladle and showered Dookhi. 'That's us washed. At least we'll smell like farmers should.'

'You're going to Gath? To the metal smiths?' asked Obed, picking up his milking pail and handing it to Dookhi, who tipped the rim to his lips and drank deeply. He closed his eyes at the pleasure of the warm, sweet goat's milk and passed it to Dawid.

'We are,' he replied, wiping his mouth on the shoulder of his grubby tunic.

'I wish I could come. I've never been to Gath and it's not that far.'

Dookhi smiled at him. 'Another time. Right now we need you to look after the horses. Give them hay and *fresh* water. What grain do you have?'

'A little barley. I can get more.'

'Soak it well in *fresh* water before you give them any,' Dookhi repeated. 'We don't want their stomachs swelling, and you don't want your fine stable covered in slimy smelly stuff, do you?'

'Of course I will care for them well,' said Obed indignantly. 'I have done this before. And I'll exercise them one at a time, in the olive groves…'

'Lead them but don't ride them,' cut in Dookhi sternly but then, seeing the hurt on Obed's innocent face, he softened. 'There's a special reward for you when we return, if you care for them well. Can we trust you?'

Obed beamed. 'Yes, yes,' he promised enthusiastically. 'But I doubt you'll have anything of value left when you return. Word from the other farmers is that the Philistines have increased their price for repairs, and new tools are hard to come by.'

'We'll make sure we keep something back for you,' said Dookhi kindly.

Their *pe'er* head coverings wrapped across their noses and mouths, Dawid and Dookhi perched sideways on the rumps of their chosen donkeys and, with the third in tow burdened by their bundles of supplies and metalware, they trotted through the chaotic outskirts of Socoh. On the Gath road they caught up with a small group of travellers, most of them on foot although several of the older men rode in a cumbersome ox-drawn cart. Only one rode a donkey.

Dookhi exchanged pleasantries with them; they were Benjaminites from Gibeah, where Saul was building his stronghold not far from the ancient city of Jebus. They were clearly tired after travelling for three days, but despite this they seemed resilient and genuinely pleased to meet fellow farmers on a similar mission. Their leader was an old man with a proud hooked nose, a long grey beard and lively eyes who rode the cart as if it was a mobile throne. Behind him was a pile of bronze and iron farm tools for repair or sharpening by Gath's smiths, leaving little room for his fellow farmers, who turned out to be brothers and cousins, all related but working their own fields in the hill country beyond Judah's border. The younger men, mostly sons of the old man, walked beside the rickety cart.

The exception was the man riding a donkey. His stiff bearing and surly demeanour set him apart from the Benjaminites. His patterned cloak revealed that he was not a farmer, and when Dookhi politely asked where he was from, he nodded curtly in the direction of Socoh and announced that he was travelling to Gath where he had a share in a weaving business and had offered to guide the farmers.

'Are you a Philistine, then?' Dawid blurted.

'No,' he replied with a wan half-smile, 'I'm a Hebrew like you.'

'Then why...?'

'Why do I trade with Philistines? Why not? They're a proud and cultured people, and I have friends there.'

'But you live in Socoh?'

'I live wherever there are people who buy my cloth. I trade freely in Ekron as well as Socoh. I'll ride with you and explain it, if you like.'

He introduced himself as Mishon, whose father had been a successful weaver and had moved his family to Gath many years ago. As a consequence Mishon had been brought up as much a Philistine as a Hebrew, which explained the apparent ease with which he could come and go in Gath, a city closed to other Hebrews such as the hill farmers. He answered questions as he picked the easiest route along the valley towards Gath, stopping within sight of the town of Azekah as the sun rose higher, allowing the slower travellers to catch up. They were sharing waterskins and dried dates in the shade of a large fig tree when Mishon asked a question of his own.

'What do you seek in Gath?'

Dookhi sensed that their disguise had been ineffective, but he maintained their deception. 'A few tools. Ploughshares mainly. And a sickle made of iron if we're not too late.'

If Mishon thought there was more to Dookhi and Dawid's expedition, he kept it to himself. 'You may be disappointed. The smiths have been concentrating on producing weapons of late, not so many farming tools. Besides, many have been before you and the more the Hebrews buy, the higher the price. I have heard that a third of a shekel is demanded for the simplest of repairs.'

'We have silver,' said Dawid impulsively and Dookhi glared at him.

'In which case,' said Mishon quickly, 'perhaps I can sell you some linen, even some silk for your women back home?'

'But that would mean entering the city, surely?' Dookhi knew from experience that Gath's guards were notoriously brutal towards Hebrew visitors.

'I can get you in. The guards know me.' Mishon lowered his voice. 'I could even pass you off as recruits for Gath's new military.'

Dawid was drawn into the trap before Dookhi could change the subject. 'They'll be impressed by the iron sword we have.'

'And I thought you were just farmhands,' said Mishon with a wry smile.

CHAPTER FOURTEEN

The walls of Gath frowned eastwards at Judah's hill country. The city stood proud and imposing, crowning two low hills with orderly squat buildings that did obeisance to a huge palace on the highest ground. Outside the walls, black tents spread before Gath like the skirts of an old woman, fingers of smoke from charcoal furnaces supporting a murky veil that weighed heavily on the land of the Philistines. Tree stumps like broken teeth scarred vales where flourishing forests had once stood, sycamore and cypress sacrificed to the austere gods of war.

Dawid stared open-mouthed at the devastation that stretched before them, but Mishon didn't blink; in fact he seemed to visibly brighten and his donkey didn't break stride as it picked its way along a well-trodden path towards Gath. Dookhi allowed his mount to wait beside Dawid's as the youth took in the grim scenes, eventually breaking the silence.

'These are the people who lay claim to the lands of Judah,' he sighed. 'They have already taken several cities from the northern tribes and now they want Judah's hills and pastures too.'

Dawid surveyed the tents that spread outwards from the city walls. He could make out several areas where these were arranged in more orderly fashion with large numbers of people buying, selling, making and mending. These were Gath's markets, selling pottery, cloth, silver bracelets, gold rings, wine and olive oil — and iron and bronze in abundance.

'I've never seen anything like it,' he said, wrinkling his nose, 'or smelled anything like it. Do they make iron with bad eggs?'

He tapped his donkey's rump and it reluctantly followed Mishon's along the path towards Gath.

They didn't wait for the slower Benjaminite farmers to catch up, leaving them to make their own way into the land of iron foundries and metal smiths. The track they followed led around a knoll on which a few pines had escaped the axe, and for a time Gath was hidden to them. Dookhi reached out to Dawid, riding at his side, and tugged the sleeve of his robe.

'I've been here before,' he said, out of Mishon's hearing, indicating the slope of the hill they were passing. 'We'll get a better view from the top, and there's something I want to show you.'

He whistled to catch Mishon's attention, signalling their intention to climb the hill. Mishon shrugged and shouted that he'd wait for them on the other side, so they eased their tired donkeys off the track and picked their way upwards towards the summit. It wasn't far but it was steep in places, a deterrent to the woodcutters of Gath. They passed among the trees, startling hares and a pair of bee-eaters that took off in a blur of blue and yellow, trilling a warning to their chicks. The vista opened before them, the city much closer now, shimmering in the merciless heat. But Dawid was looking beyond Gath with its obstinate walls, tents and makeshift shelters.

He saw the sea for the first time.

Beyond the city, beyond the verdant coastal plains, it was a wide sweep of silver-blue, as if a creator-god had become bored with fields, trees, rivers and cities and commanded them all away with a wave of his mighty right arm. What the god had given in their place was, he thought, mysterious and enchanting.

'It's so big.' It was all he could think of saying as he surveyed the sea's hazy horizon.

'You've never seen the sea before?' asked Dookhi.

'No. Never. Have you?'

'A few times, yes. But I've never been to the shore. Never actually touched it.'

'So the Philistines control all this land, between here and the sea?' Dawid asked, thinking how fertile and green the plains beyond Gath looked compared with the less prolific hill country around Beth Lechem.

'It's said they came from across the sea.'

'It's also said that we Hebrews came across the desert. That's a bit like the sea, only drier...'

'And now we meet in the middle,' said Dookhi. 'The Philistines have been pushing further into Hebrew lands, bit by bit, and someday soon they'll march on Judah.'

'Unless we march on them first,' Dawid replied. Without taking his eyes off the sea, he thought about the Philistines with their chariots and giants and for the first time questioned why the Hebrews were so fearful of them. Hadn't Saul's army defeated the Ammonites and Amalekites? Why not the Philistines too?

Mishon led Dawid and Dookhi straight to a makeshift stable, where they hobbled and tethered the donkeys near a heap of rotting vegetation. The animals stood with their heads bowed and their tails twitching weakly at determined horseflies, sensibly ignoring several richly adorned camels that lay on folded legs nearby. Dawid slung his shepherd's pouch around his neck, unable to resist looking again at Rachael's precious stone that nestled safely inside with his pipes, sling and hunting knife, while Dookhi strapped the cloth-wrapped Philistine sword to his back.

Mishon showed them where the best ironmongers were and left them to explore while he went into the city. 'I'll speak to the guards and bribe them if necessary to let two young Hebrews in,' he told them. 'I'll be back well before dusk to collect you.'

For a while, Dawid felt lost in this jostling world of loud taskmasters yelling at slaves, and traders pushing their wares. He saw women in colourful robes, their rich, dark hair wound and pinned to stand proudly above their painted faces and elegant necks, chattering and laughing with servant girls carrying the day's bargains in baskets balanced on their heads. In every tent, wares were stacked high — copper pans, strangely decorated jugs and bowls, cane cages in which brightly coloured birds chattered and sang, rows of bronze fertility gods and a fish-tailed figure that Dookhi explained was the Philistine god Dagon. In every tent were displays of bracelets and jewellery to adorn the pampered women of Gath.

Dawid stopped to examine a silver armband in the shape of a coiled snake, with a single red gem for an eye, but Dookhi swiftly dragged him away.

'Remember why we're here,' he snapped. 'Show an interest in anything like that and these merchants will have all of our silver before we've even looked at any Philistine ironware.'

Chastened, Dawid followed Dookhi closer to the city wall, where the smiths worked in the open air. A crowd of Hebrew farmers was watching tools being fired and beaten while others were admiring a stockpile of bronze and iron implements, trying a sickle for balance, admiring the bulk of an iron ploughshare or haggling over the price of an intricate ox bridle.

'Come, friends,' said a gruff voice behind them. 'What interests you today? I have some fine mattocks that will till your land until it begs you to stop.'

They turned to see a short man with broad shoulders and thick, muscular forearms. His hair was oiled and tied at the nape, a leather patch covered one eye and a gold tooth peeped through a false smile framed by his beard. Dawid stared, wondering by what miracle a tooth could be gold.

It was Dookhi who replied. 'We need sharper tools. Our bronze blades blunt too easily and we've heard that iron is better for the harvest.'

The man raised a bushy eyebrow. 'Is that such a blade you carry on your back?'

'That? Oh, it's just an old bronze sword,' said Dookhi dismissively. 'For now, it's more important that we see your sickle blades.'

'Hmmm,' the smith said thoughtfully. 'I have a few, of both types.' He put a powerful arm around Dookhi's shoulder and ushered him towards a makeshift hide shelter that had been crudely attached to the city wall. Dawid followed. Inside, two boys in loincloths worked goatskin bellows beside a ring of stones filled with glowing embers. A third poked at an axe head half-submerged in the fire.

'Hotter,' the smith said sharply and slapped one of the boys on the back of his head. He turned to Dookhi, whose face was already reddening in the heavy air. 'That's iron in there, but it has to glow red before I can do anything with it.' Several tongs and a heavy hammer lay scattered on the earth floor, and around the perimeter a variety of tools for cutting, digging and chopping were stacked haphazardly.

'Which is best, bronze or iron?' asked Dawid.

'Depends what you're using it for,' replied the smith without hesitation. 'Iron is too brittle for my liking, although I know how to strengthen it, but then bronze blunts easily and sharpening it is like trying to teach a goat to sing. Better to recast it.' He reached for a sickle that lay among the finished tools. 'Now, this is iron. Feel that … but be careful.'

Dookhi took the sickle and touched the blade with his thumb. It was very sharp. Very sharp. If the sword was like that… He chose his next words carefully.

'Would that our men had blades as sharp to fight the Hebrews…'

The smith's jaw dropped, the gold tooth showing again. 'You're not Hebrews, then?'

Dookhi narrowed his eyes as if weighing up the man who stood before him. 'Hebrews by birth, yes. By choice, no. We have many followers who will gladly fight for you Philistines against our oppressors…'

'Which is why you bring a sword instead of ploughshares?'

'Yes, and more. We want to buy weapons.'

The smith took a step backwards. 'I cannot help you,' he said, almost pleadingly. 'We have no weapons this side of the wall, and even if we had I could not show them to you. It is forbidden.'

'Then who should we see?' Dawid cut in. 'Where can we find the armoury?'

This disturbed the smith even more. 'No … no,' he stammered.

Dookhi calmly lifted the wrapped sword from his shoulder and held it out like a peace offering. 'This was made by one of your people,' he said reassuringly. 'At least do us the honour of looking at it to see if it can be restored.'

The smith took the sword and slid the cloths from it. He studied it for a moment, peering at some markings near the hilt, then looked from Dookhi to Dawid and back again. 'This sword was made by one of Gath's smiths,' he said with a hint of suspicion. 'Where did you say you got it?'

'I didn't say,' said Dookhi firmly. 'It was made here, if you say so. We bought it from one of your officers for three shekels of silver. Now then, can it be sharpened?'

'Yes, easily.' The smith turned the blade over in his hands, studying its condition. 'But not by me. It's more than my life's worth to do this for a Hebrew, whether or not he wants to march with our army. I'm sorry.'

'Then where can we go?' asked Dawid.

'Into the city,' said a voice behind them. It was Mishon. 'Give the sword back,' he told the stunned smith.

'What were you thinking?' demanded Mishon as he led them towards Gath's main gate. 'I told you I could get you into the city, but you go blundering along on your own with questions that just arouse suspicion.'

Dookhi ignored him, wrapping the sword in its cloths and attempting to conceal it beneath his loose robe.

'So where do your loyalties lie?' asked Dawid.

Mishon stopped abruptly and turned to Dawid. 'Perhaps first you should ask that question of yourselves,' he said firmly, then put a finger to his lips. 'No, don't say. All I care about is that you come to my shop and see the fine cloths I have there. On the way, I'll show you where the weapons are kept and the blacksmiths who forge them. If you want to put your heads into a lion's mouth, that's up to you.'

Not waiting for their reply, he marched off towards the gates. Dawid and Dookhi had to break into a trot to keep up with him.

All three slowed as they climbed the earth ramp towards the gates, taking care not to bump into the numerous locals and visitors coming and going under the scrutiny of two guards, who carried short spears. They wore the same blue-plumed helmets Dawid and Dookhi had seen when they had despatched the four Philistines on the Socoh road.

Mishon spoke to the guards while the young Hebrews hung back. He seemed to be familiar with them, laughing as he put his arms around their shoulders. The guards casually looked across at Dawid and Dookhi, then nodded animatedly as Mishon slipped them some small reward. When at last he beckoned, they followed him through the great stone gateway.

The guards ignored them as they walked into the cooler air of an enclosure between the inner and outer gates. Here the walls towered to three times the height of a man, casting the approach into shadow, its paving stones worn and rutted in the narrow space. Dawid sensed that here an attacking force would be squeezed into a small area to be bombarded with arrows, spears and rocks as they faced a second gate to force open. But now that, too, was open and welcoming.

They walked beneath imposing towers and into a city far beyond the poverty and desperation of Beth Lechem's crumbling alleys or the simple life of Adullam's caves.

Gath was a labyrinth of stone houses and shops, not the precarious shacks of Judah's untidy communities, but squared stones chiselled by slaves to give each building solidity and durability. There were probably more people living outside in haphazard shelters and tents, but inside the city everything seemed different, organised yet joyfully chaotic. Mishon led them through crowded, narrow streets, past potters and silversmiths, weavers and dyers, and an old man playing a wailing tune on pipes just like Dawid's while a flat-headed cobra coiled lazily in his lap. Here was a new world, far more than he could have dreamed since running from Beth Lechem's squalor. He stopped to watch the curious snake, and out of the corner of his eye noticed something unusual about the movement all around him.

Or rather, a lack of movement.

While most people were hurrying in different directions, he sensed that two swarthy men had stopped in midstride and deliberately turned their faces away, pretending to study some large clay pots overlaid with intricate bird designs. While they weren't looking in his direction, Dawid studied them. Their untidy long hair and beards, roughly woven tunics, sword belts and heavy iron-studded sandals did not set them apart as admirers of the potter's art. Nor did the swords sheathed under their left arms.

The snake charmer stopped playing and coughed, and when Dawid looked back to him, he nodded towards a frayed alms basket. Dawid shrugged, trying to indicate that he had nothing to give, and glanced around for Mishon and Dookhi. He couldn't see them.

He ran to the corner of the street and saw them walking into an open square surrounded by several large buildings, far bigger than any he had ever seen, possibly palaces or temples. He looked over his shoulder to see if the two men were following; this time, they held his gaze and strode deliberately after him.

He panicked and sprinted away from them, clutching his shepherd's robe to free his legs, and called to Dookhi as he ran. His eyes prickled with sweat, but he saw Dookhi turn with a look of surprise, then Mishon. In that moment, he saw Mishon's lips curl in a tight, triumphant smile, and he knew they had been betrayed.

'Run, Dookhi! Run!' he cried.

Dookhi hesitated, seeing the two men who were now chasing after Dawid, then looked into Mishon's eyes with an expression of sudden understanding. He swept the Philistine sword from his back, tugging the concealing cloths free.

Mishon folded his arms across his chest and smiled, then grunted as Dawid ran headlong into him, both sprawling on the ground in a cloud of dust. His hands clutched at Mishon's hair and he spat and cursed, trying to find the traitor's groin with his knee. But he was not dressed for fighting; his arms and legs were tangled in his robe, and the pouch swinging around his neck hampered him.

Strong hands grasped Dawid's shoulders and lifted him off Mishon, who sat on the ground, dusting himself down. Still Dawid kicked and cursed, and spat feebly at Mishon, but he was held firm. He realised with despair that around them were more men — tough, fighting men with the same unruly beards as his pursuers, one of them carrying what at first sight looked like a thick-trunked golden mace. It had a narrow axe head at one end, and a jewelled globe at the other.

Gradually, Dawid relaxed, realising that escape would now depend on a silver tongue, not fists and a useless iron sword. The grip on his shoulders was unrelenting, but he twisted his head to see Dookhi backing away, holding the sword in two hands. In a circle around them, six expressionless Philistines held out straight iron blades, ready to deal swiftly with any further aggression. Mishon stood, flapping angrily at the dust on his tunic, and turned to the soldier with the mace.

'These are the Hebrew spies,' he said dismissively, holding out a soiled hand to a young officer who was studying Dawid and Dookhi carefully.

'They don't look like threatening enemies to me.' He tapped his golden mace. 'They're only boys, and they look like simple farmers.'

'Don't be deceived,' said Mishon, still holding out his hand as if expecting payment. 'They came to Socoh on fine horses, and I have heard them conspiring together.'

Trying to calm his racing heart, Dawid began to realise that the betrayal had begun with the greedy innkeeper at Socoh, Naboth, and probably his son.

Dookhi was a step ahead of him. 'We're here to join your army,' he said, without taking his eyes off the two men he faced, holding the old iron sword towards them.

Most of the Philistines laughed at this, and Mishon began to doubt that his reward was imminent. He moved closer to the officer. 'Look,' he began, 'you wouldn't expect the Hebrews to infiltrate your city dressed in armour and calling on the name of their god, would you?'

The officer looked into Dawid's eyes. 'So, farm boy, which god do you call upon?'

Dawid's mind raced. The only gods he knew about were Shemu'el's Yahweh and Rachael's Ashtoreth. He couldn't even remember the names of the Philistine gods, and he didn't like the look of this soldier with his mean, narrow eyes and pretentious mace. Neither was he sure that Dookhi's announcement that they were here to fight Hebrews would remain convincing for long. He made up his mind to win over this seemingly powerful officer.

'Tell your man to let go of me and I'll show you.'

The officer nodded to the soldier behind Dawid but tightened the grip on his mace in readiness. He was suspicious of the zeal he saw in the young man's eyes.

Dawid flexed his shoulders, relishing the prickling sensation as his blood coursed freely again. Keeping his eyes on the officer, he reached into his pouch, felt for the gemstone and allowed it to slide into his fist. He withdrew it, keeping his fist closed.

'Come closer,' said Dawid. 'It is a small god.'

The officer looked at his men beside him and, deciding that he faced no threat, stepped closer to Dawid and reached out his hand.

'Let me see,' he said coldly.

Dawid held his gaze. He moved his fist nearer to the officer's face, savouring the moment when he saw a flicker of doubt in the Philistine's eyes.

'My god is wealth,' said Dawid calmly. 'This should convince you to believe us.'

He turned his fist over and slowly unfurled his fingers. The large *sappir* stone, envy of the rich and powerful, shone with myriad shades of blue. The gold flecks in it winked a thousand greetings.

But the officer did not widen his eyes with greed. He did not shower Dawid with blessings and welcomes. He no longer wanted to hear a Hebrew farmer offer his services to the noble and powerful ranks of Philistia's armies. He only wanted to know how Dawid had happened upon a great possession that he had lost in the border regions of his patrol as a tax collector. He picked up the stone and held it before his eyes.

'You've come back,' he said to the gem. Then he looked at Dawid coldly. 'Where did you get this?'

'From the moon goddess. It is she who sent us to you.'

'And this "moon goddess",' he said, snorting, 'did she tell you how she came upon the Eye of Dagon?'

Dawid felt his bowels go weak. *Eye of Dagon*? Rachael had said nothing of this, but then why should she? She had torn it from her attacker as the giant held her.

'Do you know it?' he asked quietly.

'Do I know it?' the officer echoed, staring at the stone. 'It is mine.'

'Where did you lose it?' Dawid asked, his voice still gentle, coaxing.

The officer looked into Dawid's eyes and saw accusation there. He grinned. 'In the arms of a Hebrew maiden, as I recall.'

Dawid hit him, his fist flashing out, splitting the officer's lip.

Everyone, including Dookhi and Mishon, gasped in disbelief. The officer staggered backward, dabbing at his bleeding mouth. Dawid hit him again.

Then Dookhi's blade flashed in a great arc at the nearest Philistine, crunching into his knee, the cry of pain stirring the others into action. A sharp longsword entered Dookhi's ribcage from one side, and another stabbed through his neck. Bright droplets of blood sprayed over Dawid and his rapist adversary. Mishon ran away.

Dawid threw himself at the officer with a vicious, blood-curdling scream, but he didn't know if he managed to hit him again. The blow to the back of his head sent Gath and its soldiers into a blur.

He collapsed, unconscious before he hit the ground.

CHAPTER FIFTEEN

Dawid was woken by the pounding in his head. He opened his eyes slowly and thought he was blind because he could see nothing, so he closed them again. The pounding worsened. When he opened his eyes a second time, he thought he could see a dim light on the periphery of his vision, so he tried to turn his head towards it. He vomited sticky bile that made his throat burn and decided to lie still, trying to understand where he was and why his head hurt so much. He moved his hand tentatively and felt something large with numerous legs run across his arm. The air was humid and smelled of urine and sweat. A low moan outside his head told him he was not alone, and when he concentrated on the sounds around him he realised someone was snoring. Further away — outside, perhaps? — he could hear voices in muffled conversation.

Another wave of nausea churned in his gut as he remembered the shock on Dookhi's face as the blades ripped into him. Dead, surely. Nobody could survive that. He vomited more bile, gasping for breath, and the demons pounded with renewed vigour. If only he had kept quiet, hadn't tried to bribe the officer, hadn't lashed out at Rachael's rapist, Dookhi might still be alive.

He opened his eyes again and strained to see if there was light somewhere nearby, anything to chase away the horrible vision of Dookhi's face. There. No more than a faint glow, not much to focus on. He tried to crawl towards it and realised his right foot seemed heavy and ached. He felt for his ankle and touched cold, hard iron. It was not attached to anything, allowing him movement, but he was hindered by the weight.

Beneath it his leg was raw and bleeding. He pulled feebly at the shackle but immediately let go as a sharp pain shot up his shin to the knee. He remained still until the pain subsided, then crawled on until he felt something blocking his way, something soft — a body, perhaps? He poked at it and was rewarded with a gruff protest and someone's hand pushing at his chest.

'Who…?' His throat was dry and his voice sounded scratchy. The hand pushed harder, but there was no reply. He tried again, louder and firmer. 'Who are you? Where am I?'

'Keep away, snake.' There was no mistaking the menacing tone.

Dawid recoiled, and other voices nearby demanded quiet. He realised it was night, which explained why there was no light. *Why didn't they kill me like they did Dookhi?* he thought. He resigned himself to keeping still while awaiting the dawn; perhaps there were windows to let in light, though the fetid air told him otherwise.

A distant cackling made him jump, and the prone figure that had refused him help let out a groan. The cackling turned into some kind of song, a lone voice, strong and deep, though not tuneful. The faint glow he had seen earlier was growing, dancing on damp stonework and what appeared to be a large iron grille. The singing became louder and clearer with the strengthening light, the words strangely guttural but sung in the common tongue, repeated over and over as shuffling footsteps drew nearer.

'*Sleep my angels, sleep*
Dream your dreams while you can
For soon Gol-ee-yat comes
To bite off your balls
Bite, Bite, BITE!'

Dawid heaved himself to his feet, stumbling with weakness and the weight of the unfamiliar metal band around his ankle, and lurched for the grille, tripping over bodies as he went. There were howls of protest.

The singer was repeating 'Bite, Bite, Bite' as he neared, his lamp now revealing another grille opposite, behind which more prisoners languished. Dawid looked around his cell and saw at least ten others. He grasped the grille with both hands and shook it, realising it was a large door made entirely from iron bars and bolted from the outside. No one in either cell made a move as the singer approached.

Dawid peered through the bars as his gaoler came into view.

Melek hated everyone who was taller than himself, except his friend and avenger of life's injustices, Golyat. Even most children of ten winters were taller than Melek, and he hated them too. Some had made the mistake of goading him about his lack of height, and they had soon realised that the small can be quick and the ugly sharp-witted.

As he had aged, his shaggy head sinking lower and lower between his shoulders so that he appeared to have no neck, Melek had become increasingly bitter. When Gath's king, Akish, appointed him as gaoler of the city's scum, Melek took his chance and began a regime of cruelty that soon developed into a sport. He took his ideas to Akish, reminding him that the royal company of Invincibles, the huge warriors that won most of Gath's battles for him, needed to be kept amused and fit. The giants were bored with throwing spears at straw targets and in those times when there was no war, Melek had said, why not give them something a little more *interesting* to do and at the same time give the nobility and people of Gath some entertainment?

Akish had beckoned the dwarf to his table, popped a honeyed almond into his mouth as if he was feeding a tidbit to a pet, and asked Melek to tell him more. Gath's ruler had been so impressed with his little gaoler's scheme that he rewarded him with a golden girdle and a beautifully fashioned bronze dagger with a jewelled scabbard that hung like a battle sword at Melek's side. And he appointed him commander of his Invincibles.

Dawid looked down at the dwarf. By the feeble lamplight, he saw the gold sword belt and impressive dagger. He also took in the man's short, stocky body and the glazed eyes of a dangerous if inebriate opponent.

Melek's beady eyes looked up at him and saw his fists curled round an iron bar. With the speed of a chameleon catching a fly, he thwacked the impudent knuckles with his cane. The way Dawid withdrew his hands and shook them, then sucked at his smarting knuckles, delighted him. Melek watched him, hoping the new prisoner would offer his cane another target. Instead, Dawid stared back at him, his hands tucked under his armpits to ease the pain. Melek held the lamp higher to study him.

'You're the Hebrew rat they dragged in last evening, the spy.'

'I'm not —'

'Silence!' Melek yelled, and several of the prone prisoners in both cells stirred to watch. Melek narrowed his eyes. 'Come closer,' he snarled. 'Let me look into your eyes. Melek sees the soul. I can see the truth.'

Dawid obeyed, hesitantly moving closer to the grille and stooping as Melek glared up at him.

'Now show me your hands.' Melek had suddenly adopted a more reassuring tone. 'Hold them out. Let me see if they're a farmer's hands or the soft hands of a traitor.'

Thinking this might save him, Dawid held both hands through the grille, palms up. The cane flicked through the air, catching both hands on soft flesh. This time he screamed as much in frustration as in reaction to the fire shooting up his arms.

Melek cackled with delight. 'You like pain?'

Dawid backed off, cursing. Melek turned to goad the prisoners in the cell opposite.

'Ignore him.' A quietly authoritative and vaguely familiar voice spoke out of the darker recesses. 'He likes to cause pain. Just stay out of his way.'

The fading lamplight flickered across the form of a hooded man leaning against the wall. Dawid stepped over prone bodies and moved carefully closer. At that moment, Melek moved his lamp higher to give him a better view of his prisoners. The light illuminated the man's bearded face, and Dawid saw twin flames in his eyes.

'Welcome to Sheol,' said Elhanan.

After the shock, and Dawid's involuntary cry of surprise, the familiarity of Elhanan's presence calmed him and the pounding in his head stopped. Even the sting of Melek's cane eased. But the gaoler had heard his exclamation and now he heard words exchanged. He raised his lamp in his hunt for more victims. He saw how the youthful spy was engaged in an excited conversation and made a mental note that this one would need special treatment if his spirit were to be broken.

'Silence!' he yelled at Dawid, who turned, allowing the lamplight to play on the hooded man.

Elhanan looked straight at the malicious dwarf. The humid air seemed to crackle as Elhanan held Melek's stare and gradually, like a serpent squeezing the life from a rat, he forced the Philistine to give an almost imperceptive nod of respect and turn away. Melek shuffled off; his song resumed with less gusto this time as the lamplight faded.

'But why are you here?' whispered Dawid. He heard Elhanan take a deep breath.

'For you,' said the hermit after a few moments.

'Me? Why?'

'Because your destiny is here. In Gath.'

It was Dawid's turn to pause. He slapped absently at whatever was biting his ankle and his fingers brushed the iron bracelet, reminding him of his predicament. How could a shepherd boy's destiny be in a stinking Philistine dungeon?

'Let me explain,' continued Elhanan. 'I know more about you than you realise. I've always known you would be given something special to do.'

'You're beginning to sound like Rachael. She thinks I've been chosen!'

'Rachael?'

'The priestess at the Adullam caves.'

'Ah, given to Ashtoreth.'

Dawid wondered if he had offended Yahweh's holy man and decided to defend her. 'She's very...'

'Beautiful? It's strange how priestesses are always perfect to behold and Yahweh's priests look like camels with toothache.'

They both laughed, bringing protests from those nearest who were trying to sleep in such uncomfortable conditions.

'You say my destiny is here,' said Dawid.

'Not just yours.' The joviality had gone from Elhanan's tone. 'The whole of Israel's. And Judah's. Our people.'

'Oh, you mean the war. I was sent here to find out about their chariots and weapons.'

'Yes, yes. There will be a war. Maybe not until after the winter, the next campaigning season. There have always been wars, and there will be many more. But after this, none that involve the offspring of the Shining One.'

'The Shining One? I don't know what you mean. Is he some kind of warrior? I have heard about the giants of Gath, this Golyat and the Invincibles. Is he the one you refer to?'

As the grey dawn stalked hesitantly behind the barren hills of Canaan, Elhanan told Dawid about the coming of the Nephilim. How, when man used flints for axes and stone to till the land, the Great Ones had looked on the children El had made from the dust of earth and envied them. He told how they had come among men, chosen themselves wives, and got themselves children in their own image.

'The greatest was Abaddon, the Shining One, and his servants were the lesser gods Moloch, Anak and Kerek.' Elhanan's voice was a respectful whisper. 'These are the immortals, but their offspring are mortal, the children of the Nephilim. They were driven out of Canaan by our ancestors when Moshe led them out of Egypt. Now they are a shadow of what they once were, mere relics of a once-great race, but they retain great power.'

'So Golyat is more than a man, but he can be slain?' Dawid dared to hope that this might be the course he had been chosen to follow.

'If you can take the head of one such as this, you destroy him,' replied Elhanan solemnly.

'Is it true that they stand higher than a camel's shoulder?'
'Much higher.'
'And that they have the strength of ten men?'
'More.'
'Then how can they be defeated?'

Elhanan snorted. 'They are like a bear with an ant; they don't even see those they scythe down.'

'Then how? There must be a way.' In the murky dawn light, Dawid could see Elhanan's proud features. He saw again the wisdom in those young-old eyes, glowing like the embers of Gath's iron-smithing fires.

'With belief. Faith,' said Elhanan.

'What's that?' asked Dawid.

'You'll find it.' Elhanan tapped his temple. 'There. You can think; you have choices. The Nephilim don't.'

Dawid thought about that, and hoped that whichever god had chosen him, he would be able to use the gifts he had been given. 'How do you know this?' he asked.

'Because,' said Elhanan slowly, 'I have fought him. I have faced Golyat.'

Dawid looked at him with new admiration. 'Then ... forgive me, Barak, but I must ask...'

'Ask. I have no secrets from you.'

'You have fought Golyat and you are alive. Why didn't you kill him?'

Elhanan smiled. 'I will,' he said. 'Or you will.'

CHAPTER SIXTEEN

The pails were placed by guards outside the grilles of each cell, a signal for the despondent prisoners to find the resolve to face another day of Philistine cruelty. Both cells were so cramped that bodies writhed and tangled to reach for water and food like maggots on a rotten carcass. Grimy hands thrust out between the bars to scoop precious water and grasp handfuls of grey mash from the pails beyond. Dawid fought his way forward, slipping on filth, retching at the foul stench, reaching his goal only by elbowing an old man in the face to lever himself close enough to drink and eat. He looped an arm through the grille to maintain his position, using his free hand to scoop the dirty water to his lips and lick tasteless grain mash from his fingers.

When he looked up, Melek was watching him, tapping his cane on the palm of his hand as if deciding whether to lash out again. He held the dwarf's gaze. Melek grinned, a look that told him the gaoler was planning far greater horrors for him than a stick across the knuckles. Dawid heaved himself between the struggling mass of unfortunates to stand so he could look down at Melek. Slowly, deliberately, he extended his hand through the grille and held it out to Melek, palm up. Melek's grin widened and his cane twitched. Dawid held his hand still, daring his adversary to strike. The cane twitched again, a feint, but still he didn't move, his eyes locked on Melek's. The nearest prisoners watched, intrigued.

The cane hissed through the air, a whisker from its target as Dawid countered with the slightest of movements, still looking at Melek. He saw there the briefest flicker of disappointment before Melek regained his composure and began to turn away. Dawid kept his hand outstretched, knowing that Melek would strike again. The cane hissed a second time and again he moved his hand just enough to avoid the blow. The watching prisoners found their voices and cheered as Dawid grinned triumphantly at Melek, slowly withdrawing his arm to safety. Melek glared at him, then thrashed wildly at the hands reaching for food and water, silencing the celebrations and forcing the prisoners back. Dawid remained standing, watching Melek as the others cowered. The gaoler's angry eyes flicked past him and then widened in understanding as he saw the lone figure of Elhanan, sitting with his back to the far wall of the cell. Dawid followed his gaze and realised Elhanan had not joined in with the frenzied scrabbling for food and water.

'You should be careful who you listen to in here,' said Melek, still looking at Elhanan.

'I don't know what you mean,' replied Dawid calmly.

Melek turned his grey, calculating eyes back to Dawid and ignored the other prisoners as they reached through the grille for more food and water. 'I mean there's one in here who has ideas above his station. Now it looks like there are two.'

Dawid just smiled, knowing it would infuriate Melek further. It did.

'You won't be smiling when I've finished with you,' snarled Melek.

Melek smiled to himself as he stomped away to his lavish parlour to enjoy a pleasant morning in the company of his slave girls — perhaps a little pampering with aromatic oils, some wine and those delicious spice cakes.

He deserved it. Akish said he deserved it. The nobility and the people of Gath, not to mention the royal visitors from

Ekron and Ashdod, had all been delighted when at last Golyat had been defeated fair and square. Perhaps the people were tiring of ritual slaughter, the Bull God's club crushing skulls, his golden axe severing limbs and heads. How unusual to see a naked Hebrew man leap with astonishing speed and in the blink of an eye make the hits with his dye stick. Though what all that staring and chanting was about, Dagon knew — better be careful with these foreign holy men. *Yes, what the people want is more spectacle*, he thought, *more courage, more skill.*

But what to do with the holy man now? Set him free as custom demanded? Have him sent to the stone quarries? Perhaps that would be best, before he fed too many rebellious ideas to that cocky young spy. Ah yes, the new Hebrew youth. How he ached to teach the brat a few lessons, see him suffer in the arena, but … maybe he could use the lad's speed and cockiness. Why not give him the tiniest chance, feed him up, train him? Golyat would relish the challenge. He'd get him in the end, but not before the crowds had had their fun.

And Melek knew exactly the right man to whip the youngster into shape.

Uriah the Hittite.

The guards came for the prisoners that same day, just as Elhanan had said they would after witnessing Dawid's deft baiting of Melek, but not before he had told those willing to listen about the combat ordeals some of them would face. Like Dawid, many were new arrivals, but all had heard of the bloody spectacle that Melek organised on a regular basis for the pleasure of the royal court and the people of Gath.

'Is it true that Golyat is half bull, half man?' asked a young Phoenician. 'We have heard stories in Tyre that he breathes fire.'

Elhanan laughed. 'Do you see my hair singed and burns on my skin? No, he does not breathe fire. The fire is in his eyes. Is Golyat a bull? Are his brothers and cousins unworldly animals? You will see. If they are, you have dominion over all animals. Look at me, unmarked and unharmed. Now you know they can be defeated.'

More prisoners came closer as Elhanan spoke. Dawid sat near the Phoenician, greeting him with a nod, noticing the rich embroidery on his ripped tunic and wondering what fates had brought a wealthy young man to Gath's pit. Others sat despondently apart, deserted by their gods and resigned to their lot.

The ones who listened to Elhanan were mainly young and raw, though an older man with a grey beard and thin arms drew near. Not even Elhanan's faith could see a long future for such a frail creature. The old man knew what the others were thinking. He spat. 'I've killed a man,' he scowled, 'and I'll kill this bull man too. Save you a lot of effort.'

'Only a few of you will face the giants,' said Elhanan, giving the old man a warm smile. 'Most will go to the ore quarries, and some will remain in the city to drag the great stone blocks to build the walls and palaces.'

None wanted to know about the quarries: it didn't take a lot of imagination to realise that labouring under a hot sun and the soldiers' whips would mean a slow but inevitable death. Somehow Elhanan's calm assurance and mysterious inner strength inspired hope in them, lifting them above their despair.

He faced a barrage of questions about the arena of the giants and when Dawid quailed at his description of the Invincibles with their fearsome axes, he reminded them that their weapons were balance, speed of thought and self-belief. He was so convincing that Dawid and the Phoenician even laughed when he told them that the only weapon they would be given was a short stick, padded at one end, which was to be dipped into a pot of blue dye made sticky with pig fat. Always pig fat, said Elhanan, because they knew it was unclean for Hebrews.

'They hate Hebrews,' Elhanan emphasised, looking at Dawid.

'They don't like us very much either,' said the Phoenician.

'Well, you have something in common then,' Elhanan smiled.

When Melek and his guards came with drawn swords, whips and spiked clubs, they found a small group of prisoners sitting at the feet of the ridiculous holy man. He scowled, and for a moment studied the impudent young Hebrew, imagining the look on his handsome face as it was severed from his body. Then he looked at the others, sensing the energy and hope inspired by the Hebrew mystic, and decided that yes, some of these pathetic wretches just might provide the sport the Invincibles and the people craved.

Dawid blinked in the bright sunlight. Like the others in the column of twenty cowed prisoners, he had been stripped almost naked, his hands bound before him and his ankle roped through the iron cuff, allowing barely enough room to shuffle forward under the watchful eye of Melek and his glowering soldiers. All the prisoners were unshod, the stony ground cutting and bruising their feet.

Melek rode beside them on a richly adorned ass, his dumpy body cushioned in a high-sided wooden saddle under a goatskin canopy that lurched comically with the animal's lazy gait. He sucked noisily at pomegranates, targeting prisoners with discarded skins, chuckling to himself and occasionally breaking into a taunting song about the doubtful future of his sorry charges.

Dawid closed his eyes and thought of Rachael. He saw her laughing eyes and felt the light touch of her hair, the exhilarating brush of her lips on his. He saw again the mocking face of the Philistine rapist and hoped he had inflicted severe harm on him before he had been overcome. Slowly, agonisingly, the image in his head morphed into Dookhi; he could see the awful look of surprise on his face as the Philistine swords stabbed mercilessly into his neck and chest.

What lay ahead now? He was bound, hungry and thirsty, a youth among the crushed and the beaten, his friend's lifeless body no doubt tossed among carrion in a rocky canyon — yet he felt strangely energised, resolute. Was this the power of Elhanan's god, or Rachael's? Both, perhaps. Or merely his own indomitable spirit, honed by the years of enmity with his half-brothers and the injustices meted out to him and his mother.

This is the bottom of the pit, he thought, *and I can cope with it.*

He guessed Elhanan was somewhere near the front of the column. He could see the Phoenician and the thin old man further ahead in the line, but Elhanan had been the first prisoner manhandled from the cell at spear-point. He made his own choices as to where he wanted to be and why, and Dawid could easily believe that he had allowed himself to be incarcerated in a Gath dungeon simply to provide succour and encouragement to a failed Hebrew spy.

The column halted at a well surrounded by a few acacia trees, their discarded blooms a rust-coloured carpet on the hard ground. Near the well was a row of makeshift shelters, each with a large stone firepit where virtually naked slaves worked bellows to fire charcoal and ore. Beyond the furnace pits was a thick, yellow dust cloud and from within it came the unmistakable sound of hundreds of axes picking and chipping at a rock face, slaves scrabbling for ore to feed to the ravenous furnaces.

Melek urged his ass towards the shade of the trees and held out an imperious hand for the water ladle. The nearest soldier ran to obey the unspoken command. The prisoners watched as he splashed his face, the clear water running down his thick beard, twenty thirsty men not daring to move but hoping beyond hope that there was a mote of kindness in their hateful overlord.

There wasn't.

The ladle was refilled and Melek drank deeply. He belched, glanced up at the hazy sun as if gauging the hour, and looked around expectantly. For an age he sat under his shade while the prisoners and the guards stood sweltering in the heat, the sounds of picks and forge hammers merging with the softer rasp of overworked bellows and the hiss of hot iron being plunged into water. Savage flies feasted on the flesh of slaves.

The long wait was ended with the sound of approaching riders. Dawid willed himself not to turn his head to see who had dared keep Melek waiting, knowing that a whip or a cudgel would swiftly punish any unbidden movement, but he could see Melek stir himself to greet his visitors. There were two men, one dressed in a leather jerkin and breeches and riding a horse that was bigger and sturdier than Morning Star, the other flabby and well-groomed in a more traditional tunic with a ram's horn slung across his chest, riding a mule — probably a servant. Two spears and a long sword strapped to the horse's flank set the powerful-looking man apart as a warrior. He was young, probably no more than twenty-five, his trimmed beard emphasising his firm, jutting jaw while his head was shaved apart from a long strand of dark plaited hair that hung to the small of his back. He was muscular, his upper arms tattooed with intricate patterns, but he was also lithe and supple, at one with the animal he rode.

He greeted Melek formally and dismounted in one graceful movement, landing lightly on the balls of his feet as if the ground was privileged to receive him. His servant remained mounted, as did Melek. Dawid couldn't make out the conversation that followed, but it obviously concerned the prisoners as several times both the newcomer and Melek turned to look at them. They pointed at individuals, sometimes nodding in agreement, more often shaking their heads in disappointment. Dawid was convinced at one stage that they were looking directly at him.

Their discussion seemed to reach a conclusion and Melek impatiently waved one of his guards to the nearest firepit, where he stooped to wrap a cloth around the handle of an iron rod and withdrew it from the coals. The squared end, in an unmistakable serpent shape, glowed red. Melek laughed when he saw fear on the faces of the foremost prisoners. The guard knew Melek's preferred routine and walked briskly to the back of the line while two other guards took up station on either side of the first prisoner to be branded. None would see the hot iron as it seared their flesh.

'This is my mark on my property!' Melek shouted at the prisoners. 'Anyone bearing this mark who is found outside the quarry or the slave enclosure will be fed piece by piece to the fires, and you will watch your balls roast before your eyes are gouged out.'

The warrior laughed at Melek's fanciful threats. He, like the prisoners, knew they wouldn't have the energy to run, even if they lived long enough to find an opportunity to make the attempt. But most of the prisoners stared at Melek in disbelief, dreading what was about to happen to them.

'Do you hear me?' Melek asked more softly.

No one moved or spoke.

'*Do you hear me?*' the dwarf yelled.

Some of the prisoners murmured and some nodded, but Dawid stared defiantly at Melek and hoped that others would show the same courage. Their eyes locked, the moment laden with tension, broken only when the warrior strolled across the ground between them and stood close to Dawid. He looked him up and down, wrinkling his nose at the stench.

'Begin,' ordered Melek, and the first agonised shriek pierced the dusty air. Dawid flinched at the sound and the warrior calmly studied his reactions.

Desperately, he tried to recall how many were behind him. Was it three? Or four? He dared not turn to watch, knowing that Melek wanted any excuse to prolong his agony. Instead he held the warrior's gaze, determined not to show his fear.

Another scream. And another. Still youth and warrior looked intently at each other.

Dawid sensed the two guards move up beside him and tried to block out the whimpers he could hear. The men seized his arms and held him. His whole body tensed as he felt the heat from the branding iron hovering close to his shoulder, but he wouldn't let go of the warrior's gaze.

'Not this one,' said the warrior and suddenly the soldiers loosened their grip and the heat moved away. The warrior winked at him and moved to study the reaction of the next prisoner. The man was shaking and whimpering and wouldn't look at the warrior. Dawid saw the iron pressed onto the shoulder in front of him, the prisoner crying out in agony and trying to twist away. He choked on the acrid smell of burning flesh, grateful that it wasn't his.

A guard approached with a heavy chisel and mallet, and another dragged Dawid's foot roughly towards a flat rock. While he stared blankly at the blackened snake shape as it blistered the poor wretch's shoulder, two blows at the rivets of the ankle band freed him from the line of prisoners.

He stumbled as the guards dragged him away, looking back with disbelief at the horrors inflicted on his fellow prisoners. He was still watching as his bound arms were lifted over a sturdy post, just too high to free himself without assistance. He was left standing in dazed uncertainty as the guards strode back to free other prisoners who had been saved at the whim of Melek and the strange warrior — first the Phoenician and, surprisingly, the thin old man.

The branding was almost at an end. As he watched, Dawid realised that the warrior was talking to Elhanan while the soldier held the branding iron ready at his shoulder. This infuriated Melek, who screamed 'Get on with it!' at the soldier, knowing how quickly the iron would cool.

The warrior calmly held up his hand to stay the brand. 'Free this one,' he called to Melek over his shoulder. 'I can use skills such as his.'

Melek shrugged and spat. 'Train them well,' he said. 'They'll need all the help they can get.'

CHAPTER SEVENTEEN

The chosen four were left clinging to the stake while the warrior watched the depleted slave line trudge wearily into the dust cloud to give their lives to Dagon and Philistia. The cords chafed their wrists as four pairs of arms jostled for space, their bodies thrust close together, splinters from the rough wood pricking their chests and arms.

'What was that all about?' Dawid mused, looking from the calm assurance on Elhanan's face to the lofty contempt of the Phoenician and the indifference of the old man.

'Perhaps we have been saved from this just for something worse,' said the old man with a grimace. 'I don't care. There's nothing they can do to me that they haven't already done.'

The Phoenician gave a hollow laugh. 'I count two arms, two legs and one head — and you've probably still got a shrivelled worm with two balls. Maybe they'll chop them off.'

'That would be welcome,' snarled the old man, 'as long as they start with my head.'

Elhanan, who had listened to the exchange with his eyes shut as if in prayer, smiled. 'This is different,' he said without opening his eyes.

'What do you mean, Barak?' Dawid asked respectfully.

'I mean, when I faced Golyat before, they took me straight to the arena, a great pit that has been dug near the palace of Akish. Now we are outside the city. And this strange warrior is not like Melek, or any Philistine. He is not a man of the city, and I sense that he is not cruel like Melek either. Perhaps Yahweh has something different for us.'

'Or Dagon has, more like,' growled the old man. He was skin and bone, his cheeks hollowed by the ravages of time. His grey beard and what little hair remained was wispy, barely covering several black scabs on his skull that were testament to the rough handling of the guards.

'We'll find out now,' said Dawid, who was watching the warrior walk purposefully towards them, his servant, now dismounted, hurrying behind at a trot.

The others twisted in their uncomfortable bonds to see what fate approached them. The warrior stopped an arm's length before them, folded his arms and studied them. The corner of his mouth twitched in what might have been a smile.

'I am Uriah,' he said. 'Uriah the Hittite.' He spoke with the quiet confidence of a man who expected his audience to recognise his name, but of the four prisoners only Elhanan responded.

'From the land of the Hatti? You're a long way from home.'

'This is my home now.' Uriah eased a curved dagger from his belt.

'Like us,' said Elhanan easily, 'strangers in a strange land.'

Uriah looked from Elhanan to the other three, smiling at the old man's defiant grimace then holding Dawid's gaze for longer as he looked into his eyes for the second time that day.

'But unlike you,' he said slowly, his voice almost a whisper, 'I have my freedom.'

'And you have us at your mercy.' Elhanan commanded Uriah's attention again. 'Yet why do I think you are not going to cause us harm with that weapon you hold?'

'I am a soldier. I fight fairly.'

Elhanan held the warrior's gaze, but next to him the frail old man snorted. 'You want to fight us? Cut me free and I'll show you what freedom means.'

Uriah's blade moved so swiftly that all four were still looking at him as the old man's bonds were cut cleanly and dropped away. He held his hands before his wizened face then looked around in disbelief. He backed away from the post to which he had been bound, away from his fellow prisoners and away from Uriah. Then he turned and ran, making for the open countryside away from the squat walls of Gath and the stinking Philistine foundries.

For a few moments Uriah watched him. Then he simply said, 'Ishbi.'

The servant fumbled for the horn, raised it to his lips and sounded a single, clear note. It wasn't obvious where they appeared from, but suddenly they were there, cloaked and hooded men rising from behind boulders, crevices, whatever hiding place they had found, like wild creatures surging from their lairs to snatch their prey. The old man stopped, his freedom cut short as he was surrounded by ten armed warriors, each of them young and strong and certainly faster than he was. Panting, he looked around for somewhere to run. The ten men calmly removed their hoods and closed in on him.

The old man began to back away, back towards Uriah and his three fellow prisoners. Realising that he was trapped, he seemed to suddenly make up his mind and with a scream of defiance charged headlong at the nearest warrior who, with an economy of movement, simply stepped aside and tripped the old man as he hurtled past, sending him sprawling to the ground in a cloud of dust. Strong hands picked him up, pinning his flailing arms, lifting him off the ground then placing him down again facing the way he had come. The message was clear, even to a desperate old man who didn't care whether he lived or died. Slowly he walked back to Uriah, who was having difficulty suppressing his amusement. The ten warriors followed him at a safe distance.

Uriah looked him up and down. 'Old man, you left without the courtesy of telling me your name. Well?'

'Mut...' said the old man, still struggling for breath. 'Mut-Ba'al-Ishim-ben-Azni.'

'That's too much to chew upon,' said Uriah. 'Perhaps you'll allow me to call you Muti? It's much easier.'

Muti nodded.

Uriah turned to the other prisoners. 'I'm going to cut you free, too. And as I do, I want you to tell me your names as I have told you mine. In telling me your name, you are making a covenant with me that you will not run as Muti here did. Not now, not ever. Does this seem fair to you?'

They all nodded, including Muti.

The Phoenician's bonds were cut first. 'Habib of Tyre,' he said. 'Taken when your raiders attacked —'

Uriah held up a hand to stop Habib. 'I don't want to know about the injustices of your predicament. Just your names.' He turned to Elhanan. 'You I know, though I do not know your name. I have seen your skills in the arena and I have seen what little of your spirit you have allowed me to see.'

'Elhanan,' said Elhanan.

'Elhanan of...?'

Elhanan shrugged, then looked up at the sky, which was scored with an unusual pattern of thin clouds. 'There is my roof,' he said, 'and you and I share the same hearth.'

'Elhanan of Nowhere, then?'

'No,' replied Elhanan. 'Elhanan of Everywhere.'

Uriah smiled, cut the holy man's cords and then rested the knife on Dawid's, one eyebrow raised to form the unspoken question.

'Dawid, shepherd of Beth Lechem.'

'Why do I sense that it is you, more so even than Muti here, who will cause me grief? There's a fire in you, something that rages out of control, I think. You are no shepherd boy. Melek tells me you are a spy. Well, I don't care whether you are a shepherd or a spy. If you can control whatever it is that drives you, you will live and, who knows, perhaps even you can achieve greatness.'

Dawid looked Uriah in the eye. 'Perhaps, then, you can tell us why you have given us our freedom?'

'Oh, you're not free,' said Uriah. 'My men are your prison walls. They have orders to cut down any of you who strays from my sight or crosses the boundary of my encampment.'

'Your encampment?' Dawid was intrigued.

'Gath is too soft for my men. Hittite warriors look after themselves outside the city walls.'

'And we are going there? Why?'

'Because Melek wants something more than crushed skulls and severed limbs in the royal arena. The court of Akish demands a better spectacle. They want to see you slaves put up a fight instead of bowing the neck to accept death at the hands of the Invincibles.'

The word hung in the air like a gathering storm, demanding their attention, a stark reminder that Yahweh sought champions to fight the sons of Abaddon. Dawid looked at Muti's fragile frame then considered his own limited experience of warfare. He didn't know anything about the Phoenician's skill as a fighter, doubtless as limited as his. They would be relying on Elhanan, who in turn would be relying on the good fortune bestowed by his god Yahweh.

'You want *us* to fight the Invincibles?' Dawid was incredulous.

Uriah laughed. 'Yes, you're going to fight the Invincibles.'

The small group of prisoners, guarded on either flank by Uriah's caped warriors and led by the Hittite himself, approached the base of the white cliff that stood sentinel over the westernmost approaches to Gath. At its summit were the sheer walls of the royal palace where no invader could approach, commanding sweeping views of the coastal plain and the sea beyond. At the cliff's base there were more of the brooding black tents that nestled all around the city. Dawid could see the difference immediately: these tents were not the haphazard shanties of smiths and traders. They were ordered like a rank of disciplined soldiers, arranged immaculately around a square of cleared ground from which every rock and gorse bush had been painstakingly removed. A military barracks.

As they approached, a series of commands was shouted and men ran everywhere, taking up positions to welcome their commander or rushing to prepare his quarters. Dawid looked for soldiers of huge proportions but was disappointed to see none taller than average.

Uriah led his column past a weapons store containing tidy stacks of oval bronze shields, racks of spears and swords of every shape and size. They then passed the stables, where at least thirty horses nosed at shaded hayricks, and the biggest tent of all, in which men stripped to the waist were assembling chariots, carpenters were shaping and dowelling wooden parts, smiths were hammering iron rims, axles and bosses, and others were smoothing and painting. There were no women to be seen, and Dawid wondered if these soldiers were skilled in the art of cooking as well. The Philistines were very organised, he realised, because they had hired a small Hittite army — a far cry from the motley band of Hebrew hill farmers at King Saul's disposal.

The column halted beside a spring that burst from the base of the cliff, skilfully channelled by the Hittite engineers to form a drinking supply and a large washing pool. A system of clay half pipes took the overflow from the washing pool some distance to a roofless mudbrick building that Dawid guessed might be a latrine.

Standing in their own filth and sweat, thirst raging, the prisoners eyed the water eagerly as Uriah dismounted and murmured a few commands to his servant, Ishbi, who trotted off on his new mission. Then he looked them over, clearly offended by their stench.

'You can thank Dagon that I wasn't looking for clean volunteers,' he began, then smiling at Muti, he added, 'or good runners.' He looked each man in the eye. 'I have chosen well. In each of you I see many qualities, but chiefly this: you all have *spirit*. You have been beaten, but you are not bowed. You have been threatened, but you are not afraid.' Behind him the spring gurgled and splashed invitingly. 'This is your new home, and these men —' he indicated the soldiers who stood patiently in position — 'are your brothers. But make no mistake: if you run, they will kill you.'

Dawid tensed and stole a glance at the soldier nearest him. Beneath his cape he wore a leather jerkin and breeches similar to Uriah's and carried a short thrusting spear, iron-tipped, but no shield or armour. His beard was not trimmed as close as his captain's, but he had the same mane of dark hair, like the tail of a horse. Unblinking, flinty eyes were fixed on his leader.

'You are weighing him up, Dawid of Beth Lechem.' Uriah had seen the movement of Dawid's eyes. 'You are wondering if you can outrun, even outfox him. Perhaps. But he has brothers who will die for him and for me, each of them able to survive out there —' a lazy sweep of his arm indicated the inhospitable terrain towards Judah's hills — 'day after day until they have their quarry cornered like a terrified hare.'

Dawid looked down in thought. Perhaps the Hittite camp wasn't so bad after all? He had woken in a fetid cell, marched in bonds to the diabolic Philistine mines and narrowly escaped the agonies of a branding iron. Now his wrists were free and before him was the promise of cool, fresh water — but for what? Why were they here?

The answer to his unspoken question came immediately. 'The three of you will train to fight in the arena.'

Three?

All four prisoners looked quizzically at each other, then at Uriah.

'Elhanan of Everywhere has already fought with Golyat,' he continued, pleased that he had taken his charges by surprise. 'He was the first slave to question the right of the giants to call themselves "Invincibles". Therefore, he will be your trainer. When he has finished this task, Melek and Lord Akish will decide whether to set him free.'

Uriah gave them time to let his words sink in. Elhanan nodded sagely. Dawid looked sideways at the Phoenician and wondered if he was thinking about Uriah's definition of the word "free".

Muti just grunted and shuffled his bleeding feet.

The prisoners drank deeply, washed away the filth and teased Muti while they soaked their feet in the cool water. There were no guards to silence them, no whips on their backs and no bonds to bind them. A retiring sun turned the distant sea to gold.

Ishbi brought each of them a clean tunic, sturdy ox-hide sandals and four strips of scarlet cloth.

'Uriah says you must wear these at all times so you can be seen,' said the servant, clearly pleased to have men of lower rank than he in the camp. 'Around your heads. The penalty for not doing so is death.'

He pointed to the kitchen tent where Uriah's men swarmed around the great iron pots that hung on tripods over glowing embers. 'Uriah also says you can have what's left when his men have finished their supper. But no wine. The penalty…'

'Is death,' interrupted Habib, and Ishbi glared at him.

'There are also places you must never go, on pain of —' He saw the amusement on the prisoners' faces and quickly added, 'Well, I think you understand the penalty now. Do not go within a stone's throw of the armoury, and always seek permission — mine or Uriah's — to attend the kitchens. Over there —' he pointed to a distant copse of cypress trees well away from the camp — 'is the lair of the Invincibles. Only Uriah is allowed to visit them, and of course Melek when he is here.' A look of distaste crossed his face when he mentioned Melek, as if he had chewed on an insect grub.

'Anything else?' Dawid allowed himself an impertinent tone with the servant.

Ishbi frowned at him. 'You will have duties around the camp — cleaning the latrines, washing the cooking pots, mending and digging. You will be exhausted from your exercises on the training ground, but you must also do these duties without murmur or complaint. The penalty…'

This time he broke off and looked at each of his charges with a grin. Habib smirked.

'The penalty is not just death,' beamed Ishbi. 'It is a slow death.'

CHAPTER EIGHTEEN

'You will obey me, Hittite!' Melek raged at Uriah, who smiled back at the man perched on his high seat strapped to the back of his ass, the sunshade canopy flapping gently in the breeze. Five of his sullen guards stood behind their petulant lord and master.

The Hittite captain tried not to show the contempt he felt. 'But, my Lord Melek, with so little training?' Uriah glanced across at the four prisoners who watched the exchange from a distance. 'It is just seven days since you delivered these sorry wretches to me. How can you expect your spectacle in so little time?'

Melek adjusted the folds of his favourite blue and red robe and narrowed his eyes. 'Let me remind you, Hittite, that you are a foreigner in our midst, and I have the full authority of King Akish invested in me. You will present these men to the noble people of Gath at the Festival of the Long Day tomorrow.'

'And if they die like all the others, how many more will you give me to train?'

Melek rolled his eyes and huffed. 'There are plenty more stinking heathens where these came from.'

'These are not stinking heathens. Look at them. Elhanan has trained them well these past seven days and soon they will be as fit as any of my men. They are washed and oiled, and dressed to catch the eye. But they have never seen the Invincibles, and they have not seen how they fight.'

'The Invincibles fight like the bulls they are,' retorted Melek, 'trampling what they see before them. What need have you to show these stinking heathens how they will die? Besides —' he pointed at Elhanan — 'they have that wild hermit to tell them of Golyat's terrors.'

'They have trained with bulls,' replied Uriah with a confident smile. 'They have trained with unbroken horses, but bulls and horses do not wield clubs and axes. Is it too much to ask that they be given more time?'

'Enough, Uriah!' Melek screamed, almost tumbling from his seat, his cheeks reddening with the sudden exertion. 'May I remind you that you are here at the wish of King Akish and you depend on his good grace?'

The smile slipped from Uriah's face. 'Don't count on it, Melek,' he said coldly. 'I and my men fight for whom we choose.'

Melek hesitated; Akish would not forgive him if he provoked the Hittite into taking his men to another kingdom. 'May I also remind you that I am commander of the Invincibles and the king's appointed steward of his Games? You disobey me at your peril.'

Uriah's laugh was hollow. 'Games? Is that what you call your ritual slaughter? Here I am trying to help you make something more interesting, more *entertaining*, and all you seem to want is blood and mayhem.'

Melek stared at the Hittite captain, wondering if it had been a mistake to invite the foreigner into his planning.

Uriah broke the silence. 'It is no matter, lord Melek. You will have your spectacle. The prisoners will be ready for the Festival of the Long Day, tomorrow at the feasting hour.'

'That's better, Uriah. A little humility is a good thing, eh?' Melek smoothed his robe then looked again at the prisoners. *They have been treated well*, he thought. *That's quite enough advantage.* Perhaps he should throw in a few surprises of his own on the

Long Day, maybe snatch back what little hope Uriah had given them?

'Now then, Uriah the Hittite, show me this business with the bulls.'

Uriah had chosen well, too well, perhaps. Even the old man, Melek realised, with his death wish and comical running style, would lend something extra to the show. The Hebrew spy and the Phoenician were quick and athletic, helping each other with graceful moves that confused the old bull, even daring to somersault across his back, always just out of reach of his padded horns. Melek could see why Elhanan and Uriah had chosen the bull; all of his Invincibles were as ponderous as oxen and fed on the fear they invoked to wreak their havoc, whereas the bull (had he heard that insolent Hebrew spy call him "Melek"?) was quick to react, never giving his quarry any respite.

Melek quietly admired the way the old man would distract the bull while the younger two performed their fancy footwork, even to the point of tweaking its tail if one of them stumbled. How would Golyat or his brother Lahmi react? Three fleet-of-foot prancers against one lumbering giant might prolong the entertainment — that was good, but what if it didn't end in the customary bloodshed? The crowd might turn against him.

But Golyat and Lahmi together?

Now *that* would be interesting.

Uriah played the perfect host in the comfort of his carpeted tent. He gave a skin of his finest wine to Melek and had Ishbi carve delicate slices from a smoked ham. He told jokes that had Melek and his men slapping their thighs, and flattered him with praise for his elaborate plans to amaze Akish and his court.

But as soon as Melek had tottered unsteadily into the evening and wobbled out of sight on his absurd travelling contraption, Uriah let the mask slip and spat in the dust. He fingered the ivory hilt of the knife at his belt and wondered where it had gone wrong with Melek, why the malicious dwarf had amused him in the early days of his self-imposed posting to Gath but was now like a sharp stone in his sandal. Times were changing. No longer did he, Uriah, a warrior mercenary with impeccable credentials, take orders only from Akish, once a shrewd soldier himself with courage to match. Oh, no. Almost every day there was an incomprehensible message from yet another of the king's favourites, all power-hungry and all incapable of maintaining discipline and order in the face of an enemy. Akish was losing his touch. Especially with Melek's rise to power, first as gaoler and chief torturer, then as Captain of the Royal Guard and now as Supreme Commander of the Invincibles. It was a joke for such a cretin to have power over the most dangerous killers ever seen on a battlefield. Akish would have done just as well to promote the monkey he kept at the palace to amuse his concubines.

Ishbi poured him a cup of water.

'What do you think, Ishbi?' he asked the servant.

'Of Melek? Sweeter aromas emerge from the hole in my arse.'

Uriah laughed. 'Never mind that oaf. How will my chosen three fare against the giants?'

Ishbi had known Uriah for many years and was more of a friend and confidant than a servant. He had watched the Hittite soldier climb through the ranks first in the Syrian wars and then in the unrest and migration southwards that followed

131

the uprisings in the capital Hattusa. Ishbi was no soldier himself, but Uriah knew he was a good judge of men.

'I think they will surprise you,' replied Ishbi as he placed a cloth over the remains of the ham to keep the flies off, 'especially that young Hebrew, Dawid. I sense the mantle of Enlil upon him.'

Uriah raised an eyebrow. 'Marked by the gods, eh? It wouldn't surprise me. But he is raw yet, and hot-headed. Will he fight for himself or for his colleagues, I wonder?'

'You were once like that,' said Ishbi with a knowing smile. 'I remember when you were all anger and thunder. It never did you any harm. The others will draw strength from his courage.'

Uriah nodded. 'We all have something to give, if our hearts are true.'

'A cord of many strands is not easily broken,' quoted Ishbi as he refilled Uriah's cup. 'You learned that the hard way. You'll show them how.'

'If you ask me, it's such a waste of life. They'll probably be dead come this time tomorrow.'

Ishbi frowned at his master's pessimism. 'But if they live…?'

'…then perhaps Melek will let them join the Hittites.'

Ishbi snorted. Melek's dislike of the Hittites was born out of his jealousy of their undoubted skills as a fast, effective strike force. He wouldn't agree to anything that made them more likely to catch the eye of King Akish.

'Will there be anything more?' asked Ishbi as he stacked the copper plates and meticulously tidied the floor cushions.

Uriah sighed and walked to the small shrine near the tent's entrance where Ishbi kept a lamp burning at all times. He gazed at the crude stone statuette of his ancestor Hattusilis, whose right hand clutched a curved sword, though his left had long since broken off.

'I will speak to these unfortunates about what they face tomorrow. Have them meet me by the sacred tree.'

Uriah didn't take his eyes off Hattusilis, who stared blankly at nothing as Ishbi hurried away. He stooped at the shrine, dipped two fingers into a bowl and invoked the protection of Hattusilis as he dabbed his eyes, ears, nose and mouth with the holy water.

'Be with me, Great Father,' he whispered to the unseeing figure. 'Give us your light as we enter the darkness of Leviathan and the paths of damned. Grant your strength and wit in battle to these untried youths and that brittle old man Muti.' He bowed before his forefather's image and whispered, 'Selah.' He didn't know what it meant, but he had heard Elhanan use it and he liked the sound of it.

Uriah found his charges with Ishbi at the sacred terebinth that stood near a large muddy pool fed by the springs beneath the cliff face. They had donned their cloaks and were watching a pair of oxen enjoying a mud bath, wallowing up to their haunches, each with a mottled brown sandpiper cheekily pecking at insects between the beasts' powerful shoulders. The birds hopped about on the ponderous animals, snatching at their prey in the bristles and leathery folds of skin.

'Watch them and learn,' said Uriah. 'The oxen know they are there, but they cannot touch them. If the birds feed in the shallows they will be trampled, so they find the safest place to forage.'

One of the sandpipers hopped onto its host's head, the ox twitching its ears in acknowledgement of the passenger. Dawid smiled: he had seen these crafty waders in the river shallows near Beth Lechem.

'The giants are like these oxen?' mused Dawid, not taking his eyes off the lively birds.

'Not exactly,' replied Uriah. 'An ox does not come at you with the thighbone of an ancestor and a great golden axe. But beast and bird have learned to live together — unlikely comrades, would you not say? A delicate ox-rider and a terrifying beast. Most entertaining...'

'Then we are ox-riders,' laughed Dawid, casually laying a hand on Habib's shoulder. 'That's what we should call ourselves, the Ox Riders. What do you think, Habib?'

'Perhaps we should wait a while before giving ourselves fancy names,' said the Phoenician ruefully. 'I'd like to see these great oxen for myself first.'

'You will,' said Uriah. 'Tomorrow.'

Elhanan looked askance at Uriah. Muti grunted and balled his fists. Dawid felt his knees weaken and he suddenly wanted to urinate.

'You mean we are to fight them so soon?' he asked hesitantly.

Uriah averted his eyes and nodded. 'Melek is putting the word about that he has something special arranged for tomorrow's Festival of the Long Day, and that includes you. He hopes you will prolong the inevitable like these daring ox-riders, as you call them.'

Dawid watched the oxen as they moved away from the mud pool, eyeing the wild grasses that prospered nearby, the pair of sandpipers still balancing precariously on their unusual mounts.

'Tomorrow is as good a day as any.' He felt light-headed.

'A good day to die,' said Muti.

'No,' Dawid responded immediately. 'It's not a good day to die — it's a good day to live, whatever it takes.'

Elhanan eyed him with admiration. Muti grunted. Habib clapped Dawid on the back.

'I'm with you,' said Habib. 'We thought we were dead when we were thrown in that pit, and now here we are with new clothes, good food and clean water to wash with. Perhaps the gods are smiling.'

'She is,' said Dawid, thinking of Rachael.

They all looked at him suspiciously.

'She is,' he repeated. 'Ashtoreth is with us.'

The Long Day dawned under bruised skies, the gods arguing in low grumbling voices, the distant ocean black with menace. The air was thick and tense with a storm that would not break. No birds sang as the dead stifled the breath of the living.

Dawid awoke, wondering if he could defy the demons that made his head throb and his breath laboured. He peered into the gloom and saw Elhanan sitting straight-backed against the trunk of the tree, his feet crossed, his hands limp in his lap, and his eyes rolled to the whites as he communed with his god. Rival gods flashed their complaint across swollen skies, and in the brief stab of light Dawid imagined he saw the hermit sweating blood. Beside him, Habib thrashed at his nightmare and beyond Muti snored indifferently.

He wondered if he should pray and, if so, to which god. Had Ashtoreth chosen him to be her sacrifice in the lands of another god? He thought not. And Yahweh, the god of Elhanan and the prophet Shemu'el — why would he send a wild shepherd boy into the jaws of foreign gods and demons?

He drew a deep breath of humid, sultry air and woke Habib, who instinctively lashed out at his nightmare's oppressor. Dawid caught his wrist in a firm grip.

'I can see you're ready,' he whispered. 'It's a good day to live.'

Habib smiled, the night's shadows dissipating.

'I'm ready,' he said quietly. 'And the old man?'

'Still sleeping.' They listened to Muti's irregular wheezing. Dawid let go of Habib's wrist and looked across to where the old man lay, a threadbare blanket unable to disguise his fragile frame. 'A strange choice, but I think perhaps he will prove his worth.'

'At least we'll die laughing,' said Habib. 'Let's hope he'll confuse the giant with his antics…'

'And then we can strike swiftly.'

'Exactly.' Habib looked beyond Dawid to the stormy skies. 'The gods have something planned. On a day such as this, my people would say that even Astarte would hide from the thunder god.'

Dawid raised an eyebrow. 'Do you mean Ashtoreth? You know of the goddess?'

'Of course. How else would we have the finest olives, spices and herbs? She smiles on our people.'

'But not on you, Habib, a captive in a strange land.'

'Ah, but perhaps she sent me here. To keep an eye on you.'

Dawid grinned and punched Habib on the shoulder. 'You have it root over branch; it is I who have been sent to keep you from harm.'

'We'll see,' laughed Habib, fastening the red cloth around his head and springing to his feet. 'We'll see. Now, what's for breakfast?'

A fresh breeze from the north harried the storm clouds that morning, eventually pushing them south towards the land of Egypt. The sea recovered its sparkle, a thousand gems winking on the grey water, saluting the two young Ox Riders as Elhanan put them through a series of exercises, tumbles and somersaults, while Muti scowled and scratched his crotch.

Later, as the sun bathed Gath in a golden glow, Uriah led them along a narrow path that was clearly seldom used towards the forbidden lair of the giants, pushing aside thorns and wide-leafed plants that thrived in the damp at the foot of the cliff. They began merrily enough, only Elhanan brooding as he brought up the rear with Ishbi, but when they heard the distant sounds of workmen and builders, Uriah slowed their pace to a creeping walk.

The air seemed to go cold, and a sense of dread weighed heavily upon them as they clasped their cloaks tight and tugged their hoods over their heads. The unmistakable sounds of a busy community grew louder — the chink of chisels on stone, the distant whinnies of horses, the rasping honk of mules, the faint hubbub of voices and the barking of orders.

Uriah gave a signal to halt. He brushed at a thick cobweb and gingerly pushed aside the fronds that blocked the path, revealing two skulls held aloft on poles, gruesome guards silently warning off unwelcome visitors. Dawid craned to see around him, eager for the new sights that awaited him, hoping to catch his first glimpse of the giants. He saw none: there were many slaves, labouring under the whips and harsh commands of their taskmasters, none of them taller than average height. But the stone blocks they were manoeuvring into place with ropes and greased rollers were enormous, far larger than those with which the city above had constructed.

The men shouting the orders did not look like Philistines. Dawid studied them. Even from a distance, he could see that their embroidered knee-length kilts were unlike anything normally worn by Philistine men, who preferred richly coloured robes — these were white with blue edging, matching their head coverings, which fanned over their necks and shoulders. Their faces were clean-shaven, and they were bare-chested and dark-skinned, as if used to the fiery sun and the heat of the day.

'Egyptians.' Uriah had noticed Dawid studying the strange overseers. 'Men from the south. Their king thinks this city is worthy of their skills as builders.'

'What is it they build?' asked Dawid, fascinated by how a small knot of slaves could lever stones many times their own weight into position.

'A temple, though a fortified one. For the giants and their strange rituals. It will guard their entrance to the city. Look there, within the walls they are building.'

Uriah pointed towards a stone carving of a massive solitary hand standing near the base of the cliff, its height twice that of a man. Its palm faced outwards, fingers rigid in an unmistakable command to halt.

'Count the fingers,' said Uriah quietly.

'Six, including the thumb. Why six?'

'It's their symbol,' replied Uriah. 'I've never checked myself, but I'm told they have six fingers on each hand and six toes on each foot. In Gath they say the merchants get two extra shekels for every ten sacks of grain they supply to the Invincibles! But look beyond the hand.'

Behind the statue were three wide steps leading to the dark opening in the cliff face, the soft stone on either side shaped into smooth columns. Dawid could see no guards, nor could he make out what was inside the cave entrance.

'That,' said Uriah, 'is the Gate of the Giants, their doorway to the city. They have gone before us.' He looked at Elhanan, then into the eyes of each of the Ox Riders. 'And we will follow them.'

CHAPTER NINETEEN

Dawid knew he was in the presence of dark forces the moment he followed Uriah and Elhanan up the imposing steps and into the cavern beyond. No one challenged them; the Egyptian taskmasters ignored the column of hooded men as they moved into the darkness of the Leviathans.

It took a few heartbeats for Dawid's eyes to become accustomed to the dark. Flickering torches mounted on the dank walls gave scant light, barely enough to illuminate more hideous skulls mounted on spikes, testament to the power of the giants.

Uriah led them swiftly past what appeared to be an altar, covered with dark stains that might have been dried blood. He reached for one of the torches and held it aloft. A staircase carved in the stone by hundreds of chisels spiralled upwards into the gloom. The steps were deep and worn in the centre, as if they had been used for a thousand years. More torches gave meagre light to pale plants clinging to crevices, lizards darted to the safety of cracks and fissures, huge spiders retreated and the light danced in the eyes of translucent frogs and meaty toads. Dawid thought he could hear a drumbeat, then realised it was his heart pounding in his ears. He felt crushed by the heavy, doom-laden air that smelled of blood and rotting flesh.

The men quickened their pace as they scrambled towards a faint light that grew brighter as the air freshened, their hearts and spirits lightening as they climbed away from the baleful cavern. At last the feelings of dread dropped away as they emerged into a hall, shafts of weak sunlight illuminating an armoury of weapons, racks of thick, iron-tipped spears, embossed shields that looked too heavy to be carried by a normal soldier, an array of bronze and iron swords far larger than the one Dawid and Dookhi had brought to Gath, scaled bronze shirts the size of tents and a line of fearsome crested helmets. Here was proof that the legend of Gath's giants had not been exaggerated.

There was no one in the hall, though the din of a large crowd somewhere near drifted through the high windows. They heard laughter, music and the shrill shouts of street sellers. There were three huge doors, all closed. Uriah crossed the stone floor to a door with a central grille and rapped on the sturdy oak with the hilt of his dagger. A face appeared at the opening.

'Open,' demanded Uriah.

The guard looked suspiciously at Uriah through the iron bars and peered beyond him to where Ishbi stood with the four hooded prisoners.

'Unmask them,' he snapped, 'and show me your authority.'

'You are new here, soldier,' hissed Uriah. 'I'll overlook your insolence this once, but if you ever question the authority of Lord Uriah again…'

At the mention of the Hittite commander's name, the guard flushed and mumbled an apology, unbolting the door. It groaned open on strained iron hinges. Uriah turned to his small company.

'Hoods down and stay close. Ishbi, bring up the rear.'

Each of the four lowered the hoods of their Hittite cloaks, revealing the scarlet headbands they had been ordered to wear at all times. Dawid thrust his shoulders back and lifted his head proudly, bracing himself to re-enter the city that had betrayed him and murdered his friend.

But though the sound of the crowd swelled as they emerged, they could see nothing as Uriah led them along a walled corridor, open to the skies, past two more guards who saluted him by touching bowed foreheads, and through another large doorway into a walled courtyard. From the familiar smell, Dawid knew instantly that a number of unfortunate prisoners were being held nearby, no doubt soiling themselves in fear of what was to come. But he did not look for the source of the smell. Instead he looked into the cruel eyes of Melek.

The dwarf sat on a throne-like wooden chair beneath a leafy fig tree that clung to the courtyard walls. He had been in deep conversation with two powerful-looking guards, but now he broke off to study the newcomers, especially the young Hebrew spy for whom he had high hopes of a little sport before his body was carved up by Golyat's axe.

'Get those cloaks off and stand over there,' he commanded, pointing to a corner of the courtyard where there stood several pails of dye and a number of the short, padded poles of which Elhanan had spoken. Dawid looked at Elhanan quizzically.

'*Now!*' yelled Melek. They obeyed. 'And the shirts,' he added when he saw that Uriah had given them clothing from his stores. 'You wear only those stupid Hittite breeches and your pretty headbands.'

The noise of the crowd outside surged, as if something had suddenly attracted their interest above the acrobats and street sellers.

'It begins,' said Elhanan quietly.

Melek slid from his chair and barked orders at the two guards, then turned to Uriah.

'Have your slave daub them up in different colours. I will send my guard for them when the time is right.'

Uriah bowed. 'It will be as you ask.'

'It had better be good,' Melek snorted and stomped out of the courtyard.

'It will,' whispered Uriah, though a flicker of doubt crossed his face. Then he turned to Ishbi. 'Make them look like warriors, not fools.'

Ishbi, it turned out, was quite an artist. Using his fingers, he darkened the skin around the prisoners' eyes to make them appear larger and more menacing, then painted patterns that curved across half of their faces and down one shoulder and arm: Dawid's were blue, Habib's deep red and Muti's ochre. It gave them a demonic appearance that each admired on the others. Then, with black, Ishbi traced the outline of the giants' six-fingered hand symbol on their chests, filling in the shapes with blood-red dye.

While he worked, the Ox Riders listened to the crowd gasp and cheer at the deaths of their unfortunate fellow prisoners in the arena nearby.

They stood side by side before the solid gate with heads held high, each clutching a dye-stick that had been plunged into the blue pail. Dawid hoped neither Habib nor Muti would notice his hands shaking and the uncontrollable twitch in his leg. He felt sick and tried to take deep breaths to calm his pounding heart. In front and behind, their guards stood still, waiting for the gates to swing open to reveal the killing ground and the crowds craning to see more bloodshed. They were quiet now as the herald announced this new spectacle, organised at great expense for the delight of Lord Akish and his noble court, and the people of Gath. Dawid could only make out a few of the shouted words, but it was clear that Melek's endeavours were being well received.

Someone shouted, 'Bring us Golyat!' and for a while the herald was drowned out by chants of the giant's name. The noise petered out as someone must have ordered silence. Then a lone voice shouted, 'Show us the wretches!' and again the crowd began to chant, but the herald kept them waiting, allowing the excitement to build.

'Come on, come on,' said Habib under his breath. 'Let's get on with it.'

Muti was making a grunting noise and hopping from one foot to the other.

A horn sounded beyond the gate, bringing cheers from the waiting crowd.

'We … we are the Ox Riders,' said Dawid, fighting for breath. 'Remember the birds — always riding the ox. There are three of us. We can do this together. Daub him three times and victory is ours.'

The gate opened towards them, the din hitting them like a gust of wind. A mass of people were crowded above a circular sandy pit edged with stakes twice the height of a man. Around the perimeter were more guards, sombre in their blue crested helmets, spears pointed inwards as a deterrent to desperate victims. Beyond them colourful robes and headwear blurred the faces into one grotesque being, and the crowd's voices merged into one sound that jarred every nerve and turned blood to ice. Dawid forced himself to look beyond them, to the solid palace that towered over Gath, its whitewashed walls and terraced gardens providing a steady focus.

The herald turned towards them as the gates opened fully. He was tall and angular, dressed in a robe that fell to his feet, his hair and beard groomed and his hand delicately expressive as he invited the crowd to see what Melek had brought before them. He walked elegantly towards them, picking his way carefully between the dark stains in the sand.

Dawid realised what had caused the delay. There was no giant to be seen, so there must be another exit — somewhere to take the bodies of the victims — but here and there, lying in sticky pools of blood, were slabs of fly-infested flesh.

The herald flounced through the gates with a fixed smile and nodded to the front row of guards. Dawid felt a spear butt prodding him in the back and forced his legs to move forward. He sensed Habib and Muti beside him, trying to draw strength from them though they, too, must be feeling as helpless as he. He tried to breathe shallowly as the stench of blood made his stomach heave, but then, as the guards peeled away and left the three painted slaves alone in the arena, he felt a new sensation coursing through him.

The crowd was cheering them.

He lifted his head, allowing their praise to strengthen his feeble body and ignite hope. He glanced at Muti, who was scowling and spitting, still hopping frantically, then at Habib, who raised his dye-stick to a section of the crowd where several young women blew kisses and waved.

He left his companions to their antics and looked around the arena. The gates were closing behind them. So the giant would come from there too, he thought, but when? How long would they have to await their fate? He looked again to the palace and saw the nobles of Gath massed on the terrace nearest to the arena, picking at dainties served on silver platters by their attendants. They were pointing at the new arrivals and probably making wagers on how long they would last against the power of Golyat. One of the nobles would be King Akish, but Dawid couldn't be sure which one. He stole a glance at a small knot of women standing nearby, noticing the brightness of their sheath dresses and the flowers adorning their lavish headwear. His heart missed a beat when he thought one of them, a tall dark woman whose luxuriant hair was barely covered, was looking directly at him.

He turned back to face his more immanent fears and found that his heartbeat had slowed and his legs had found new strength, his mind refreshed by whatever power the gods had provided as they had entered the arena. He took a few steps towards the people above and before him. He raised his stick as Habib had done and bowed slightly, hoping the body paint and the renewed strength he felt would have an effect. They did, and the crowd's reaction fed his spirit.

Then the gates began to grind open again.

The Ox Riders turned at the sound. The crowd hushed.

Golyat was the same height as the gate, and Dawid could see his leather girdle, studded with iron, and his black loincloth, which could barely contain the hard thigh muscle beneath. Then Dawid's eye was forced to the warrior's head. He wore the mask of a bronze bull, horns curving forwards, more menacing even than their trusty training animal in all its fury.

All three of the Ox Riders stepped back when they saw what was being revealed — Golyat, in all his power. But more than that — not one, but two giants. Behind the golden bull stood his fearsome brother, almost as tall but wider, his head crowned by a wolf mask, his body, like Golyat's, oiled and glistening.

Golyat stood before them, larger than Dagon, more terrifying than fire-breathing Moloch. In his left hand was the thighbone of his ancestor, its top carved into a skull, iron spikes set into its thick shaft. In his right hand was the bane of Philistia's enemies, a two-headed iron axe inlaid with gold, the shaft bound with golden cords. Golyat grasped its hilt with a fist the size of a boulder. Behind him was Lahmi, his forearms already stained with the blood of sacrificial slaves. In one hand was a short thrusting spear, in the other a bronze sickle sword so large that anyone with less strength would need two hands to wield it.

'By Dagon's testicles...' said Muti breathlessly, backing up until his naked back touched the rough wood of the barrier.

Habib also backed away.

Only Dawid stood his ground, unable to tear his eyes from the magnificent golden bull's head.

'Habib? Old man?' he managed, breathing deeply, unaffected now by death's stench. 'Are you with me?'

There was no reply.

Then Golyat looked at Dawid. There was fire there, yes, and more. He saw the naked power of Abaddon, all the demons of Sheol gathered together, waiting to unleash their fury.

'*Habib?*' Dawid felt the giant's eyes sucking the spirit from him, but he could not look away. '*Habib? Muti?*'

At the back of his mind he sensed the crowd had responded to him just because he stood his ground. There was a sigh of anticipation, a murmur of approval. He took a step forward. The golden axe was lifted just a little, and Dawid heard Golyat grunt, though it sounded more like the geyser of Gaylen. He watched the movement of the axe and saw that it was slow.

'Ox Riders are fast.' It was Habib, and never had Dawid felt so much encouragement as when he heard that voice in his ear.

'We are fast,' Dawid said without taking his eyes off the giants.

'Perhaps we can divide them?'

'Perhaps. We need Muti to confuse them. Is he with us?'

'He is here,' said the old man. 'Muti isn't afraid.'

'Then run at them, but do not die, old man!'

Muti proved his courage by standing on one leg and moving the other towards the giants, then repeating the movement in slow steps, all the time emitting a haunting cry like an egret in the mating marshes.

'I said run at them, not taunt them,' hissed Dawid.

His words had no effect. Muti crouched and made a low moaning sound, his thin legs snaking out beneath his frail body in an unmistakable challenge to the giants.

Golyat took a step forward and Dawid was convinced he felt the ground shake, The giant's sandaled foot sent small clouds of dust into the air and the crowd gasped, then cheered.

Muti sprang forward with astonishing speed. His blue-tipped stick touched the appalling giant on his chest just above his left nipple, and the old man was gone in a flash, high stepping around the arena and soaking up the applause.

Golyat roared and raised his axe at the strutting old man.

In a flash, Dawid ran forward and ducking below the axe, aimed a blow at Golyat just above his girdle. It left a blue stain from navel to rib.

Golyat roared again as Dawid retreated with a little more dignity than Muti had shown, looking for another opportunity.

'One more and then what happens?' he asked Habib breathlessly.

'Will he retire, or will he try to kill us?' mused Habib, his eyes flicking from Golyat to Lahmi. 'Who knows. It's my turn next, eh?'

Dawid and Habib touched fists. The crowd was amused at this and clapped wildly, but the giants at last began their attack. Lahmi's sickle sword slashed in a wide arc that would have taken both of Muti's legs had he not hurdled the blade at the last second, while Golyat roared and aimed a savage blow at Dawid's head with his thighbone club. It hissed through nothing but air as he ducked. Dawid staggered back, off-balance, and Muti again threw himself at their opponents, aiming his dabbing stick at Lahmi. Golyat's kinsman deflected the old man's thrust more by luck than anything, and Muti sprawled in the dust. Lahmi couldn't resist the easy pickings. He raised his spear and aimed it at the frail victim, who lay coughing and spluttering.

Dawid's leap was just in time. Lahmi, distracted by the small Hebrew leaping straight at him, missed. Dawid left a perfectly round blue circle on Lahmi's chest and Muti scampered to safety.

Running backwards and glancing from one giant to the other, Dawid called out to Habib.

'We take Golyat out! Then we have only one to contend with.'

Now it was Habib's turn to show the bravery of brotherhood. He had no experience of battle, only the courage of youth, and he ran straight at Golyat. Somehow the giant had anticipated his move and his skull-headed club was already sweeping in a wide arc that would crush ribs, head, anything in its way. But Habib was inspired, his perfect leap leaving the fearsome club flashing through the air. A dramatic somersault took him almost to head height with his quarry, his dye-stick stabbing downwards. Another blue mark appeared on the giant's shoulder.

The crowd was delirious, screaming their delight. Golyat was defeated at last.

Habib somehow landed on his feet, but the club had not finished its savage arc. The thighbone flashed full circle and took him in the ribs, with a dull thud that Dawid felt almost as much as Habib. He crumpled in the dust. The giant roared at his triumph, unaware that he had been marked three times, and turned to finish his victim. He raised his axe high over his head, his aim obvious. But it was Muti who saved Habib, the old man leaping to cling to the axe head, his hands dripping blood as the sharp blade sliced at them. Dawid saw that Lahmi was now aiming his spear at Muti, so he leapt wildly, his dye-stick taking Lahmi in the eye at the same time as his foot crashed into the giant's jaw.

Dawid fell heavily, the breath thrust from his lungs.

The noise from the crowd was deafening, but Dawid heard only a ringing in his ears. He saw the iron tip of Lahmi's spear held just above his eyes. He knew that he was dead. He closed his eyes and waited for the piercing thrust.

But it never came.

When he opened his eyes, he looked into the depths of Sheol. Golyat. The giant had removed his bullhead helmet, and Dawid saw that his eyes were pale blue. He looked deep into the Hebrew's soul and the youth glared back, his chest heaving with exertion.

The crowd was silent, expectant.

Golyat grunted, and a huge finger took a smear of the blue dye from his chest. He touched Dawid on his forehead.

'Warrior.'

His voice was deeply resonant and the finger had pressed with astonishing strength, snapping Dawid's head backwards.

'Warrior,' the giant repeated.

CHAPTER TWENTY

Muti's hands were bandaged and he was unable to eat or hold the wine cup to his lips. Habib was stiff and unsteady with several broken ribs. The Ox Riders sat around the crackling fire in the Hittite camp, where Dawid begged one of Uriah's musicians to lend him a reed pipe. Hesitantly at first, but then with more gusto as the wine freed his fingers and his lungs, Dawid found the right notes to match the deeper rams' horns and the goatskin drums that the Hittites favoured.

Uriah beamed his pleasure while Melek, uncomfortable among these foreigners, scowled. The ambitious dwarf had at first been fearful that the unlikely victory in the arena would end his dramatic rise to power, but then as he had soaked up the wild applause and had later been congratulated by King Akish, Melek had grudgingly accepted that popular entertainment in Gath had taken a turn for the better. Now he sat at Uriah's left hand under a lavish canopy before the fire and accepted all the traditional Hittite morsels — except those ghastly honeyed locusts — and wondered where his foresight and cunning would take him next.

'Lord Uriah...' His use of the title got the heathen commander's attention, as he had intended. Uriah turned to him with one eyebrow raised. 'I was wondering, how long until these ... these *slaves* ... are recovered and ready to take to the arena again?'

Uriah shrugged. 'They are young — well, two of them are — and will recover swiftly. The old man may not ever be able to perform again.'

'A shame. He was my favourite. Such courage, such madness.'

'Indeed. He surprised us all.'

'We need more like him, like these youths too.'

Uriah frowned. He thought he could see where Melek was leading the conversation.

'There are young men in Gath who are goaded by their fancy women to do the same, but I think that Akish would never allow it.'

Uriah was thoughtful. 'If your young nobles wish to try their hand against the giants, why not? It will give them valuable experience for the wars that your people expect when the year turns...'

'And your men, perhaps?'

Uriah shook his head. 'No. Not my men. They are warriors who follow me into battle. They do not seek the hero worship of Gath's giggling women.'

'Ha. Everyone seeks that, unless they are women themselves.'

Uriah laughed, but Melek's words had troubled him. 'My doctors will have your Ox Riders fit and ready within ten days. Look to them, and any other slaves you want to give me, but not to my men.'

'Ox Riders? What is this? And ten days?' Melek laid a hand on Uriah's shoulder and didn't notice the Hittite shudder involuntarily. 'Ten days is too long. Akish wants more, and he wants me to bring the slaves to court. His daughter Lalia and the noblewomen demand it. I think our little endeavour has pricked their fancy.'

'To answer your first question, they call themselves the Ox Riders because you give them only a dye stick to face cruel weapons of war, and still they win — by pecking at the great oxen. To answer your second, look at them. Why not show the Ox Riders to your nobles in their bandages, to show how courage can overcome any disadvantage?'

Melek ripped the tasty flesh from a mutton foreleg and chewed thoughtfully, waving the stripped bone in a circle before him. 'You know, Uriah, you are right.' A dribble of grease lodged in his beard. 'I think I will give you two days. I will send my messenger. And I will expect them to fight again in seven days.'

He spat out a glob of gristle and fat.

'Have them ready,' added Melek with a twisted smile. 'Now, let's drink to the … Ox Riders, did you say?'

'To the Ox Riders,' agreed Uriah, lifting his cup. 'May they always surprise us.'

When Melek had gone, Uriah commanded Ishbi to bring ritual offerings. Ishbi busied himself rolling five balls of beeswax and mutton fat the size of pomegranates and then summoned the Ox Riders and Elhanan.

'Come,' said Uriah, standing as they approached, 'feed the gods of the fire with me.'

He beckoned to Ishbi, who carried a copper tray laden with his five offerings. Uriah took one of the balls and held it to the stars.

'May the gods do thus to me and more, if I do not keep my word to my friends, Dawid, Habib, Muti and Elhanan.' He tossed the ball of fat and wax into the fire, where it spat and sizzled with surprising brightness. 'May my limbs turn to wax and my heart be consumed by fire if I do not hold them in honour and give them my sword.' He turned to Habib. 'Can you swear?'

Habib took one of the balls and tossed it into the fire. 'I so swear. You have my daubing stick to command as you please!'

Uriah was delighted. Ishbi seemed fearful at the irreverence, but then he too laughed nervously.

'Muti?'

The old man took one of the offerings. He held it up to the moon and muttered an indecipherable prayer, then threw it into the fire.

'I'll take that as your pledge,' said Uriah with a twinkle in his eye. 'Dawid?'

Dawid took the fat in his hand and cupped it with the other. 'Uriah,' he said carefully, 'you are not a slave master, you are a friend. When your enemies prevail, you will always find me at your side, even unto death.' He tossed the ball into the fire without taking his eyes from Uriah's.

Dawid turned to Elhanan, who was looking at him with an unfamiliar intensity.

'That is a solemn oath,' said the hermit. 'I trust you will do as you say, for you do not yet see the way ahead.' He shook his head sorrowfully and turned away, breathing deeply. Then he swivelled and looked at Uriah, his eyes catching the starlight. 'These three have given you their lives, have promised to stand with you even when you come to the very gates of Sheol,' he said solemnly. 'That I cannot do.'

Uriah nodded slowly, understanding on his face. 'Then what will you do, man of Yahweh?'

Elhanan shrugged. 'I am your man, by the command of the Philistines.'

'No, Elhanan, you are not. You are your own man. You have done all that was asked of you, and more.'

'And now?'

'Return to your people, and your god.'

Elhanan looked at his three charges, searching their souls for the true purpose of their presence among the Philistines. He took the remaining ball of wax and fat and handed it to Dawid.

'You make another oath,' he whispered, almost inaudibly. 'Decide between the many gods of these uncertain days, and choose whom you serve. And when the darkness comes and the sun is extinguished at the height of the day, you will find me and your eyes will be opened.'

Dawid tossed the fat ball into the flames and a blue flame leaped to the height of a man, before dying down to crackle and spit. 'I give myself to the god of my friend, Barak,' he mumbled.

Elhanan saw Dawid's uncertainty in the glow of the flames and knew that the youth he loved would always waver when faced with spiritual choices. He embraced Dawid firmly. Then he turned and without a glance behind him, walked into the darkness.

'Barak,' mouthed Dawid as Elhanan walked away. 'Barak...'

His sense of desolation was almost unbearable, but he breathed deeply and realised that if he was to survive in this world, he must not depend on the likes of Elhanan, Nathan, Rachael or Uriah. He had been chosen by Ashtoreth, and before that Yahweh — if Shemu'el and Elhanan were to be believed — and now he was in the realm of another god, Dagon, and the giant offspring of The Shining One, enemies of Israel.

Were there really any gods? Or was his destiny in his own hands?

Dawid let the wine blur his mind and chose to wait for the evidence to appear. Until then, he would trust in his own ability, which had been proved beyond doubt with the defeat of Golyat and Lahmi.

His mother would be proud of him.

The chariots entered the twin gates of Gath to tumultuous acclaim. Everywhere Dawid looked there was a sea of faces and the same buffeting noise that he had experienced in the arena. He stood beside Uriah, one hand gripping the ornately carved chariot, the other waving to admirers crowded on the walls and lining the streets.

Once inside the city, the route to the palace was direct, as the chariots carrying Golyat and Lahmi were so large that only the wide street that led up to the palace could take them. They passed the houses of the wealthy and the great temple of Dagon, where even the priests acknowledged the new heroes and the temple prostitutes momentarily lost their composure.

Uriah's charioteer was skilled, a squat Hittite with powerful shoulders who constantly calmed the horses with a deep voice, interspersed with shrill whistles that made them lift their proud heads and prick up their ears. Behind Uriah and Dawid came Ishbi's chariot carrying Muti, his injured hands and forearms bandaged. He was steadied by Habib, himself stiff and awkward from the battering he had received from Golyat's club. But his discomfort did not stop him soaking up the crowd's praise as Muti growled at his side.

Behind the Hittite chariots came two of the great war machines of Gath. The Ox Riders had gaped in awe when Golyat and Lahmi had arrived at the Hittite camp in their immense chariots, and Dawid had immediately understood the military might these warriors brought to the Philistine army. Like the Hittite chariots, these were built to carry three men and an array of arms that such immense warriors would use in battle, though as today was a state visit, none were to be seen. But what Dawid could barely imagine was the havoc such chariots and their powerful horses would cause if they were ever ridden at speed towards an enemy's front line. They would crush everything in their path, bringing demoralisation and bloody chaos without anyone needing to raise a spear or sword.

Now Golyat and Lahmi rode at a sedate pace in the majestic column, dressed in linen tunics bearing an embroidered six-fingered hand symbol, their heads covered in white turbans of peace. The crowds stepped back into doorways and alleyways to allow them to pass, mothers ushering their children out of harm's way as the great iron-rimmed wheels groaned solidly by.

The procession entered a wide square before the palace gardens, bordered by the royal barracks and beyond them Gath's hideous arena of death. Melek was there to greet the delegation, though even from a distance Dawid could sense that the city's favourite dwarf was scowling. He sat on his ass's high saddle under a new canopy of purple cloth decorated with silver braid, flicking imperiously at persistent flies with a horsehair swish stick, a dozen of his armed guards standing in an orderly line behind him.

Uriah motioned for Dawid to dismount. Ishbi jumped clumsily from his chariot and followed the Hittite commander, with him Muti and Habib, and together they walked proudly towards the palace gates, ignoring Melek and his guard of honour. For within the lush grounds was King Akish of Gath and his own guard, which was far more resplendent than Melek's.

Glancing over his shoulder, Dawid saw the huge turbaned figures of Golyat and Lahmi lingering at a distance, for once not the centre of attention. Perhaps Gath was becoming bored with these behemoths.

The commander of the king's guard took several paces forward and challenged the guests with ferocious words that carried no venom: tradition and common practice, Dawid thought. Uriah answered with a magnificent explanation that here were the Invincibles under the command of Lord Melek and the triumphant challengers to their invincibility, the humble Ox Riders from countries as far afield as Judah, Phoenicia and... He realised he didn't know where Muti hailed from, so he improvised. 'From beyond the Great River,' he announced, hoping that nobody would question which river he meant.

'We welcome you, Hittite,' said Akish graciously, stepping forward with his arms held wide in greeting. 'And we welcome these warriors whose courage has at last overcome the Great Ones.'

Akish was everything Dawid had expected in a king. He looked about forty years old and was not adorned with extravagant robes and jewels, but he carried himself with the poise and purpose of a man with authority. His hair was shoulder-length and had been oiled and plaited. Dawid watched him, studying his gestures and bearing. He found himself involuntarily mimicking the way he lifted his chin when he spoke, the casual twist of his wrists, the pursing of his lips and the raising of his eyebrows to emphasise his welcome. So focused was he on the King of Gath that for a few heartbeats Dawid didn't notice Gath's powerful men, the chancellors and nobles, captains and ministers, and beyond them the women of the court. When he did look beyond the king, he saw again the tall, striking woman he had noticed before his encounter with the giants. He saw that familiar haughtiness in one who had been taught to subdue emotion, her expression dispassionate and remote.

Standing slightly behind her was a girl with wide eyes, as engaged as her superior was remote, her rebellious hair refusing to be constrained by the hood of her simple cloak. Dawid realised that both were looking directly at him, but the servant shone with an enthusiasm her mistress clearly didn't feel.

He felt a tug on his sleeve. 'Do exactly as I do,' Uriah was saying, snatching Dawid's attention from the intriguing women of Gath's court, 'and say nothing unless you are commanded to speak. Make sure you pass that on to the others.'

Habib heard Uriah's commands. 'Which way to the harem?'

Dawid suppressed his amusement and noticed that Muti for once seemed to be about to laugh. Uriah silenced Habib with a glare.

The Hittite commander strode forward, the Ox Riders following obediently, and they knelt before the king to clasp the hem of his robe. It was pure ceremony, Dawid thought, and told himself that he would do the same, hoping that Muti and Habib would have the sense to do likewise. While he waited his turn for ritual obeisance, Dawid glanced around at the magnificent palace and terrace gardens, noticing that a detail of around twenty slaves was working on a tower not far beyond the courtiers, overseen by one of the Egyptian taskmasters as they positioned stones that had been lifted using a sturdy tripod and ropes. Three of the slaves were hauling an ox-hide bulging with stones, easing it slowly upwards to the platform where they worked.

Dawid knelt before Akish and touched his hem in the same way as he had seen Uriah perform the Philistine ritual. But his thoughts were racing. He hesitated at the feet of the king, closed his eyes and examined the image in his mind: weakened, sweaty slaves, their bodies streaked with grey dust, their laboured movements, their faces etched with hate and hopelessness. Probably Hebrews. They obeyed the commands of these colourful people and the rich, demanding king whose hem he now clutched in homage. He realised how thin was that line that set him and his Ox Riders apart from those miserable wretches and determined that never again would he bow the knee to a Philistine, be he the King of Gath or the gaoler Melek.

Dawid was still kneeling when Habib tugged his sleeve. The king had gone, his courtiers and his attendants strolling casually towards the palace, the women following dutifully. He looked blankly at Habib and Muti, and then at Golyat and Lahmi, who stood tall and detached behind them, arms folded, patient.

'We're meant to follow,' said Habib. 'Are you all right?'

Dawid nodded and glanced again at the slaves high on the wall, heaving their precarious load. The taskmaster had resorted to using his whip as the ox-hide snagged on a protruding stone below them. The renewed efforts of the slaves freed it, and once again it edged towards their platform. Only Dawid noticed the tear in the ox-hide.

The Ox Riders hurried to catch up with the entourage, the tall, haughty woman and her lively servant girl not far ahead, their two guards keeping pace on either side.

The Egyptian's whip snaked out again, too far above them for anyone in the royal train to notice, but Dawid saw it. He saw the red welts on a slave's shoulders, the flash of anger on his face, the redoubled effort as the load jerked free from another hindrance. He heard the sound of ripping leather as the tear widened, felt the strain of rope and pulley and sensed that inevitable moment when the gods would intervene in the lives of mortal men.

Without thinking, he rushed forward and careened into the tall woman, his right arm gathering the smaller servant as he flew into them. Both shrieked with surprise as they fell into the bushes that lined the palace path. The nearest faces turned in shock and outrage, then watched with horror as the stones fell around them, instantly crushing the skull of one of the guards. A cloud of dust enveloped the confused and terrified courtiers.

Dawid didn't feel any pain, only the whistling in his skull as he passed out.

CHAPTER TWENTY-ONE

The voices sounded distant and Dawid couldn't make out what was being said. He opened his eyes slowly. The room was dark; it was not a tent, so he assumed he had not been taken back to the Hittite camp. Was he in the palace? He lay on something soft, more comfortable than any bedding he had known, and he could make out the silhouette of two people in conversation near a large window shrouded by drapes that moved gently in the late summer breeze. He tried to move and grunted when a sharp pain shot across his shoulders. The voices stopped and both heads turned towards him. In the gloom, he made out the portly figure of Ishbi, but he didn't recognise the other man.

'At last, the patient stirs,' said Ishbi, crossing the room to Dawid's bedside.

He tried to speak, but the effort made the pain worse.

'Lie still and say nothing,' said the second man, who had ambled over. He was old. There was more hair in his nostrils and ears than on his head, and Dawid immediately saw through the grumpy expression on the man's lined face.

Ishbi made the introduction. 'This is the king's personal doctor,' he said. 'You are in good hands.'

The doctor huffed and scowled, which made Dawid attempt a smile. He put a shaking hand on the patient's brow and grunted. 'The fever has gone,' he pronounced and prodded Dawid's shoulder. This time the pain shot through his chest and he winced.

The doctor turned to Ishbi and spoke to him as though Dawid wasn't there. 'You were right to believe he would live. I have not seen this in one who bleeds from the mouth. He is not to be moved, and I fear he will find it hard to eat.'

'I doubt he can move with his legs strapped,' said Ishbi, and Dawid realised that he couldn't move his legs. He wasn't even sure he could feel them.

'We should try to give him food,' said the doctor as Dawid tried to speak. 'Bring some broth from the kitchens. He is very weak after so long without nourishment.'

'What...' Dawid eventually managed, halting Ishbi, who was leaving to obey the doctor's command. 'What happened?'

Ishbi turned to him and smiled. 'It all happened so fast. I saw you throw yourself at the king's daughter like a demented bull, but before anyone could react there were stones and rocks falling right on the spot where she and her servant had stood. They fell on you in their place. They would have been killed, the Princess Lalia...' His voice trailed off, as if the consequences were too awful to think about, then he added, 'You, young man, are a hero.'

The doctor frowned and tugged rudely at Ishbi's sleeve. 'Go, get some broth.'

Ishbi obeyed, casting a happy glance over his shoulder as he left.

'What about my legs?' Dawid asked the doctor, wincing at the effort. 'Why can't I move them?'

'One is broken,' replied the doctor, as if it was nothing. 'I have strapped both together with a splint between them so the bones can mend, but you have so many cuts and bruises that the dressing will have to be changed.'

'Honey and thyme,' muttered Dawid through the pain.

'What?' The doctor looked confused.

'Honey and thyme,' he repeated. 'Stops infection. Ask the priestess.'

'Priestess?'

Dawid realised his thoughts were in rebellion and Rachael, Sparrow and Ashtoreth were in another place and another time. He slowly moved his head and looked around, taking in the sight of a familiar silver pendant, a six-pointed star hanging by a leather thong that had been hooked over the back of the chair next to his bed.

'What is that?' Dawid indicated the star with his eyes.

'That?' The doctor reached for the thong and held up the star. 'This is the Star of Anak. A gift from one of your visitors.'

'Golyat?' Dawid whispered the name.

'The giant, yes. I think he likes you. You have had many well-wishers — your fellow warriors, the princess and her father — but the giant stayed longest.'

'Why did he leave the star?'

The doctor watched the star as the heavy silver amulet twisted before them. It was a simple design, two solid triangles overlaid to form six points.

'I am a doctor — to me it is just a trinket, though surely a valuable one. But to them it is the symbol of their ancestors.'

He was still studying its crude workmanship when Ishbi returned, carrying a bowl of steaming broth. The rich aroma made Dawid realise much of his pain was caused by a ravenous hunger. He forgot about the Star of Anak as the doctor helped to raise his head onto a firm cushion to enable Ishbi to feed him more easily.

'Word is out,' said Uriah's servant. 'I have told them in the kitchens that you are yet weak, but I think you can expect visitors soon.'

'Is he going to live?'

Dawid heard a young woman's voice at the door — gentle and enticing, like morning rain. The pain as he lifted his head was worth it. He took in the wide, inquisitive eyes of the servant girl, her freckled face framed by dark hair as she peered into the room. And behind her was the tall, aloof woman, presumably this princess of whom Ishbi had spoken, but now she was not so aloof and he could see what he hoped was concern in her expression.

The doctor and Ishbi bowed.

'He will live, noble lady,' said the doctor, ignoring the servant's question as he looked to the princess, 'but he will be a long time in my care.'

Absently, Dawid stored the thought that he might be trapped in an unfamiliar palace among Israel's enemies and studied the two women, so different in appearance and aura. There was no denying the princess was striking — tall and thin, her body sheathed in a shimmering ankle-length garment that was unlike anything worn by Hebrew women. Her braided hair was unusually short, her silver bracelets sparkling in brilliant contrast to her kohl-darkened eyes. Her pale skin was pure marble, hidden from Philistia's sun, her gaze coldly divine as she masked the hint of sentiment that had momentarily slid into her face.

But the servant girl's beaming smile was the warmth to melt the royal frost. Dawid grinned back at her. For a moment nobody moved, the smiling girl's eyes locked on the stricken hero, the princess standing tall with unblinking disdain, the doctor fidgeting nervously, Ishbi hovering behind him as servants should.

Dawid summoned the effort to speak. 'I hope you will forgive my rough treatment of you both,' he said quietly, 'but I am just a humble shepherd from a foreign land.'

Forgetting herself, the servant girl squealed with delight and ran to Dawid's bedside. Then she hesitated, looking back to her mistress. She returned to her side, took her hand and coaxed her towards the patient.

'This is Lalia, daughter of King Akish,' she said formally.

'I am honoured,' said Dawid, equally formally. 'I am sorry that I cannot bow, but my head hurts.' At last Lalia smiled, just a flicker of movement at the corners of her mouth.

'We are both in your debt.' Her voice was rich and deep.

Dawid tore his gaze from the darkened royal eyes and looked at the mischievous servant. 'And you are…?'

'Naomi.' Naomi blushed but didn't look away. 'I am Hebrew, like you.'

'Hebrew? Are you a slave?'

'She is no slave,' Lalia interrupted severely. 'She is here by her own choice.'

Naomi, who was crouching at Dawid's side, lifted her mistress's hand to her cheek. 'I am sworn to my lady,' she said softly. 'She plucked me from the market when I feared for my life and my honour.'

The doctor suddenly snapped out of his subservience, remembering his sworn duties to the king. Wringing his hands, he stammered apologetically that the young Hebrew was in his care and was in no fit state to receive guests at this time.

Dawid glared at him. 'The princess and her handmaiden are all the medicine I need,' he said with as much charm as he could muster through the fog in his head. Naomi giggled and again the princess showed just the smallest hint of a smile.

'We understand,' Lalia said to the doctor without looking at him. 'We will leave our hero to recover and return when he feels better. My father also wishes to see him to express his gratitude, perhaps in a day or two? Longer, if necessary. He is a patient man.'

The doctor bowed his acceptance of her suggestion. The women turned to leave.

'What happened to the slaves?' Dawid asked.

'The slaves?' asked Lalia, turning back to him.

'The ones who were working on the palace wall, when…'

'Oh, them. Put to death, probably. How should I know what my father decrees?'

Dawid wondered if the princess was as innocent as the expression she wore. 'It wasn't their fault,' Dawid said as the women retired.

The princess wasn't listening, although Naomi turned briefly and shot him a look that warned him against getting involved in the ways of these people and their politics.

When they were gone, Dawid found himself longing for their return.

Dawid's broken bones healed far quicker than the pessimistic Philistine doctor could have dreamed. The first rains of Tishri were awakening green shoots on the surrounding hills and replenishing the Elah river when Dawid took his first tentative steps with the aid of a crutch that Ishbi found in the well-stocked healing tent of the Hittites. He staggered to the palace terrace and lifted his eyes to the swollen skies, savouring the gritty wind from the sea on his face. Ishbi hovered nearby, ready to call for the doctor if he cried out, stumbled or even complained: Akish had ordered that nothing was to be denied the young Hebrew, and if any harm was to befall him then

167

those responsible would pay with their lives.

And nothing was denied him, save his attempts to dismiss the claustrophobic presence of guards, servants, the doctor and Ishbi whenever Lalia and Naomi visited. A Hebrew hero was still a Hebrew and not to be trusted. Yet almost daily gifts of fine clothes, rings and bracelets were brought to him. 'From the king,' said the servants as they presented them, though Dawid suspected they had been chosen by the princess and her maidservant.

Uriah brought honey cakes from his kitchen tents, accompanied by Habib, who ate them all while animatedly describing the latest triumphs in the arena. Muti hopped and fidgeted, uncomfortable in the magnificence of the rooms where Dawid recovered. Naomi began to run out of excuses to attend her countryman, always bearing food and wine from the palace kitchens, occasionally bringing Lalia, who sat apart, silent and expressionless. Once Dawid caught her studying him while Naomi chattered, her eyes guarded. He held her gaze until she looked away with a momentary flash of anger at her unexpected weakness.

To alleviate his boredom, Habib brought knucklebone dice and before long the guards and servants, and even the doctor, had joined the long sessions in which Dawid lost and then won back many of his new trinkets. Once, Golyat entered the room, unarmed and wearing a black turban and loose robes made from the same material. He stood apart in a darkened corner and watched Dawid with hooded eyes. The huddle of gamblers was subdued in the giant's oppressive presence, and they returned to laughter and ribbing only when he left.

As Dawid's winnings mounted, Ishbi found a wooden chest in a nearby storeroom and brought it to the invalid's room. In this, Dawid hoped to amass enough silver and gems to buy him respect and honour when next he could walk the streets of Gath.

Or even Beth Lechem.

CHAPTER TWENTY-TWO

King Akish of Gath chewed thoughtfully on one of the latest sweetmeats to have arrived with a caravan out of Egypt.

'Tell me, Melek,' he said, a sticky morsel clinging to his bottom lip, 'how does the Hebrew youth fare?'

Melek shifted on the royal cushions and eyed the pile of delicacies before him, uncertain whether to reach out for one without Akish's express permission.

'He is recovering speedily, my lord.'

'So I hear. Perhaps it's time for me to receive him?' Akish popped another of the delights into his mouth and stretched his legs across the intricately woven carpet that covered much of the stone floor. A fire blazed in the hearth, dulling Melek's senses just when he needed of them most. Akish looked across at Melek and indicated that he should try the food. 'Eat,' he ordered. 'It's very good, very sweet. You'll like it.'

Melek reached greedily for a confection. He didn't have to pretend to be amazed at the explosion of spicy sweetness and made a mental note to spend more time with visiting traders from the south. Akish watched him coldly and wondered why, with all the privileges he had lavished on the uncouth dwarf, Melek had adopted so few of the manners that Philistine society demanded.

'Tell me what you know of him.'

Melek swallowed hastily. 'He's a spy, my lord. An enemy of Gath. He is worthless. As soon as he is mended, he should return to the arena.'

'And will Golyat kill him?'

'Of course. No one can stand against Golyat.' Melek realised that was exactly what the spy had done and hastily added, 'If not the arena, send him to the mines. He is not fit to live.'

'That's not what I am told.'

Melek shifted uneasily, realising that the king was probably well informed about this youth. 'But, my lord, he cannot be trusted.'

'My daughter owes him her life. She tells me he is an innocent, yet a strange fire burns within him. Does he sound like a traitor to you?'

'It is possible he deceives her. But he cannot deceive me. These Hebrews, they are uncivilised zealots.'

'Then why does Lalia visit him?'

Melek squirmed under the intense questioning. 'Your daughter has visited only a few times, to express her thanks, I expect. And I have my informants, who will tell me everything about this Hebrew worm.'

Akish reached for another sweetmeat and inspected it thoughtfully. 'My daughter tells me he is just a youthful adventurer.'

'As I said, a clever guise.'

The king bit into the delicacy. 'I'll tell you what I think, Melek. I think your games in the arena have given us a new hero, Hebrew or not. The others fight and entertain well, but the word is that this youth, this Dawid of Beth Lechem, is special and the people want a hero. When he walks again, I have it in mind to elevate him to my court.'

'Lord…?'

'He has an energy that we need. The nobles grow fat and lazy. When the spring comes, we will prepare for war and I want young men like this Dawid in our ranks.' Akish ate the rest of the delicacy and reclined on a plump cushion. 'So, my friend, I want to know the truth about who he is and why he is here. If he is a spy, prove it. If he is not, and he is just a chancer who happened to seek adventure in Gath, then we will humour him.'

Melek nodded, thinking fast about how he could put an end to his king's foolish plans.

'But I don't want my daughter involved,' Akish added. 'The servant girl, Naomi — she could be useful to us.'

'Your daughter's maidservant?' asked Melek. 'How so?'

'She is Hebrew. Perhaps they could become intimate. Girls talk, don't they?'

'Indeed they do,' laughed Melek, reaching for another Egyptian delight. 'I will see to it that she has something to gossip about.'

Or, he thought with a warm glow, maybe she could be the weapon he could use to torture this arrogant Hebrew.

When Princess Lalia came to Dawid as evening fell, a log fire burning bright and warm in the hearth, the shepherd knew his destiny was about to change again. He was alone, wearing only his Hittite breeches as he gently exercised his muscles back to firmness, when the princess of Gath approached unannounced. She pulled the hood from her brightly braided hair, revealing collarbones that shone like polished marble and the slender neck of a swan.

'My lady,' he breathed. 'Where is Naomi? Your guards?'

'I do not need guards in my father's palace,' she replied, her eyes offering no hint of softness. 'And Naomi is on an errand for me.'

Dawid smiled and reached for his shirt, but Lalia was there first, placing a foot on the crumpled garment to prevent him from picking it up. She towered over him where he sat on the hearthrug.

'Lady…?'

'You intrigue me, Hebrew.' Lalia's eyes lingered on Dawid's chest and shoulders, admiring the youthful muscle and the shimmer of sweat. He began to rise, but she stooped and, placing her hand on his chest, pushed him down upon the rug.

'You have once before handled me roughly; now is my revenge.'

She kissed him, hard. Her tongue snaked like a viper's and she moaned throatily when he responded, crushing his lips to hers. She was surprisingly strong.

Confused, Dawid yielded, allowing her to straddle him, his heart pounding as she tugged feverishly at his breeches. He helped her remove them, then she pulled her tunic above her hips, grinding downwards, the muscles of her thighs taut with ardour. Dawid felt himself glide into her and bright lights flashed behind his eyes as he climaxed. His eyes were wide with pleasure, yet he knew he had proved himself inexperienced and immature. Still she pressed down hard, and he felt himself aroused again.

He threw his arms around her neck and kissed her. She moaned, and with a long, breathy sigh she called on Dagon, Ba'al and Astarte, swore on the heavens and the fiery breath of Moloch. Then her body went limp. For a long moment she lay above him, panting, her breath hot and damp in Dawid's ear.

'Breathe a word of this and I'll have you sent to the mines.'

'I love you too,' he croaked.

'Your first time… Don't they teach you anything in Judah?'

'Only shepherding,' he said.

Lalia laughed. 'And how do I compare with your sheep?'

'It's a close thing, but they are more compliant.'

She bit his chin.

'Ouch. Stop it. I surrender.'

'Weakling,' she hissed, and began to move her hips again.

Dawid gambled with anyone in the palace who was foolish enough to risk their possessions. He swiftly stockpiled a hoard of useless things, from pottery buttons to rusting daggers and even a pair of shoes. He stowed them in his trunk with his other treasures, always lingering over the hefty Star of Anak that Golyat had given him.

Ishbi visited often, the doctor less and less, Habib frequently — his luck was on a par with Dawid's — and Muti occasionally when the old man wasn't pursuing his new career as a storyteller in the marketplace. Uriah came often, but only to talk of life in Judah.

Dawid saw Lalia only one more time before Philistia marched on Judah, and that was when he was summoned to the king's private chambers to talk of gods, the Hebrews and his personal impressions of Gath. She floated across the terrace attended by her handmaidens, seeming not to notice him. But one of her handmaidens took the opportunity to steal a shy glance at her favourite Hebrew youth.

As warmer winds from the south overcame the chill of winter, Naomi invented a hundred excuses to visit Dawid and found it amusing to lose her mistress's rings, bracelets and necklaces to his relentless advance on the wealth of Gath. She even brought him fashionable high-necked tunics, breeches, goatskin boots with garish lacing, silver bracelets (not that he needed more), jaunty headgear and a wolfskin cape that gave him a warrior-like appearance.

But his greatest gift was not the jewellery or the ostentatious clothing. It was the precious time he snatched with Naomi, whenever she could leave the princess without drawing attention to herself. There were moments of laughter as they explored mutual beliefs, and the world around them came alive with their love. Dawid forgot Rachael's vulnerability and the fierce grip of Lalia's thighs, such was the excitement of Naomi's innocent chatter, her impertinent questioning and, when the time came, the tenderness of her embrace.

Neither of them noticed the silent figures in the shadows, the look of a guard or the discreet glance of a clerk.

All of them reported what they saw to Melek.

CHAPTER TWENTY-THREE

Dawid always considered himself a year older when the hillsides around Beth Lechem blushed pink with almond blossom; the month of Adar brought the same promise to Gath's palace gardens as it did to Judah. Even the periodic rains had the smell of new warmth about them.

So by his own reckoning he had seen his eighteenth winter. His beard now demanded the attentions of the palace barbers, and his shoulder-length hair was sleek, oiled and perfumed by Naomi whenever she could find an excuse to visit him, or by other palace servants lured by a gift from his growing store of valuables. He bathed daily and delighted in selecting the most outrageous tunics and cloaks from his lavish wardrobe, with bracelets and gold necklaces adding to his peacock appeal. He was a favourite among the court's women. Only the nagging ache in his slowly recovering leg, causing a slight limp, reminded him of his imperfections.

King Akish found Dawid's behaviour faintly amusing. He even harboured secret thoughts that the young man might fill the aching void left when his only son had died in the plagues that had cursed the whole of Canaan a decade ago, taking the child's mother in the same night, leaving him bereft of life and spirit. Now the king allowed Dawid to sit with him when merchants or foreign emissaries came to the palace. He even welcomed him onto the royal terraces to watch the games in the arena, now bloodless performances, except when there were slaves and enemies to be executed.

Dawid was at the king's side discussing the differences between their respective traditions when a panting messenger brought news that the first of the season's caravans had been observed to the south, flying the colours of Ashdod. In that moment, the lethargy of winter was dispelled. The lords of Philistia were coming to Gath to plot the downfall of Dawid's people.

Hadad of Ashdod claimed the choice position for his palatial tent close to the eastern gate, and for the next seven days the tents of the *seranim* of Ekron, Ashkelon and Gaza jostled for flat ground in the wide valley as far as Gath's ore mines. Each of the four royal tents competed in their elaborate colours and gay pennants, surrounded by a host of more functional tents for the attending clerks, merchants and soldiers. The palace buzzed with anticipation as servants hastened this way and that, carrying great bolts of cloth to decorate the halls, and ushering acrobats and musicians to their rehearsals then chasing them away again to make way for the next troupe of dancers or singers. All the while, the kitchens were a noisy hell as an army of cooks prepared dishes designed to show the royal visitors that Gath was still the most important city within the Philistine alliance.

In the chaos, Gath's peacock hero was instantly forgotten.

Dawid wandered the palace, dodging frantic servants and industrious decorators, uncertain whether he should make himself useful. He resented being ignored by everyone. He looked for Naomi but couldn't find her or any of the princess's entourage, nor the doctor or Ishbi. Golyat, who could never have made himself invisible, was nowhere to be seen. Dawid took advantage of the turmoil stirred by the arrival of the Philistine warlords and, hiding his chest of possessions in a dusty storage room, walked calmly through the palace towards the bustling city. That was when he saw a familiar face and felt hatred welling up with the recognition.

Mishon.

The weaver of Gath and the traitor from Socoh who had delivered him to the dungeons, and Dookhi to his death, was among the city's traders remonstrating at the palace gates with a clerk, watched by several bemused guards. Mishon had three bolts of cloth and was clearly arguing that his material was worth far more than the paltry price being offered. The clerk was having none of it.

Dawid studied the traitor's face as it reddened in desperation and wished he had brought a weapon with him. He took a step towards the small group, the urge to take revenge coursing through his veins. Then he stopped and forced himself to think. Had not the gods smiled on him since his capture, given him privileges and good fortune? He was a man now, dressed in fine clothes and living in luxury, no longer a hot-headed shepherd boy from beggarly Beth Lechem.

He calmed himself and walked slowly through the gates, ignored by the guards. Mishon glanced at him as he sauntered past and for a moment Dawid's anger surged, but he forced down the emotion and looked away. He walked past the group. He sensed Mishon's hesitation as he searched his memory for a familiar face, but then the bargaining, shouting and pleading resumed.

Mishon had not recognised him. Dawid smiled and promised himself that one day soon, when Mishon least expected it, his moment would come and Mishon would suffer.

He walked away from the palace, his step light with newfound confidence, towards the gates of Gath. He had decided to visit Uriah, not as a slave or an Ox Rider, but as a palace favourite.

While the city and its palace had been in a state of scrambling confusion, the Hittite camp was ordered and precise. The weak sun cast its watery light over two rows of Uriah's men, who were facing each other, about fifteen on each side of a wide track that had been cleared and swept smooth. It was some kind of military parade, Dawid realised as he leaned on a tree trunk to observe, taking the weight off his injured leg. The Hittites were silent, disciplined, waiting patiently in their light leather uniforms, each with a sheathed sword at his hip and a spear in his hand, shafts planted on the soft ground beside them. They were helmetless, attired for ceremony and not war. Uriah was nowhere to be seen, nor Ishbi.

Dawid sat beneath the tree, unobserved, convinced something was about to happen.

A distant horn wailed, and as one the guard stiffened. Then there was a shouted command from somewhere in the direction of the Invincibles' cliffside temple, the whinny of horses, and the rumble of iron-rimmed wheels as Gath's formidable chariot force approached. But the first chariot to come into view contained no giant and needed only a pony to draw it. It had Melek's trademark canopy of gold and red with an array of outlandish tassels and ornaments, the dwarf imperious in black robes with a heavy gold chain about his neck. The chariot was driven by a horseman who had clearly been selected for his small stature. Behind followed Uriah and Ishbi on horseback, both traditionally dressed in Hittite riding clothes.

Though Melek's transport brought a smile to Dawid's face, the chariots that followed inspired awe and fear. He counted ten high-sided chariots, each drawn by four horses abreast, the finest beasts from the Hittite enclosure. These chariots were much wider, expertly controlled by a skilled horseman, each carrying a fully armed giant, Golyat to the fore. His bronze scale armour glinted in the pale light, the fanciful bull's head discarded for a conical iron skullcap to which was attached a shoulder-length neck guard of polished bronze mail. A burly shield-bearer, dwarfed by Golyat, stood at his side, both hands holding the rim of a gleaming shield, an ornate bow slung across his shoulder. Tied to the chariot's runner were five iron-tipped throwing spears, shafts as thick as a weaver's beam, and resting in Golyat's folded arms was the huge golden axe that the giant had wielded in the arena. Dawid found himself back on his feet, as if ready to flee from the might of Gath, for behind Golyat rode Lahmi and eight more warriors, none quite as impressive as Golyat, but each twice the size and bulk of any of Uriah's renowned soldiers.

Melek led the procession between the two rows of Hittites, his pony skittish at the sight of armed men to either side, but Uriah's warhorse and the animals behind him were seasoned in battle and high-stepped their way between the warriors. As soon as the last chariot had passed, the Hittites turned to follow, closing ranks to march in time to the music of their jangling ankle bracelets. Dawid ducked behind the tree as Melek's chariot passed. Melek did not see him, but Uriah did, throwing him a smile and a wink. Dawid studied the Invincibles as they passed, each stone-faced beneath their iron helms, broad-shouldered and so muscular that their scale armour must have contained half of Gath's bronze. A formidable fighting force.

He watched the procession disappear in the direction of the Philistine camps, no doubt to show off the core of Gath's military might to the visiting warlords. He wondered whether to return to the city or look for old friends in the Hittite camp — perhaps he could make himself useful in the kitchens or even learn something among the iron smiths. He chose the latter.

He was snooping near the armoury when he heard a familiar whistle. He looked up and saw Habib sitting cross-legged in the entrance of a dormitory tent on the edge of the camp, a fire blazing in a ring of stones before him. The Phoenician beckoned and Dawid limped to him.

'Well, aren't you the fancy cockerel among the hens of Gath?' laughed Habib as he embraced Dawid and felt the quality of his tunic with his forefinger and thumb.

'You're not doing so badly either, by the look of you,' replied Dawid with a grin as he admired Habib's jewelled necklace. 'Putting what I've taught you to good use, I see! Got any wine?'

'None that I could steal without a full military enquiry,' chuckled Habib, 'but the men of this tent had just drawn a pitcher of beer when they were so rudely summoned to their duties.' He stooped into the tent and emerged clutching a jug of ale and two clay cups. He handed one to Dawid and poured the murky liquid. 'Let's drink to freedom.'

'To freedom,' echoed Dawid, 'sudden and unexpected as it is.'

They both took a draught. 'You just walked out of Gath? Without permission?' asked Habib.

'Yes. It was most peculiar. It seems everyone is preoccupied with the royal visitors.'

'You are going back to Judah?'

Dawid shook his head. 'I like it here.'

'Ah, I see.' Habib raised a suspicious eyebrow. 'Who is she?'

Dawid gave himself away by blushing and swiftly changed the subject. 'What about you? Will you go back to Tyre?'

'Not if your lady has a sister,' said Habib with a wink and gulped more beer. 'Tell me.'

'No sister. She's only a servant girl. But there's a certain royal lady who would love to sample a bit of Phoenician manhood…'

'What? Akish's daughter? Dawid, don't tell me you —'

'I'm telling you nothing. Find out for yourself.' He held out his cup for more beer and they sat by the fire, enjoying its warmth.

'Perhaps this would be a good time to run,' Habib said thoughtfully, 'but I agree with you that Gath isn't a bad place to enjoy the pleasures of life. My home city stinks of rotten fish, and anyway my older brother stands to inherit my father's wealth. I'm rather hoping that Uriah will let me ride with his men when war comes. I can't see anyone standing up to the might of Gath.'

Dawid frowned. 'I agree. But it seems likely that the Philistines will march on my homeland next. They'll march east, and when they've conquered Judah they'll sweep through Israel and north to your lands. Doesn't that worry you?'

'It hasn't happened yet, and if it does it'll be many years in the making. By then I'll have made my fortune and will be siring a family with all my pretty young wives.'

'You don't worry for your own people then?'

'No. Do you?'

'Why should I? My brothers hated me and my mother. There's nothing there for me. And I'll wager it stinks worse than your city. But I don't think I could march against them with the Philistines.'

Habib studied Dawid. 'You, me and old Muti made a great team, even if we only fought together once. Just the three of us, each from a different land with different gods. What does it matter where you come from? We are brothers now. Ox Riders.'

'I'll drink to that,' said Dawid, staring into his empty cup. 'Any more beer where that came from?'

The Phoenician disappeared into the tent to search for more beer and quickly returned with a replenished pitcher. 'As soon as we hear them coming back, we'd better make ourselves scarce,' he said. 'The men will be thirsty when they return from showing off their marching skills, and they won't take kindly to finding an empty barrel!' He poured two generous measures and Dawid realised he was beginning to feel light-headed.

'Give them that girl's necklace you're wearing. Worth a month's wages, I'd guess.'

'They'd rather have this,' said Habib, chinking his cup to Dawid's. 'Uriah looks after his men well.'

'Now there's a man who knows how to lead,' agreed Dawid.

'I don't think Akish realises how lucky he is to have Uriah and his Hittites with him.'

'But surely they're paid well?'

'Oh, it's not a matter of silver and gold,' said Habib. 'It's Melek. The little runt drives Uriah mad. Wouldn't surprise me if Uriah led his men out of here and attached his pennant to some other cause.'

'Melek? Surely Uriah could just slit his throat and be done with him?'

Habib savoured Dawid's suggestion. Both knew the wisdom of avoiding the cruel dwarf at all costs — he seemed to be in the king's favour and wouldn't look kindly on the apparent successes of two former slaves from his dungeons. 'That's not Uriah's way. He's an honourable man. Powerful, yes, but honourable to the core. He'd rather ride away and offer his sword and his men to a nobler cause.'

'And you'd ride with him?' Dawid asked quietly.

Habib nodded. 'Would you?'

Dawid shrugged, thinking of Naomi. If it wasn't for her…

Habib read his mind. 'So, my friend, tell me about this servant girl.'

The solitary drum sounded a slow and mournful beat as the chief priest of Gath held the ceremonial knife to the ram's throat. It struggled in the powerful grip of the attendants, twisting its head frantically, but their hold on its horns was too strong. The drum quickened, the huge stone god, half man, half fish, seeming to grow larger with every beat as Dagon cast his shadow over his supplicants. With a deep breath, the priest turned his head away and cut deep. Warm blood ran freely over his hands and arms, a crimson spray arcing across his white robe. The ram went limp, one leg twitching in sudden death. The knife was slippery in the priest's hands as he cut into the animal's warm underbelly. Four other priests stepped forward and peered at the gory mess, poking at the white of entrails.

'Clean?' asked the chief priest.

'Clean,' confirmed the priest of Ekron.

The others nodded to each other, and together they turned to face the lords of the five Philistine cities. Their long robes trailed in the ram's blood, and their hands shone red. Gath's priest spoke to Akish, who stood slightly apart from the other Philistine warlords.

'It is done,' he said solemnly. 'Dagon is pleased with this offering.'

'What say you?' Akish addressed his allies in a voice loud enough for all of his courtiers to hear. 'What say you, Abimelech of Ekron?'

The oldest of the five stepped forward to Akish's side and placed a hand on his shoulder. 'Ekron agrees,' said Abimelech.

'Hadad of Ashdod? What say you?'

Hadad cleared his throat and paused for effect. 'Agreed,' he said after a few moments.

'Aga?'

The lord of Ashkelon, younger than the others but the only one with a gold headband to emphasise his authority, also stepped forward. 'War,' he said a little over-eagerly. 'Agreed.'

Akish turned to look at the last of the warlords, a careworn man with an untidy grey beard. 'What does Gaza say?'

Hanno of Gaza nodded slowly, not wanting to be the only one to dissent. 'The god and the lords of Philistia have spoken. It is war.'

The chief priest turned back to the stone god, his blood-soaked arms outstretched. 'Great Dagon,' he cried, 'Lord of the seas and the storms, lead us to victory, for you are greater than all other gods!'

'And,' muttered the young warlord of Ashkelon, 'we have the Invincibles.'

CHAPTER TWENTY-FOUR

'When?' Dawid's question was abrupt and Naomi pouted. He tried again, stroking her shoulder. 'My little bird, when do they say the army will march?'

'Don't stop. Please...' She edged closer, hoping his hand would continue its exploration.

'When?' His eyes teased her.

'Ziv. At the moon's renewal. I think that's what Lalia said.' She brushed her lips against Dawid's. 'Now, please...'

Dawid obeyed.

Later, they talked until the sun rose, the signal that Naomi must return to her mistress. They had stolen a rare night together, a night in which neither slept and between passionate moments they had told each other about themselves. Naomi was honest and open about her young life, Dawid more guarded as he struggled to answer her questions about his childhood, his dreams, his intentions — and his loyalties. 'You look and sound like a Philistine, but this says you are a Hebrew,' she chuckled at one point, caressing his most sensitive place to remind him of the distinctive mark ordained by Yahweh's law.

'So are you,' he breathed in her ear. 'Yahweh's beautiful angel. Or are you Ashtoreth come among us?'

Naomi laughed. 'Yes, I was born a Hebrew and in my heart I am a Hebrew. But I have no people, no family in Israel.'

'Neither do I.'

'But you have your mother in Beth Lechem,' she chided.

'True,' he confessed.

'And those people in the caves — what is the place called? Adallah?'

'Adullam.'

'Yes, Adullam. You speak of them as if they are your family. Surely you want to warn them to flee? It's only one moon until the army marches. You could easily leave Gath and warn them. Nobody would notice.'

'And leave you? I think not.'

'Oh, Dawid, how sweet. You should go. You can come back when it's all over. I think King Akish rather likes you. He would maybe give you a position here in the palace, and we could be together.'

'There's no need for me to go. The Hebrews already know the Philistines are coming. They knew a year ago. It's obvious, anyway; the Philistines have always wanted more land, and now that the Israelite tribes have a king of their own, they're even more determined to wipe our people out.'

Naomi pinched him playfully. 'You know, I think that underneath your skin you're just a little bit selfish.'

'What do you mean, little dove?'

'You'd rather stay here where everything's soft and comfortable, so *easy*, than go back to that rough old life of yours to defend our people...'

'If I did go back, I'd go wearing my new clothes and some of my choice bracelets! Show them that I'm no clod under Jesse's plough!'

Naomi pinched him again. 'You're no clod. You never were. There was always a warrior prince underneath that shepherd's mantle!'

They made love again, slowly. But this time, Dawid was not quite so attentive as he had been previously that night. He allowed Naomi's words to float in his mind, saw himself riding

Morning Star into Adullam, Beth Lechem, even Saul's stronghold at Gibeah, the ragged people cheering the new hero — the warrior prince.

Naomi had to summon all her composure when she was seconded to serve wine and pomegranate juice to the war council in the great hall. Her hands shook when she offered the city's best wine to the youngest of the warlords, the haughty and mean-looking Aga of Ashkelon. He frightened her and made matters worse by deliberately brushing his hand against her breast when he took his goblet from her tray. She lowered her eyes demurely and fought against the disgust she hoped did not show on her face, grateful that Akish was speaking to the whole assembly of city kings, their clerks and captains. She glanced at Melek, the only commander allowed to stand close to the huge cloth map that had been spread on the stone floor — it was obviously the only way he would see the Philistine plan. She hoped he would not notice her presence, as he had recently taken to studying her intently on the rare occasions they brushed past each other in a corridor or found themselves in the same room.

The last of her goblets was taken by the untidy Hanno of Gaza, and she rushed to the kitchens to fill a pitcher. Planning a war was thirsty work. When she returned, Akish was still speaking. She concentrated on his words as she poured, intrigued to know what fate awaited her people, though what she would do with the information other than report it to her beloved Dawid, she did not know. Her devotion to the princess brought her inner peace and made her more Philistine than Hebrew, but in her heart she knew that the ancient gods were stirring, and when the gods fought each other there could only be upheaval and terror in their tidy, organised world.

Akish was speaking slowly and loudly enough for all in the war council to hear. Apparently it was important to find flat terrain to fight the Hebrews, land where the chariots could operate, and the best place to drive home this advantage was in the Valley of Elah at its widest. Akish stabbed his royal staff on the map as he shared this information. Naomi was pouring wine into a goblet clutched by one of the lesser captains and was too far away to sneak a look at the chosen battlefield, but then she distinctly heard Akish mention Azekah, which she knew to be the city closest to Gath, and Socoh, which she thought was somewhere further afield but in the same valley. She noted the names as she smiled at the officer and moved closer to the centre of the room, hoping for a clearer view of the map.

Akish was saying that his spies reported recent activity at Gibeah, where the Hebrews were gathering to the standard of their king, Saul — his staff prodded the map again — and therefore, in order to draw them to the chosen killing ground, their advance would be gradual, the taking of Azekah slow and deliberate with much threatening and cruelty. They would allow prisoners to escape with news of the advance, to draw this Hebrew rabble onto the spears and chariots of the Invincibles. His staff swept across the map. Defeat them here — another decisive prod — and the lands of Judah and Israel would be undefended and at Philistia's mercy... Naomi lost track of his words as an officer's hand roughly squeezed her buttocks. She pretended it delighted her, laughing with her eyes but backing away from him. She stumbled into another, turning with horror lest she had caused a noble to spill his wine, and found herself looking into the cold, accusing eyes of Melek.

For a moment she read his mind as he stripped away her innocence, finding beneath her gaiety and devotion to her mistress a steaming morass of guilt and shame. His eyes said she was a Hebrew, with no right to be in the presence of superior Philistine lords, and she shuddered involuntarily as the dwarf's menacing gaze tore her apart like a wolf disembowelling a lamb. The moment was brief, but it was enough to let her know that she must at all costs avoid this man of hideous self-importance. He had the power to make her — and Dawid, if he could — suffer far beyond the common indignities of a soldier's groping hands.

It was Abimelech, the warlord of Ekron, whose authoritative voice snatched back Melek's attentions to the weighty matters of war when he mentioned the dwarf's favourite subject: intrigue. Only Abimelech, as a longstanding friend of Akish and the oldest of the *seranim*, could interrupt the king of Gath, and Naomi struggled with the shock of Melek's silent assault as she tried to understand what the new voice was saying. She heard the words 'Jebus' and 'the Jebusites will rise up' and though she had no idea where this Jebusite city was, she understood perfectly that these were enemies within Israelite territory, and Abimelech would persuade them to attack the Hebrew army in the rear as they faced the Philistine invasion.

This latest strategy brought a murmur of excitement that swelled as the inevitability of success dawned on the Philistine leaders. Naomi wondered how the Hebrews would ever survive such overwhelming odds, but as a child she had heard the legends of great warriors like Yoshua and Samson. She hoped their spirits would rise from Sheol and guide the new king to achieve similar feats to bring a swift end to all of this warlike posturing by her Philistine masters. She walked briskly towards the kitchens, desperate to get away from an atmosphere now thick with bloodlust, but hesitated when Akish, demanding silence, called on his commander of the Invincibles, Melek, to speak in conclusion to their deliberations.

She felt a surge of sickening panic but forced herself to listen, busying herself near the door.

'My lords have been patient,' said Melek gruffly, 'and I will not detain such great nobles for longer than is necessary. But there is one matter that remains, and for this I crave your indulgence.' Naomi's heart pounded. 'There are Hebrews working in this city, even in this very palace, and we should be aware that the enemy is already among us.' A gasp escaped Naomi's lips, but no one noticed as Melek had their full attention. 'They are untrustworthy scavengers and have no right to be among us.' There was a murmur, mostly in agreement.

'What exactly are you suggesting?' asked Akish, polite but firm.

'The gates should be closed, and all Hebrews rounded up and put to death.'

The council's response, still largely in agreement, was louder.

'Why?' demanded Akish. 'I see the sense of this, but if the gates are closed, none can escape.'

'We cannot be too careful. Especially now that my lord Abimelech has informed all of us —' he looked around for Naomi, but he could not see past the burly captains nearest him — 'including, ah, servants of questionable lineage, that our allies the Jebusites will fall upon the Hebrews from the rear.'

Naomi edged towards the door as several of the nobles looked around at the servants with pitchers of wine and trays of food.

'What you say is quite right,' said Akish. 'We cannot be too careful. Let it be done swiftly and cleanly. Anyone who gives a Hebrew into our hands is to be rewarded with a shekel of silver from the treasury.' Naomi thought she would faint as she backed slowly through the door. 'But none of the palace servants is to be touched.'

'But, my lord —' Melek protested.

Akish silenced him with a withering glare. 'I repeat, none of my servants or those of my family are to be harmed, though they will be confined to the palace. That is my will in this matter. Now, I want numbers of chariots, horses, riders, archers, slingers and spearmen by sunset. I have spoken.'

The lords and captains began to leave, chatting as if they were planning an afternoon's entertainment, while Melek made haste to do his bloody work.

'Akish said we would be safe in the palace. That's what you told me,' said Dawid when Naomi had shared all that she had learned. 'Why worry?'

'Dawid, it's only a matter of time before that evil Melek gets his way! I saw it in his eyes.'

Dawid yawned. 'Maybe tomorrow. I'm tired.'

Naomi gave an exclamation of frustration. 'You have to warn them. They're our people and they don't know that the Jebusites will attack them from behind!'

'Of course they know. Doesn't the prophet Shemu'el know everything?' He eased his head towards the soft pillows.

'Do you really believe that?'

Dawid shrugged. Perhaps he should play the hero; there would be untold riches if he proved his worth to the Hebrew king. But not today. 'Come to bed,' he said.

Naomi couldn't help the tears. 'Oh, Dawid, don't you see? They're going to start killing all the Hebrews in Gath, and they've probably started arresting them already. It's a sickness that will soon spread inside the palace, and before long Akish will go with the army and probably many of the guards. He won't be here to protect you.'

'Or you.' Dawid reached out and wiped a tear from her cheek. 'If I go — when I go — you will come with me. Or I won't go at all.'

Naomi shook her head sadly. 'I can't come with you,' she whispered.

'Why?'

'Because I have to look after Princess Lalia.'

'But she has any number of women to look after her. She wouldn't even miss you.'

'But I promised to stand with her. We Hebrew women are renowned for our skill as midwives and...'

'Midwife? You? But Lalia has no husband!' He narrowed his eyes, thinking fast. 'Is she ... she's not with child, surely?'

Naomi nodded, and he grew dizzy with sudden fear.

'When, how ... who...?'

'I think you know how,' Naomi said with a hollow laugh, wiping her damp cheek with the back of her hand. 'When — that's anyone's guess, but Lalia is a woman and she knows the signs. As to who, she won't say. She is entitled to her secret.'

'But ... I mean...' he stammered.

'Don't be embarrassed, Dawid. These things happen all the time.'

He calmed himself, forced a weak smile, and thought furiously. If he asked too many questions, Naomi might guess what he suspected. But he had to know what the Philistines did to foreigners who interfered with their noblewomen.

'Is she not betrothed?' he asked, trying to keep his voice under control. 'To another king, or a prince perhaps?'

'Oh, I think the kings and lords of many lands near and far would seek the hand of the lady Lalia,' laughed Naomi. 'But not now. Perhaps it was her way of avoiding an awful fate far away from here. I hope the man she bedded was highborn, or someone's in for a slow death!'

Instantly, Dawid made up his mind to leave.

CHAPTER TWENTY-FIVE

On the day of his departure, Dawid threw on his finest tunic — Philistine blue embroidered delicately on the sleeves and neck with fine silver thread — and tugged a pair of leather breeches over his silk underwear. He laced up knee-high goatskin boots that the palace cobbler had soled with tough ox-hide, while Naomi rummaged for a dark but practical hooded cape and handed him a leather belt to which was attached a traveller's pouch large enough to carry a few necessities.

Suitably attired to make a good impression as well as a potentially long journey, Dawid threw open his chest of valuables. A curved dagger with a honed iron blade, sheathed in jewel-encrusted leather, was swiftly strapped to his thigh, while a braided headband gave him a princely air. He wanted to look like a Philistine in a city that hated Hebrews. He foraged for bracelets fashioned from gold and silver and rings flashing with rare gems, placing the largest on his forefinger. He would part with them reluctantly and only to stay alive. Food he would find on his journey, acquired with a gift or a threat.

Lastly, reverently, he took the Star of Anak, snapping it free from its leather thong, and secured it in his pouch.

Naomi held him at arm's length, looked him over, then threw her arms around him. 'Go carefully. And when this is over, come back to me.'

'I will,' he smiled. 'And you, keep yourself hidden from Melek. If he or anyone so much as lays a finger on you…'

'Shh, Dawid. I know. I'll be safe, don't worry.'

She kissed him passionately, then slowly pushed him away and walked to the door. It was fashioned from heavy oak, with a square hole through which the iron latch could be lifted. She dipped her fingers in the bowl of oil and myrrh attached to the wall, laced the metal to ease it open without a sound, and peered left and right along the torchlit corridor. There was no one to be seen. She touched his lips with fragrant fingers and murmured, 'Go with the lightness of Ashtoreth and the strength of Yahweh.'

He smiled at her and was gone.

No one challenged the Hebrew who looked like a Philistine lord as he walked calmly past the kitchens, the bedrooms, through the great hall where the *seranim* of Philistia had plotted the annihilation of his people. He strolled across the terraces in the fading light of dusk and down wide stone steps to the palace courtyard as if he was the son of Akish himself, nodding to guards and ignoring servants as a noble should. In the distance he could hear the commotion and upheaval in the streets as inflamed commoners sought potential victims for the merciless blades of Gath's soldiers, betraying Hebrews and hated neighbours alike, the cries of the victims mingling with the impassioned shouts of their hunters.

The palace gates were closed, reinforced by a line of fully armed guards under the control of a young officer who looked worried by the small crowd that pressed against the iron grilles, some even offering valuables as a bribe to gain entry before the half light of dusk gave way to night. He slowed his pace, weighing up the scene before him. The officer was pacing behind his soldiers, evidently confused by his new orders to admit none save those with business inside the palace. He had to get *out*, and logic told him that the guards were more intent on stopping anyone coming *in*, so all he had to do was wait for the gates to be opened enough to allow him to squeeze through and lose himself in the busy streets. Leaving the city itself was another problem, as he expected the same if not more security at both of the main gates.

Close enough now to see the pressing supplicants, he studied their faces and saw one he recognised. Mishon was forcing his way to the front of the crowd, his attention fixed on the officer, trying to attract his attention. He held aloft a gold medallion similar to those used by the palace architects and clerks as a badge of authority but, Dawid thought, it could easily be a fake or stolen. He decided this was the moment to exact his revenge.

'You!' he called to the officer, who turned and on seeing the richly dressed youth who summoned him, immediately approached. He had the look of a man who needed some authoritative help.

'My lord?' The officer's respect gave Dawid the impetus he needed.

'That one, there. The one holding up a palace seal.' Mishon had turned his attention to one of the guards, remonstrating with him.

The officer studied Mishon, who was becoming abusive in his desperation. 'I see him. What of him?'

'He is a Hebrew.'

'My orders are to admit Hebrews if they can prove they have business in the palace.'

'This one is dangerous.' Dawid decided the more absurd his story, the more likely the impressionable young officer was to believe him. 'He is an assassin sent by the Hebrews to kill King Akish.'

The officer looked at Dawid with alarm, then back to the scene at the gates.

Dawid didn't hesitate in sealing Mishon's fate. 'Lord Melek's men were following him, but they lost him in the market two days ago. There is a reward of ten shekels of silver for his head.'

'I have not heard this,' blurted the officer, 'and my orders came from Lord Melek himself...'

Dawid could see greed wrestling with common sense and interrupted. 'Melek's orders come from me.' He held up his right hand so that the gold ring with its oversized, blood-red carnelian stone was just a hand's breadth from the officer's face. 'Of course you recognise this,' he blustered, removing his hand before the officer had time to react, 'and when you have done what I am about to order you to do, you will report to Lord Melek to tell him that you have obeyed the son-in-law of your king and receive your reward.'

'Yes, my lord.' The officer began to bow, but Dawid stopped him with a hand on his shoulder.

'Come now, we will be friends. But first, loosen your sword, have your men let this Hebrew assassin through the gates, and despatch him immediately. Do it yourself, and be wary of his guile. Do not hesitate.' He hardened his eyes as he spoke, seeing the young officer draw strength from such a firm-handed noble. 'Be strong. I will be at your side.'

Both turned and the officer pointed to Mishon. 'Let that one in, and no one else,' he commanded.

Dawid edged closer to the guard who was freeing the heavy bolt, and stole a glance at Mishon, who stared at the officer with a look of relief on his face. The thought flashed through Dawid's mind that a man like Mishon would have many enemies in Gath if he cheated his customers with the same relish as he betrayed simple Hebrew farmers. Then Mishon looked at him just as a burly guard grabbed his robe and pulled him through the small gap; was there sudden recognition there? Dawid hoped so but wasted no time in sliding his body behind Mishon to stumble through the gates before they closed. Mishon sensed something was wrong and began to protest as he saw the officer tense, his blade bared, pointing at his chest. Dawid turned to see the determination in the officer's eyes, and sensed the wave of panic in Mishon and the astonishment of the watching crowd. The sword found no resistance between Mishon's ribs, his death cry cut off by a brief gurgling sound. The crowd backed away from the gates, no longer so enthusiastic about seeking asylum.

Dawid did not allow himself the luxury of gloating. In a few moments the only light would be the moon's, the darkness his friend, but first he had to find his exit from the city — definitely not the city gates. He walked briskly past the arena and, in the fading light, studied the line of the inner city wall, looking for a door, a window, steps perhaps that would lead him to the giants' chambers where the Ox Riders had been taken on the day of that first fight against Golyat and Lahmi. It was quiet here, the city and its soldiers preoccupied elsewhere as Gath stirred itself against the Hebrews and prepared for war.

Dawid found a recess in the bulky stonework and peered into the gloom. A solitary skull watched, sending a shiver down his spine. It was the unmistakable marker for the giants' domain, the spirit guard that no citizen would pass for fear of a greater curse than a swift death. He hesitated, gaze locked on the hideous skull, and muttered a prayer he only half believed. *Though I walk in Sheol's shadows, I fear no evil...* He wasn't sure to which god he spoke, and it didn't make him feel any more courageous, but he reminded himself he had been here before and was even considered a friend of Golyat himself, demon or not.

He stepped into the crushing gloom of the recess and made out the blackness of a narrow corridor. It was just wide enough for his slight frame. The air was dank with the smell of death. Cobwebs brushed his face and he felt the crunch of cockroaches under his boots. He crept blindly on, sensing the ground sloping downwards, hearing the echo of distant voices, indistinct words becoming louder as he descended, the flicker of torchlight reflecting off damp walls somewhere ahead.

He stopped when he reached an opening into what he guessed was an anteroom near the top of the giants' steps, which led down to their cave with its new fortified temple at the base of the cliff. He peered around the stonework. He could see no guards, though he could hear ribald laughter and the clatter of dice. He guessed the guards must be in another room. He glanced around the room and saw that the door leading to the stairs was ajar, his escape from Gath beckoning.

This time he had no light as he felt for each step and descended into Sheol, moving slowly, fighting the familiar feeling of dread. Calling on his memory of the Ox Riders' ascent so many months ago, he felt his way down, grateful for weak lamp flames here and there, past the unearthly chambers of the giants and their blood-stained altar, stopping frequently to listen for any following footsteps. There were none. Eventually he made out the soft moonlight that marked the giants' gate, their entry to the city, his exit from it. He sensed the movement of cooler air and saw the torch flames that marked the cavern entrance dancing with more energy than those few inside the caverns. He made for them quickly and quietly.

Outside at last, he took a deep breath of fetid air and walked as calmly as he could away from the temple of Sheol. Believing his good fortune would run dry at any moment, he hurried into the night. His over-eagerness to leave the cavern would have been his undoing had not Uriah's men been posted outside the Gate of the Giants to prevent anyone *entering*, with no orders to impede anyone *leaving*. By the light of the torches they held aloft they recognised Dawid, the young leader of the famed Ox Riders. Several gave low whistles at the fine quality of his clothing.

'Well, if it isn't the Hebrew champion,' said one, flashing a toothy grin.

Pushing the horrors of the cavern from his mind, Dawid forced a knowing smile. 'Just passing through,' he said nonchalantly. 'Looking for Uriah with a message from the palace.'

'He's in the camp,' replied the first Hittite. 'Know the way?'

He nodded.

'Here,' said another soldier kindly. 'Take my torch. We've got plenty to spare.'

Dawid muttered his thanks and decided not to push his luck by engaging in soldier's banter with the guards. He took the flickering torch and headed for the track close to the base of the cliff that led to the Hittites' tented barracks, casting an appreciative glance over his shoulder as he went.

He broke into a jog. The ground was soft after the winter rains but not treacherous, and as he went he reasoned with himself. Would Uriah try to prevent him leaving? He was convinced that the Hittite commander was not enamoured with Gath's nobility, particularly Melek, but would he allow a Hebrew to leave, knowing that Philistia's enemies might be forewarned of the invasion plans? Perhaps he should skirt around the camp and melt into the night, gone forever.

But something told him that Uriah was not an enemy, and with a bit of luck, Habib would be eager for a fresh adventure. He thought ruefully that although he had escaped from Gath and managed to pass through the unholy caverns of the giants on his own, it would be better to travel with a friend if he could. Yes, it was worth the risk if Habib agreed to come with him.

CHAPTER TWENTY-SIX

Uriah the Hittite tossed a stripped bone into the fire's embers and broke away another hind leg from a herb-roasted hare. He chewed thoughtfully, looking from Dawid to Habib and back again.

'Let me get this right,' he said through a mouthful of the tender meat. 'You want to just walk out of Gath as if you are a free man?'

'I've already walked out and now I am free,' replied Dawid swiftly. 'No-one has tried to stop me.'

'Hmm. Dressed like that, I'm not surprised.'

'I'm leaving tonight. And I'm not coming back.'

Uriah understood. 'Where will you go? To warn your people, perhaps join their army?'

'I'm not interested in the war between my people and the Philistines. I'm hoping Habib will show me the way to Tyre.'

Habib shook his head. 'You don't want to go there. It smells like rotting fish guts.'

Uriah waved his hare bone at Dawid. 'You don't fool me, Hebrew. You know too much. You'll run straight to that arrogant new king of Israel and tell him all you have heard in the palace.'

'But I don't know anything,' lied Dawid, his face a picture of indignation. 'And even if I did, why would King Saul listen to me?'

'Come now. The whole of Gath is like a flock of sheep bleating about marching up the valley and taking Azekah, then Socoh, and massacring an inept band of farmers armed with nothing but sickles and hoes. Personally, I'm not sure it will make any difference if you do tell them. They might see sense and withdraw to the hills. It's mostly barren scrubland anyway, no use to anyone.'

'That's not how we see it,' said Dawid, betraying his true feelings for the first time.

'Aha, you give yourself away!' For a moment Dawid held Uriah's fierce gaze, but then the Hittite relented. 'Go on. You go. I'll tell Melek I haven't seen you.'

'And Habib?'

Uriah looked at the Phoenician. 'What about you, Habib? What do you think?'

'If Lord Uriah permits it,' Habib said slowly, 'I would go with Dawid. Whether to his dusty wastelands, or north to my people, or south to the land of the Nile.'

Dawid embraced his friend. 'Habib, I've got sights to show you that will make your hair curl.'

'It's already curled, and oiled if you hadn't noticed.'

'Then there's many a Hebrew girl who would like to run their fingers through it!'

'Enough of that,' laughed Uriah. 'Gath's maidens will be glad to see the back of both of you. Now get going before I change my mind.'

The mule Uriah gave them was strong but slow, not varying its plodding pace from dawn until the noon hour when they reached the well at Azekah, where they accepted bread and cured olives from the women in return for hauling up several pails of questionable water.

Dawid and Habib sat on one of the great stones that legend said fell from the skies when the Hebrews put the local kings to flight, and the Phoenician scoffed at Dawid's fanciful notion that the Philistines would suffer the same fate. They gazed at the hilltop town with its meagre defences and agreed that Azekah would swiftly fall, especially as the well was outside the main settlement and the brook was separated from it by fields of barley and wheat.

'We should warn them,' said Habib firmly.

'Warn who, exactly? Azekah is probably as much Philistine as it is Judahite, it's so near to Gath.'

Dawid recounted how at Socoh, half a day's ride along the valley, he and Dookhi had encountered Mishon, who had been in league with the Philistines all along. By declaring themselves fugitives from Gath, they risked being taken as hostages and offered to the invaders in the inevitable negotiations that would take place.

'But on the other hand,' Dawid went on, 'if we are to warn the Israelite king or the prophet Shemu'el, we have to make our way to Gibeah, and I don't know the way. Do you?'

Habib shrugged. 'Never heard of it.'

'So we'll have to ask. Pretend we're traders.'

They did, but the area around the well was the domain of Azekah's womenfolk, who stared blankly at the finely dressed young men, or giggled as if they had made a lewd suggestion. Habib quickly decided he might get something more than information and set about charming the younger women. Dawid left him to it, gazing along the valley that he knew led to Socoh and Adullam, and beyond to Beth Lechem. These were the only places he knew in the whole of Judah, let alone Israel to the north. Should he return to the caves and entrust Rachael and Martha with the details of the Philistine plans? Perhaps Nathan would be there. Or should he just forget about it all, find a town far away from the imminent conflict and make his fortune and a name for himself? He thought about Naomi begging him to do the right thing for his people, and he wondered what Rachael would expect of him.

Then he remembered an old friend he had left behind at Socoh so long ago — Morning Star, and Dookhi's horse, too. Would the innkeeper's son have kept his word and looked after Morning Star against the promise of silver when he returned? The original plan of just a day or two in Gath had turned to months, and it was likely that the fat innkeeper had sold their horses long ago. But he had to find out. And there was another matter to settle, almost as important as getting the horses back, and that was retribution against the innkeeper, Naboth. It could only be him who had betrayed them to Mishon, and if his son, Obed, had been involved too…

Dawid whistled to Habib, who reluctantly dragged his attention away from a group of heavily veiled young women who seemed more interested in his colourful clothing than any favours he might be suggesting.

'Come!' Dawid called. 'If we're going to reach Socoh by nightfall —'

'Do you really think that old mule can manage it?' laughed Habib as he waved his farewell to the girls of Azekah.

Melek, Commander of the Invincibles and favoured by King Akish, fingered his new chain of office and frowned at the severed head. The expressionless eyes stared back at him. It was a thin face, a pallid grey colour, its wispy beard and hair matted with black gore. He thought he recognised the slightly bent hooked nose and those sleepy eyes set too close together, but he couldn't be sure.

'A Hebrew?' he said to the young officer without taking his eyes off the fascinating trophy. 'Trying to get into the palace, you say?'

'Yes, my lord.' The officer felt uneasy that Melek hadn't immediately congratulated him on executing an enemy assassin.

'And you beheaded him on whose orders exactly?'

The uneasiness mutated into the kind of foreboding that twisted the gut. 'I … uh … well…'

'Spit it out, man! Whose orders?'

'Yours, my lord. At least, that's what he said —'

'He?'

'Yes, my lord. The young noble who pointed him out to me. He said your men had been following him and there was a reward for his head.'

Melek stroked his beard and ordered his thoughts. Why would one of Gath's nobles make up such a tale and have this obscure Hebrew randomly executed? Unless… He fixed the officer with a menacing glare.

'What you tell me next will decide whether I have your skin flayed from your back before you beg for the mercy of death,' said Melek coldly. 'Describe this noble.'

'He is the king's son-in-law. He said —'

'*The king has no son-in-law!*' Melek shouted and the officer jumped back a pace. 'I said describe him, not fiddle around for excuses.'

The officer did his best. He described the magnificent ring and the youth's fine clothes and, as a trickle of sweat ran between his shoulder blades, the shock of reddish hair, the impossibly handsome features — surely a mark of nobility in the immaculate court of Gath, he thought — and yes, the distinguishing scars on his face. And he walked with a limp…

Melek's eyes glazed over as he remembered the dirty Hebrew spy and his taunting speed when he avoided the cane on his knuckles, the impudence of his success first with the Hittites and then in the arena. His refusal to succumb to an agonising death, or even an instant one, the favours shown by Akish and his daughter in the palace, and yes, oh yes, the secret tryst between Princess Lalia's Hebrew servant girl and the unclean foreigner. He breathed his name in a moment of revelation. *Dawid.*

'Sir?' The officer was beginning to hope that Melek's deliberations meant he had earned himself a reprieve for whatever mistake he had made.

'Hmm…?' Melek waved him away impatiently. The officer almost tripped as he backed away with undue haste, but Melek didn't notice the indiscretion. *Where will you run, you heathen spy? Straight back to your pathetic rabble and that feeble king to warn them that the Philistines are coming? I'll find you, and I hope your luck keeps you alive until I do…*

Socoh had aged. The slum tents outside the walls were eerily quiet as the mule picked its way between miasmic latrine pits and discarded animal carcasses, ignoring the skinny dogs that scavenged for decaying scraps and yapped at the strangers. The gates were unguarded and inside the city the streets were quiet. No traders displayed hopeful wares and the beggars seemed resigned to another night of hunger and want.

Naboth's inn was bereft of life. The wooden gates hung askew on rope bindings rotted with neglect, and there were no animals housed beneath the sparse hatch of Obed's stable. No Morning Star. Not even a goat to milk. Dawid left Habib to tether the mule and called for the innkeeper, noticing movement from within the darkened building and seeing the haunted look in the eyes of one of Obed's sisters.

'Tell your father he has guests,' he said softly.

The young girl stared vacantly, but a gruff voice — Naboth's — came from somewhere inside the inn.

'We're full. Go away.'

'We've returned to pay what you are owed,' Dawid said more firmly into the darkness.

The mention of the words "pay" and "owed" brought a response and the innkeeper appeared at the door. He looked older, with less hair, and perhaps his clothes hung a little looser around his ample frame. Naboth peered at Dawid as he stumbled into the courtyard, remembering the half shekel of silver, the fine mounts, his small windfall for information given to the secretive Mishon and, more importantly, the half shekel more he had been promised in return for looking after the horses. He fidgeted, shuffled and began to back away.

'Where are they, old man?' said Dawid, aware that his appearance contrasted convincingly with the shepherd's mantle he had worn on his last visit to Socoh and that now he struck fear into Naboth's heart.

'Gone.' Naboth sighed and wrung his hands, searching for an excuse.

'Where is your son, Obed? He swore to look after the horses.'

'Gone.'

Dawid unsheathed his dagger and stepped closer to Naboth, whose back now touched the inn's wall. He had nowhere to go. Dawid enjoyed the smell of fear as the innkeeper stared at the knife's curved blade.

'You don't have very long to live old man, unless you tell me where the horses are.'

His brow beaded with sweat, his hands shook and his reply was tremulous. 'They took the horses … and Obed went with them.'

'They…?' Dawid's blade twitched under Naboth's nose. The girl watched impassively.

'They said they came in King Saul's name. Look, I was paid nothing…'

'And Obed?'

'He would not leave your horses. He cared for them better than he cared for us.'

'I'm not surprised,' said Dawid. 'Horses don't cheat and betray you.'

'What do you mean?' Naboth's eyes were darting now, looking from Dawid to the point of the knife before him.

'Tell me, Naboth,' said Dawid coolly, 'have you seen your friend Mishon recently?'

Naboth went white. 'Mishon…? I don't know anyone by that name.'

'Liar.' Dawid cut Naboth's earlobe and the girl screamed as the innkeeper pushed back against the wall.

'All right, leave me be. I'll tell you what I know.'

'Go on.' Dawid smiled at the girl, knowing he couldn't cause any more harm to her father than a small cut to the ear, though they'd see enough terror when the Philistines came to Socoh.

'Mishon let it be known he would pay for information, but I swear I didn't know what he did with it.'

'You can guess.'

Naboth nodded. 'I know, the Philistines. Mishon often went to Gath. For his business.'

'And also his death.' Dawid, who had been looking at the girl while Naboth spoke, now turned his flinty eyes back to the innkeeper. 'He died last night, in Gath. I ordered his execution personally.'

'You…?' Naboth quaked. He had the look of a man who knew he was going to die.

'And now you can convince me not to cut your throat. Where did these Israelites take my horses?'

'They're building a fortress near here — about a hundred men in all. It's not far, and their leader chose your grey mare for himself, so find him and you find your horses.'

'What's this place called?'

'Ephes-Dammim. It's on the ridge above the Elah brook, near where the valley turns towards Azekah.'

Dawid studied Naboth's face and decided the old man would suffer more through self-imposed misery and greed. 'I'm going to let you live, Naboth, for the sake of your son, who I happen to like. But first you have to answer one more question. What is the name of the thief who stole my horse?'

Naboth dribbled in his relief. He knew the name, as did any Hebrew who listened to the tales of heroism in the halls and taverns of Israel and Judah.

'Yonatan,' he said softly. 'Yonatan, the king's son.'

The meteorite storm that lit the clear night sky could be seen from Dan to Beersheba. In the port of Sidon, because the lights that flashed across the dark expanse came from the west, the priests rent their clothing and wailed about impending disaster from the sea.

The hail of shooting stars caused a small war in the east where the Moabite king saw the display and concluded that the gods had chosen him to destroy the desert tribes that competed with Moab for trading rights on the King's Highway.

In the fortress of Jebus, the old king Elyizedek was reading a message from the Philistine coalition of warlords. He put down the clay tablet and marvelled at the way the gods, silent for so many years, should speak in so clear and timely a fashion.

In Gath, King Akish walked the upper terrace of his palace alone, looking out at the thousands of twinkling fires in the valley where the men of Ekron, Ashdod, Gaza and Ashkelon camped, and knew that the time was right. Dagon was with him.

On the ridge above the Elah valley, Yonatan and the young warriors of The Fist dismissed the sign as nothing more than confirmation of what they already knew, but two days' march to the west, at Gibeah, Yonatan's father King Saul railed at the prophet Shemu'el because Yahweh was sending them an enemy that numbered more than the stars. Shemu'el told him to pull himself together.

Dawid and Habib were exhausted after their travels and slept through it, curled together for warmth in a deserted shepherd's lodge well away from the stench of Socoh.

At the Adullam Caves, the priestess Rachael and Nathan's mother, Martha, watched the night's display in awe.

'They come,' said Rachael.

It wasn't a difficult sign to read.

PART THREE: THE VALLEY OF ELAH

CHAPTER TWENTY-SEVEN

The seeping cold of dawn woke the two youths, who pulled their cloaks tight around their shoulders. Dawid filled his lungs with Judah's sweet air and gazed absently at lazy columns of woodsmoke drifting above Socoh. A fragile mist clung to the valley below, obscuring the barley fields, nudging the wooded slopes that concealed the Hebrew prince's camp opposite. They watched a pair of graceful buzzards circling above and debated whether to return to Socoh in search of food or to scavenge in the woods for nuts and, hopefully, wild berries. Or they could even make the short journey to Yonatan's camp, where there would be a plentiful supply of provisions, however unappetising.

Growling stomachs were hastening their decision when they heard the shouts of hunters violating the valley's peace. The hobbled mule, which had been grazing nearby, snorted as it looked for danger, ears twitching in alarm. In one bound, Dawid was beside the mule to free its bonds in case flight was their safest option. He calmed the animal by blowing into its nostrils. They listened, trying to learn numbers, direction and intent. Several men, mostly on foot, with two or three horsemen, were coming uphill towards them through the woods. And there was another sound, a heavy beast grunting with effort, crashing recklessly through undergrowth.

'Boar,' said Dawid. 'Wounded, by the sound of it.' He looked around. 'It's safest if we stay behind a tree. The beast is running, so it will slash at anything in its way.'

The boar stormed into view. It was a male, moving with surprising agility for such a large beast, its angry eyes inflamed with the pain of two black-flighted shafts embedded deep in its flank. Three riders emerged from the woods at a canter, keeping pace with their prey. Half blinded and wheezing blood from punctured lungs, the boar sensed Dawid's mule in its path and swerved away from it, presenting a target for the lead rider, who hurled a spear as the beast turned. It was a powerful throw, the bronze point taking the boar below the shoulder, piercing vital organs. Its forelegs crumpled instantly and it slid through pine needles and rotting leaves to lie heaving just five paces from where Dawid and Habib stood.

Dawid had already recognised the hunter's mount, and Morning Star had recognised him. The rider, too tall and muscular for the mare, dismounted and moved swiftly to the boar to despatch it with his knife, ignoring the two observers. Two more riders reined in their horses, one of them whistling and calling to the less fortunate hunters who followed on foot. Dawid willed Morning Star to come to him, and his heart beat faster as she obeyed, trotting to his side with a small whinny to nuzzle his chest. The hunter looked up from his bloody work.

'My horse likes you.'

This was said softly, as if the man did not consider Dawid and Habib to be enemies.

'She is not yours.' Dawid looked into the hunter's brown eyes, knowing this was the son of Israel's king, yet he somehow warmed to this adventurer with his untidy hair, lopsided grin and thick, bull-like neck.

'Do we ever *own* an animal such as this?' mused Yonatan, striding powerfully to Morning Star's side and slapping her neck firmly as if he appreciated her efforts in the hunt. 'Perhaps it is the other way around.'

'In which case, she appears to have chosen me.' Could a shepherd boy turned Philistine courtier take such a fine creature from the Prince of Israel? He would do so even if he had to fight, but he knew that he had something of great value with which to bargain.

'Or perhaps she likes the smell of goat?' Yonatan studied him to see if he would rise to the insult, but Dawid laughed and Morning Star nuzzled him again.

'Do we fight or talk?' It was Dawid's turn to watch for a reaction, though he had to look up to Yonatan, who was a head taller and in the prime of manhood. There was silence between them, a moment in which he smelled blood and sweat and knew he would not defeat Yonatan in combat, but he held the older man's gaze.

'We talk,' smiled Yonatan. 'Then we let the mare decide who rides her.'

Habib had watched the exchange with a mixture of trepidation and amusement, but he understood that the gods of time and place had yet again been with Dawid and now he was face to face with one of the most powerful men in Israel. This was the warrior prince Yonatan himself, a Hebrew whose father had been chosen by their god to rule.

'Are you going to eat that or do you only want its tusks?' he ventured cheekily, pointing to the dead boar.

Yonatan and Dawid stared at him incredulously, and the other men, a dozen in all, muttered to each other in disbelief.

'I mean,' Habib went on boldly, 'if you're all Hebrews and forbidden to eat pig meat, how am I going to manage it all on my own?'

Dawid, who knew the Phoenician's daring as well as his own, was quick to react. He introduced him to Yonatan. 'This is Habib of Tyre, of a race of lesser mortals without wit or ability.'

'Yonatan,' said Yonatan with a courteous nod, 'son of a farmer with no manners and a general ignorance of the laws of the land. Yes, we are going to eat this beast, extremely tasty when roasted with herbs and onions, and its mate which lies speared somewhere in the valley, and —' he pointed to the hares hanging at the flank of one of the horses — 'those we trapped earlier. We have a lot of mouths to feed and too little time to ask Yahweh which animal we should eat, but all, including the geese and grain we have been, ah, given by the generous farmers of these parts are eaten with a prayer of thanksgiving!' He turned to Dawid. 'And who are you?'

'Dawid of Beth Lechem and lately of Gath.'

Yonatan raised an eyebrow. 'A Hebrew, then? Why in Gath?'

'Imprisoned. We both were,' he replied, indicating Habib as his fellow unfortunate.

'Imprisoned, yet so finely dressed, even if you could do with a wash! You have some explaining to do, I think.'

Dawid decided to reveal his bargaining position. 'We have information about the Philistines that may interest you.'

Yonatan nodded, eyeing the two youths suspiciously. 'Freely given, as the farmers give us food, or at a price?'

'At a price.'

'Name it.'

'My horse. Morning Star.'

Yonatan laughed. 'Agreed.'

Obed was in the camp at Ephes-Dammim, the "boundary of blood" as Yonatan had named it, like a line in the sand across which the enemies of Israel could not pass. Obed was just one of several Dawid knew as he rode between the ditches that Yonatan's men were digging at the summit of a long ridge overlooking the Elah valley. Ari, the chubby youth who had faithfully handed over Morning Star all those moons ago in Beth Lechem's stables, was with him. Obed and Ari were good friends, united in their love for the winsome mare. Both were suspicious of the prestigious character Dawid had become. But for now, Morning Star was Yonatan's property, and until the Hebrew warlord said otherwise, they obeyed his every whim.

The men cheered Yonatan into the camp, knowing they would feast well after their labours that day. First to greet the king's son was the eldest of Dawid's half-brothers, Eliab, flanked by the leaders of The Fist, Oren and Rimon. These Dawid greeted warmly, but he eyed the haughty Eliab with trepidation. It took an age for Eliab to recognise him, and Dawid realised that it was not just his outward appearance that had changed in the year since he had left Beth Lechem. Now he had become a man, fought giants, known two women and was trusted by the king of a city. No longer could anyone treat him as if he was dog's dung on the sole of a sandal. He caught Eliab eyeing him and chose to ignore the man at whose fists he had suffered many a beating.

But Oren and Rimon he did not neglect. He embraced them as equals, enjoying the scowl that Eliab gave him, then turned to laugh and chat with the Prince of Israel. How he relished the feeling. Better than a gratifying fist to the jaw of Jesse's eldest son.

Oren was now the leader of The Fist as Nathan had been injured in a fall and instead was given to learning the mysterious ways of Yahweh at the feet of Shemu'el. Oren's troop of horsemen, now numbering more than twenty, had been commandeered by Yonatan who understood the value of swift horses and riders. With an arm around Dawid's shoulder, Oren plied him with questions about Gath, Dookhi, and his experiences among Israel's enemies. Dawid was guarded, saving the best for the conversation that would soon come with Yonatan. But when he told Oren and Rimon about their comrade Dookhi, all three wept at his untimely death, and swore they would each take ten Philistines in retribution when they joined in battle, as they surely would before long.

And they welcomed Habib among them, proclaiming him an honorary member of The Fist as he had fought with Philistines twice his size and lived.

Dawid placed a large pebble in the pouch of Oren's sling. One end of the leather cord was looped around his wrist, the other held between forefinger and thumb.

'Balance is important,' he told Oren, proud to have been asked to demonstrate the art of using a sling. The round stone, of a size to fit in a man's palm, nestled comfortably in the soft goatskin pouch. 'Here, you try it.'

Oren fitted the loop over his wrist as he had been shown and placed the pebble. He swung it gently.

'That stone is deadly only if you swing it fast,' Dawid told him, 'and only if you release the cord at the right moment. Try it. Hit that tree over there.'

Oren swung the sling behind then over his head. The stone dropped harmlessly behind him.

'Here,' Dawid laughed, taking the sling back. 'Watch my hand carefully for the moment when I release.' With a practised movement that flowed behind him then over his shoulder, the missile thudded into the tree trunk, leaving a greenish gash in its bark.

Oren whistled, impressed, and ran to retrieve the pebble. He was searching for it in the undergrowth when a spear flashed past him and embedded itself in the tree a hand's breadth from the mark made by Dawid's throw.

'Now that's a killing weapon,' said Yonatan.

Dawid turned, surprised that such a big man had approached unnoticed. 'And now you're unarmed, but I have more stones in my pouch.' Dawid knew he was being cocky, but he was confident that Yonatan did not demand airs and graces.

'Your little pebbles will just bounce off,' said Yonatan smoothly. 'It's like being stung by a bee — unpleasant but not fatal.'

'Ask the thieves that came for my flock. Or the wolves and wild cats that got in the way of such little pebbles!'

Yonatan went to the tree and freed his spear. Dawid noticed how his shoulder muscles stood out with the strain as he withdrew the weapon. 'You have a point,' he said, tapping the spear's bronze tip on the ground before him. 'Can these slings be used on horseback?'

'I have managed it,' Dawid replied, remembering the encounter with four Philistines near Adullam. 'But I think it would be less accurate, and difficult, if riding at a gallop.'

Yonatan turned to Oren. 'How many riders do you command? Twenty?'

Oren nodded. He was as tall as Yonatan, and Dawid sensed in him a self-assurance that had grown with his command of The Fist.

'And could your men learn how to use slings?'

'It's not as easy as it looks,' replied Oren. He hesitated, then added, 'But yes, we can.'

'Good.' Yonatan turned to Dawid. 'How are these weapons made? Can you show us?'

'We'll need skins, which have to be scraped and soaked.'

'Soaked? In what? Water is scarce up here.'

Dawid laughed. 'Not water. Piss! There should be plenty of that as long as we have pots to piss into!'

Yonatan slapped him on the back. 'So we'll have to drink more wine.'

'And we can use the skins of those beasts you hunted…'

'The skins of unclean animals?' Yonatan exclaimed in mock protest. 'Don't ever breathe a word of this to my father or that crazed prophet of his.'

He sent Oren to acquire the skins and organise a small team of tanners, then he beckoned Dawid to follow. They walked past several of the makeshift shelters his men had made to a fenced enclosure where twenty horses grazed on new grass or nosed at a trough of mashed grains.

'They are cared for better than my own men,' he sighed. 'And for good reason. Until now, we have had to make do with mules and ponderous oxen to supply our men. We're a rabble. When our enemies come with chariots and proper weapons, we run to the hills. If the enemy follows, they die, because we know the mountains and valleys better than they. But now, look at these horses…'

Morning Star spotted the two men at the fence and trotted over with an excited whinny. She nuzzled Dawid, looking for some treat, but was content with a reassuring ruffling of her mane and a scratching of her nose.

'Mules are stubborn, but these are clever,' Yonatan continued, admiring Morning Star's bright eyes. 'And they like nothing better than to be ridden hard. Would that we had more and could try them in battle.'

'The Philistines have horses, but they use them to draw chariots.' Dawid knew that the traditional preamble was over and now the serious talk would begin.

'You have seen these chariots?'

'Yes, and the mighty giants that ride in them.'

Yonatan's eyes sparkled. *A man who yearns for a challenge,* thought Dawid.

'I have a feeling that when you have finished speaking, this mare will be yours,' said the Prince of Israel.

CHAPTER TWENTY-EIGHT

Yonatan clarified each point concerning the enemy's plans and plied Dawid with questions about numbers and weapons, especially the huge chariots. He swiftly grasped that a Hebrew army would stand no chance if it engaged these war machines on the flat barley fields of the Elah valley, and appeared shocked on hearing of the alliance between the Philistines and the city of Jebus. Dawid watched Yonatan's face as he grappled with the horrific images of Israelites being smashed down from the front and simultaneously attacked in the rear.

When he had wrung every detail from Dawid he studied the horses in silence, then pointed to Morning Star.

'She's yours,' he said, surprising Dawid with a kiss on the cheek and an embrace. 'If I had more to give, it would be yours too,' he whispered in his ear, 'but for now, I have only my friendship to offer.' He stepped back, squeezed Dawid's shoulders then turned abruptly, striding into his camp and calling for his trusted commanders. They came running, as did most of the camp as Yonatan's troops were inquisitive to a man and eager for action.

He drew a crude map in the sandy ground with the tip of his spear, pointing to the Elah brook, Gath, Azekah, Socoh, Jebus and Gibeah. He told them that it was likely a large and well-organised army was marching from Gath right now and the main Hebrew army was at least two days distant. He told them about the Jebusites, silencing an officer who began to curse his own people's tardiness in not taking the walled fortress years ago. He raised their spirits by telling them the good news — thanks to the horses of The Fist, Saul was no more than a day's ride distant and the sooner he was informed, the sooner the Hebrew host could march to meet the Philistine threat. Then he issued his orders with calm authority.

Yonatan chose a grizzled veteran, Eleazar ben Dodai, to ride with Rimon east along the Elah valley then sweep north to Jebus and Gibeah, watching for a force of Jebusites. If they saw the Jebusite force, Rimon was to return to Ephes-Dammim to inform Yonatan, leaving Eleazar to continue alone to Saul's camp at Gibeah. If the Jebusite raiders had not left their city, then both must implore Saul to send a small force to blockade Jebus while marching west along the Elah valley with his main army.

Another rider was sent to summon Abner, Saul's most trusted general, who was stationed near Ekron with a small but ferocious force to watch for possible Philistine incursions.

'This leaves us with seventeen horses and nearly a hundred men,' said Yonatan after the three messengers had hurried away to their tasks, 'and maybe three days until our army is assembled here. You don't need me to tell you that the Philistine horde could be marching up this valley before our soldiers arrive in force. So we must find ways to delay them, even fight a rearguard action to hold them if possible while we wait for the king and Abner. And the prophet Shemu'el, of course.'

Not one of the men flinched at that, as if they were used to following Yonatan on suicide missions. They waited patiently for their orders, though Dawid noticed several of the warriors glancing at him, realising that all this information about the enemy had come to Yonatan's attention with his and Habib's arrival in the camp. Dawid felt a surge of pride and fidgeted where he stood next to the king's son.

'We are fortunate to have been given such valuable information,' Yonatan continued, placing a hand on Dawid's shoulder. 'This man has fought Gath's champion warrior and lived, and has feasted with Philistine nobles.'

Dawid stole a glance at his half-brother Eliab, the one man in this company from whom he expected trouble. He was staring at him quizzically, surprisingly without any hint of hatred. And it was Eliab who spoke, voicing the concerns of perhaps several of the men.

'If this young man has feasted in the halls of Gath, how can we be sure he is not feeding us a lie and the attack will come from elsewhere while the host of Israel waits in the wrong place?' It seemed like a sensible question, but it angered Dawid. He took a step forward, fists balled, and was about to answer when Yonatan gently pulled him back.

'Eliab makes an interesting point,' he said, 'one quite rightly put. But to you all I say this. I have questioned this youth and he convinces me. If I am wrong and the Philistines sweep through our lands from the north, or further south, then my friends, look where we are. Gath lies not far from here —' he pointed west — 'and it will be undefended. We will take it. But believe me, this man speaks the truth and we will soon be in a fight to the death. If we live, if we are victorious, we will drink to Dawid, son of…'

Yonatan cursed himself for not having asked the traditional courtesy of Dawid's lineage. Dawid was about to reveal that he did not know who his father was when he heard Eliab's voice again.

'Dawid ben Jesse,' said Eliab loudly. 'Youngest of the eight sons of Jesse of the line of Boaz and the Moabitess Ruth.'

Dawid's head swam. What was Eliab saying? That he was a real person, with ancestors? Not the son of a whore, hated and spat upon all his life, like his mother? Eliab was his brother, not his half-brother. And Abinadab and Shimea, whose disdain had crushed him as a child. And Raddai and Elihu, both treacherous and cruel in their different ways.

'Dawid?' said Yonatan.

Dawid realised Eliab's words had plunged him into a world of his own. He shook his head and looked at Yonatan.

'What is your answer, Dawid ben Jesse? Can you train these men as slingers?'

He nodded, his mind still spinning.

'And to use these slings while riding horses?'

Suddenly Yonatan's plan became clear. He wanted to use the riders of The Fist to assault the ponderous Philistine army like wasps whose nest had been poked with a stick. A hail of slingstones could do so much damage even to armoured foot soldiers, and unless the Philistines unhitched the chariot horses, it was unlikely that the Hebrew riders could be caught. It would be enough to demoralise the Philistines and send them scurrying for cover.

'Of course,' he beamed.

It was obvious to Dawid that Yonatan wanted to take personal charge of training the slingers, but there were two obstacles to this. Firstly, Yonatan was not born to the saddle. He was powerfully built and muscular almost to the point of being clumsy, though his sword drill showed he did not lack technique and he carried a fine horn-tipped bow that gave his arrows considerable range. Secondly, he concerned himself with watching for the invaders, not simply by standing on the highest point at Ephes-Dammim, staring towards Azekah and Gath beyond, but by sending out riders with orders to return by nightfall. This further depleted the number of horses at

Dawid and Oren's disposal for practising slingshot riding, but it did bring him news that Dawid's report was true and the Philistine host was mustered at the walls of Gath.

So Yonatan had appointed an officer with experience in warfare to oversee the training — Eliab. But if Dawid thought this would provide an opportunity to find out what Eliab meant by his revelations, it was not to be until dusk fell the next day. Eliab proved to be a hard taskmaster, firm in his drill without being frantic, given that time was short and an army could easily march from Gath to Socoh in a day. He was probably as good as Dawid with a sling, having spent much of his youth tending Jesse's flocks, and he immediately took a team to the brook to select a store of similar sized stones, ideal for distance and accuracy yet not too large for the riders to carry in the tough goatskin bags all Hebrew conscripts bore with them on military campaigns.

But Dawid and Eliab were not the only seasoned slingers among the hundred. Yonatan had handpicked a number of men from among his native Benjaminites, a tribe that traditionally supplied slingers whenever the call to arms had been sent throughout Israel. While Yonatan had poured scorn on the primitive weapon, instead arming his men with swords, spears and bronze farm tools, many had secretly retained their faith in their favoured weapon and brought their slings with them. It added a competitive edge to Eliab's practice sessions, the Benjaminites trying to outdo the two Beth Lechemites from Judah.

But none of the Benjaminites had ever ridden a horse before. Eliab and Yonatan saw the hopelessness of asking foot soldiers to attempt to ride bareback while keeping an arm free to use their slings. Only Oren, Dawid and the riders of The Fist succeeded.

It was Dawid who saw the solution. Providing the Benjaminite slingers and those others who had mastered the art were slight, the horsemen of The Fist could carry them to a position where they could dismount, fire a volley at the massed ranks of Philistines, then remount to retire before the enemy could catch them. That way, there would be twice the number of slingers harrying the advancing army, but in carrying two men, the horses would be slower.

'We risk much,' said Yonatan when he saw what Eliab, Dawid and Oren were planning. 'Thirty men against the Philistine host. Now those are odds to contend with!'

The cooking fires were lit at dusk when Dawid sought out Eliab, bringing him a wineskin as a peace offering just in case the old enmity between them was rekindled. But Eliab had changed and invited him to sit by his fire. *Like a brother*, he thought ruefully.

Eliab talked with fondness of their mother, Nitzevet, a woman of peace and love and the cherishing wife of a powerful man. He then described how Jesse had listened to the sordid words of the priests, hearing their judgment that he, descendant of the heathen Moabite Ruth, was not worthy to be married to a Hebrew and he should put her aside, banishing himself from the purity of Yahweh's perfect seed. So, Eliab continued sadly, Jesse had sent away the woman he loved and married his handmaiden, the Canaanite Kerith, in her place. Then he had turned to wine, becoming so inebriated he didn't know his own sons or his wife. Kerith was the innocent in this sorry time, said Eliab, and Nitzevet saw this.

'It wouldn't have surprised me if our mother had become bitter and filled with hatred for Kerith,' said Eliab, staring into the flames. 'But she didn't. She had such strength and wisdom.

I wish I had seen it before, but we were all so young and believed the idle gossip about her, fanned by those evil priests. She befriended Kerith and helped her, a terrified servant elevated to such an exalted position. And none of us knew of this friendship and their plotting together…'

'Plotting?' Dawid interrupted. 'You make our mother sound like an idle old woman with nothing better to do.'

'No, it wasn't like that. I realise that now. Kerith was unable to give Jesse any more sons, and she knew that Nitzevet wanted to bear one more child. She must have been disappointed in all of us — we were so cruel to her and we weren't any kinder to Kerith. These two women supported each other through their misfortune and knowing that our mother would never go with another man, Kerith begged Nitzevet to take her place in Jesse's bed. The old man was so drunk he could not tell a perfect Hebrew woman apart from a Canaanite servant girl.'

Dawid understood. He was a secret child, the son of Jesse, not the unwanted child of some wastrel passing through Beth Lechem.

'But how do you know this?' he asked as Eliab used a stick to stoke the fire. 'If it was such a secret, why have they told of this now?'

'Because…' Eliab threw the stick into the flames and covered his face. He tried again, his voice muffled. 'Because they stoned our mother.'

'*What?*' Dawid leapt to his feet and looked down at his guilt-ridden eldest brother. 'Stoned? You mean they killed her? Who? Why…?'

Eliab turned his tearful face to Dawid and tugged at the hem of his tunic. 'Sit. Be calm. She is not dead.'

'I will go to her at first light tomorrow. But first you will tell me who is responsible.'

'Who is responsible?' Eliab gave a bitter, humourless laugh. 'The priests maybe, with their greed and hypocrisy. Nitzevet herself, perhaps, and Kerith, for keeping silent all these years. Our father — a pitiful drunk, but at least now he is trying to do right by her. All of us, yes, for our arrogance and petulance. But especially Raddai and Elihu, for they weaved their lies to incite the priests and the mob.'

Dawid spat into the flames and considered Eliab's words. Until now, he had known nothing of the man save his cruelty and aloofness, but now he seemed human, even considerate. And for the first time in his life, Dawid laid his head against the breast of a man who had hated him and wept, an appalling sadness washing over him. His father was slave to the wineskin — a bloated, wealthy, highly respected paragon of the law, whose god was in the last foul dregs of the goblet at daybreak. He reached out, took the skin and poured a stream of wine into his mouth, numbing the pain. His father was probably doing exactly the same in far-off Beth Lechem. His head swam.

'I must go to Beth Lechem,' he said through his pain. 'I must go home.'

'No. Not yet.'

'But my mother…'

'No. She lives and she calls for you, but you are needed here. Judah is greater than our mother. She would tell you that. Besides, all deserters are impaled on their own spears, and Yonatan will make no exception for you, however valuable you have proved to the Hebrew cause. No, Dawid, we will return together, for this shame is upon us both and my … *our* brothers.'

'Raddai… I must kill him. And Elihu too.'

'I have dealt with them according to the law. I killed Raddai and Elihu fled to Hebron to seek refuge. Look at me, Dawid. I have killed my own brother.'

He saw the pain in Eliab's eyes and knew that he suffered too. But Nitzevet had suffered most of all. 'Tell me about her. Is she loved? Is she cared for?'

'I cannot say that she will live until you and I return. But I live in hope. Kerith is with her — she warms her and loves her soul. With Kerith by her side, she will live, I think…'

'Please. I must go to her. I will ride….'

'No. By whichever god is in this place, you must stand by Yonatan. This will all be over in a day or two. If you live, then go. And you will live — our mother believes it so.'

'I will not die,' said Dawid purposefully. 'I will see my mother before she is lowered to the grave.'

Dawid reached into his pouch and fingered the stones he had placed there next to the Star of Anak and felt the smooth leather of the sling he had put with them. He imagined using his sling against Elihu and the priests of Beth Lechem, but then decided that his brother was right — there was much to do before that day came.

He silently mouthed a prayer to the goddess. *Keep her safe. Keep my mother safe until I come to her.*

CHAPTER TWENTY-NINE

The riders of The Fist thundered towards the copse that represented the Philistine ranks. At a signal from Oren, the riders reined in their mounts and all dismounted, firing rapid volleys at the trees, which shuddered at the remorseless impacts. Then within a few heartbeats, they remounted and wheeled away.

They practised until the sun was at its zenith and Eliab ordered them to rest.

Dawid ate dried figs in sullen silence while Habib chattered, trying unsuccessfully to restore his friend's spirits. It was wasted effort. Something grew dark and terrible behind Dawid's sad eyes.

Word reached the camp that the Philistines were on the move, news that was expected but which nonetheless brought about a renewed energy. The few swords carried by Yonatan's men were sharpened, bows and bowstrings oiled and arrows gathered in bundles. Oren and Eliab spoke to the riders with urgency, their voices low as if the enemy was hidden in the woods.

Abner arrived at dusk. He and his men travelled on foot, not trusting mules, donkeys, horses or chariots. They came to the camp at a loping half-run, a technique developed for travelling long distances with speed yet maintaining stealth and silence. Their numbers doubled the troops at Ephes-Dammim. Abner's men were hardened warriors stripped to the waist, each carrying a short thrusting spear in one hand and a bow with several arrows in the other. They were greeted with enthusiasm by Yonatan's men.

When Dawid saw Abner, he put aside his misery and wondered what sort of warrior could take so many wounds yet still walk and breathe. His powerful upper body was streaked with old scars and his face looked as if it had been rearranged by a Philistine war hammer. His nose was flat and bent and one eye drooped lower, giving him a vacant look, accented by a livid scar that ran down one side of his face, leaving a gap in his beard from lip to chin. He was dark and swarthy, his hair matted and tangled, and his men smelled like a herd of goats, but Yonatan embraced them all with the enthusiasm and joy that Dawid had come to expect from this generous prince of Israel.

'Uncle!' roared Yonatan as Abner led his men to the cooking fires, embracing the sweating warrior and kissing his neck. It seemed that Saul kept his senior appointments in the family, which made sense to Dawid. But he smelled danger in this unsmiling Abner, anger perhaps, and he remained on the edge of the reunion, watching as the men told tales of their travels and their skirmishes.

'How many?' Abner asked Yonatan, holding his nephew at arm's length to look him up and down.

'Do you mean how many women have I bedded or how many men do we face in battle?'

Abner snorted. 'The women you can tell me about later. For now, how many Philistines?'

'Our rider returned today. He watched the Philistines march towards Azekah. They filled the valley, he said — perhaps ten thousand, too many to number.'

'Saul will bring that many,' said Abner. 'Maybe more.'

'It's not so much the numbers, it's who leads them into Judah.'

'Akish? An old man.'

'No, not him. The Invincibles.'

'Who?'

'The Invincibles. That's their word, not ours, obviously, as we will defeat them. But these are monstrous men with very large chariots, and there are at least ten of them.'

'Nephew, are you afraid?' Abner's expressionless eyes held Yonatan's.

The Prince of Israel smiled. 'Afraid? Perhaps. I have not seen these Invincibles. But we have one among us who has fought with them. They will come in chariots strengthened with iron.'

Abner nodded. 'Effective on flat ground.'

'And useless in the hills.' Yonatan smiled. 'We must make them leave the valley and come up to us.'

'Difficult,' said Abner. 'We can insult their mothers and bare our arses, but if they want to use their chariots they'll stay down there.'

'So, a waiting game?' Yonatan stroked his beard, an idea forming.

'Yes. They won't be able to advance into Judah because then we could strike them from behind their army. They'll have to fight us here.'

'And we choose the ground?'

'We choose the ground.'

With dawn the next day came the first refugees, filing along the valley towards Socoh. Some led carts pulled by a donkey or a mule, some handcarts, and later in the day as a pall of smoke hung over the besieged city of Azekah, there were stragglers on foot without any possessions.

Yonatan sent a man to garner as much information as possible without revealing that two hundred of Israel's best troops lay concealed in the wooded hills above. 'We cannot help them, but perhaps the people of Socoh can,' he said to his scout. 'Go now, walk with them, and find out what the Philistines have done.'

Dawid and Habib watched from within the woods.

'I think we'll fight soon,' said Habib. He didn't sound afraid.

'I hope we don't meet Uriah,' Dawid mused. 'I wouldn't like to fight him.'

'I doubt we'll have time to think about who we're aiming at. But you're right — let's not kill Uriah.'

'I wonder if we'll see him again. I got the impression he didn't like the Philistines much, certainly not Melek.'

Dawid and Habib looked at each other and smiled.

'Melek. Now there's a Philistine I could gladly kill,' said Dawid.

The riders of The Fist dismounted and led their horses to the ridge that overlooked Azekah, the first victim in the struggle for the fertile land of the Shephelah valleys. Oren took Dawid and Habib as close as they dared to plan an attack. They could see that many of the wooden shacks that surrounded the city were smouldering ruins, the palisades torn down and used to fuel the surrounding army's night fires, now sending thin columns of smoke into the damp dawn air. Some of the Philistine soldiers slept by the fires in simple tents, while others had found a semblance of shelter inside the sacked city. Yonatan had been convinced the city would have fallen swiftly and by morning most of the Philistine army would have very sore heads. He was right. No amount of orders and threats could prevent common soldiers running amok after a battle, especially when it was so easily won.

'We could be upon them before they realise we are here,' said Oren.

Dawid and Habib agreed. The three had been chosen to ride without passengers, not just because they had mastered the use of slings while mounted, but also to pick up any colleagues whose horses had been injured.

'Where shall we strike?' asked Dawid. 'The kings and captains will all be safe inside the city, so our targets will be the sleeping soldiers.'

'We'll wait until the trumpet sounds,' said Oren. 'We need targets on their feet and closely packed, but too weary and cold to retaliate until we've gone.'

Habib pointed to the mass of tents around the city well. 'What's the first thing you do when you wake up with a sore head?'

'Take a piss,' said Dawid.

'And then?'

'Quench your thirst... Aha...'

'Exactly.'

'Pass the word to mount up,' said Oren.

A horn sounded somewhere in the occupied city, answered here and there throughout the vast camp with the sounds of horns and pipes, shouts and whistling, and the protests of men who had slept all too briefly. Eighteen riders mounted, and fifteen of them gave a lifting hand to a slinger. All wrapped their *pe'er* turbans around their faces so that only cold, determined eyes showed. They moved off between the trees and descended to the valley where it narrowed opposite Azekah, then approached the enemy camp as a tight knot of riders who could easily be mistaken for a force of mercenaries seeking employment with the Philistine invasion force. They kept their horses to a walk, chatting and laughing to maintain their pretence. They passed groups of prone soldiers, waving to those who stoked a fire, and calling jovial greetings to others. Some of the men were stretching or urinating, while the more diligent sharpened blades and polished buckles and mail. A hundred paces away, half-dressed soldiers congregated at the well to fill empty waterskins from the pail, arguing about seniority, pushing and shoving. They ignored the approaching horsemen.

Dawid eased the wrist loop of his sling into place and calmly loaded the first of the five stones he carried. He had estimated he would have time to loose perhaps three before the signal was given to retreat, more if he could. He glanced at Habib, who was readying his own sling.

Oren eased his mount into a trot, and with him the riders of The Fist. As Morning Star picked up her pace, Dawid noticed a procession of slaves making their way towards the well, carrying on their shoulders a wooden palanquin that undoubtedly housed one of Philistia's lords. It was garishly coloured with billowing yellow curtains. As the column wheeled towards the well, a gust of wind caught the curtains, thrusting them aside. He recognised the occupant instantly. The Philistine dignitary was Melek.

He couldn't resist the gesture. He loosened the cloth of his turban and showed his face.

As Oren led The Fist into open ground a mere thirty paces from the milling soldiers, Dawid watched Melek, who now saw the sudden danger. He revelled in the fury and terror that contorted Melek's features, then ignored the dwarf as Oren signalled the dismount. He picked out a Philistine soldier who was elbowing his way towards the well and in his mind's eye visualised his first missile thudding into the back of his skull. But Morning Star veered as he loosed. His stone caught the soldier on a shoulder blade, the victim spinning in agony as his bone shattered. All around there was mayhem at the well as stones rained on the enemy. Soldiers who had shown gritty resolve when taking a virtually defenceless city now screamed in agony as the missiles smashed into them.

Dawid aimed his third stone straight at Melek's eyes, but at the last minute he moved his head and the stone crashed through one of the sedan chair's uprights behind him, collapsing the canopy. A second hurled by Habib lost its power in the yellow cloth. The evil gaoler had survived, though if any of his men had seen the attack and where it came from, they would be amused. Had Melek seen him? He hoped so. Oh, how he hoped so.

The command from Oren was clear. Withdraw.

The Fist reined in, and the slingers remounted and were gone. They'd suffered no casualties and had caused untold damage, not least to the morale of Philistia's army.

They rode away from Azekah unchallenged.

CHAPTER THIRTY

The riders of The Fist took the easiest and quickest route along the valley, following the snaking brook that gave them cool water, although all the pomegranates and dates had been stripped by Azekah's refugees. They rested the horses as the sun climbed, looking back uneasily towards the fallen city in the distance, expecting pursuit but seeing none. The slingers picked out enough rounded stones from the brook for a second lightning raid, but now the Philistines would be ready for them.

'We wait and watch,' Oren told them. 'If they come, we will harry the marching ranks, try to slow them so that Saul's host has more time to join up with Yonatan and Abner at Ephes-Dammim.' He pointed to a wooded hillside where the terebinths and acacias grew thickly, where the brook snaked closest. 'We'll camp there. But no fire. We'll have empty stomachs, but I promise you a feast when we return to the camp.'

Dawid had other ideas. 'Oren, it may not be much, but as sure as the sun rises every morning I will find food in these woods.'

'Ah, the foraging shepherd boy,' Oren chuckled. 'See what you can find but take someone with you.'

Dawid chose Habib, and agreed on a signal should the enemy be spotted: the *hoop, hoop, hoop* of the *dukhifat* bird. Habib was amazed when Dawid made straight for a clump of green-leafed almond trees, all showing an abundance of soft pink blossom, as everyone knew that the almond season had passed many moons ago. Boar and other foragers had left many of the hard shells on the ground, and clinging to the branches were several more on each tree, stubbornly refusing to drop until coaxed with some vigorous shaking. They also found a few walnuts to add to the store, picking only those that had none of the telltale boreholes left by the grubs that laid eggs inside the shells.

They searched deeper in the wood, finding wild berries and fat locusts. Most of these Dawid ate as they moved upwards to denser woodland, arguing that locusts and crickets were best eaten fresh and the fruit would turn to mush by the time they returned.

In a clearing Dawid dropped onto all fours, drawing his dagger and probing the sandy loam. He found several large earthy nuggets, and exclaimed as if he had found gold lying near the surface. He wiped one and then split it with his knife, offering half of the white flesh to Habib. He then popped the larger chunk into his mouth and chewed slowly, and Habib did the same with a suspicious look. His eyes lit up.

'Gritty,' he said happily, 'but better than my mother's food ever was!'

Dawid grinned, chunks of the fungus showing on his teeth. 'Food of the gods,' he said, 'though I'm not sure the others are good enough to have some of these.'

But they resisted the temptation to eat them all and dropped several of the nuggets into their shoulder bags.

'If we could find honey, the feast would be complete,' said Dawid, patting his store of woodland delicacies. 'First we find a bee-eater and follow her. She will show us.'

'I know this bird,' said Habib excitedly. 'They hunt here too?'

'Of course,' answered Dawid and held up a hand as he listened for the throaty warbling within the cacophony of forest sounds. 'Come,' he said, 'this way.'

They ran like children through the undergrowth, the fallen foliage springy underfoot.

But they didn't find their bee-eater.

Dawid cursed when he saw the strained bow and the arrow aimed at his forehead. Habib tripped over a root and sprawled headlong before the three hooded men. He looked up, twigs in his hair and dust in his mouth, and both thought they were about to die.

'So Hebrew warriors aren't so stealthy after all,' said a familiar voice.

Uriah.

'Only one of us is Hebrew,' said Dawid calmly, hoping that friendship would bring a reprieve. 'The other is not worthy of a Hittite arrow.'

'Speak for yourself, Hebrew peasant.' Habib spat out grit and dust.

'Both peasants still,' said Uriah coldly, keeping his aim squarely on Dawid. 'We should have trained you better. Have you forgotten everything Elhanan taught you?'

Dawid watched Uriah, looking for the slightest hint of the warmth he had felt when he had last seen the mercenary commander. But the Hittite's eyes were hard, his bow steady, the arrow well aimed.

Uriah loosed his shaft.

Dawid felt the air ripple as the arrow flashed past his ear, embedding itself in the gnarled trunk of the tree behind him. But he didn't flinch or take his eyes off Uriah's.

'You're wondering,' said Uriah, 'if you are now a prisoner of the Hittites, and therefore of the Philistines.' He lowered the spent bow. 'And I am wondering why for so long I, too, have been a prisoner of the Philistines.'

Confused, Dawid said nothing, not even daring to step forward. Habib climbed to his feet and dusted himself down.

'So where would that leave me?' said the Phoenician. 'Enemy or friend?'

At last Uriah's face cracked into a smile. 'Friends, both of you. But as for warfare, I am yet undecided. What of you two sneakthieves?'

'Oh, we have already struck at the heart of the enemy,' said Dawid, hoping that he chose right in his admission. 'We attacked the invader at daybreak. A conclusive victory.'

'So you brave warriors unmanned the Invincibles and the host of the Philistine kings, just the two of you?'

'Not exactly. There were thirty of us. No more than that.'

'A great victory, then,' laughed Uriah. 'So the men of Gath are in full flight back to their city?'

'Well, we were slightly outnumbered…'

'So now you hide in the woods?'

'Only until we can attack again.'

Uriah signalled his two colleagues to lower their bows and embraced Dawid, then Habib. 'Very brave, very brave,' he muttered, 'but I think I know more than you about the true balance of this war.' He looked at Dawid, brow furrowed. 'Your king has arrived.'

'Saul?'

'Yes. He meets with his son even as we speak. My men have watched his approach.'

'How many?' Dawid was impressed, though he knew Hittites were masters at observing without being observed.

'A great host. More than the men of Akish and his allies. But they are a rabble — no match for the Invincibles and hard Philistine iron.'

'And that begs another question,' said Dawid, 'a simple one. For whom do you fight?'

'We fight for ourselves.' Uriah turned and smiled at his two archers. 'And those that pay with silver and gold.'

Dawid sent Habib back to The Fist's temporary camp with nuts, insects, *kamah* fungus and the half-eaten flat loaves that Uriah gave them. He then followed the Hittites to their camp, a hollow in the hillside where the smoke from their fire lay trapped beneath the tree line.

Once there, he understood why Uriah and his men had deserted the Philistine cause. There were seven prone figures, helpless and agonised, waiting for death. They were so exhausted, so inhumanly treated, that they could barely move. Dawid was shocked. He had seen suffering since his days in Beth Lechem, but nothing like this. Some had lost their eyes. The sockets were raw, bloodied, leaving cavernous bruising where the knives of torturers had gouged. One had no hands, just stumps bound with bloody cloths. Another had dark stains on his mantle, indicating that his genitals had been carved away.

'These are the elders of Azekah,' said Uriah in a bitter voice. 'Their crime was to be living in the path of the Philistine army. For this they have been mutilated and given to the Hittites to set free. It was Melek who ordered this. I think he wanted us to show them to Saul, and thus to say to the Hebrew host, come to us and fight.'

Dawid felt the tears on his cheeks. He had seen cruelty during his time in Gath, but he had thought Akish a kinder ruler than that. Perhaps things were different in times of war.

'And so,' continued Uriah, 'we have obeyed. We take these men to Saul, and we invite them to fight...'

He let the words hang in the air.

'…and then we fight for the Hebrews.'

Dawid wiped his face with the back of his hand. He tried to smile. 'We fight together, then?'

'Yes.'

And the haunting sound of the *dukhifat* floated across the tops of the terebinths, the almonds and the olives of Elah's vales.

A call to fight again.

When Philistia went to war, the kings were never certain which gods would support them. There had been arguments about this on many occasions, and it wasn't until Akish took control of the alliance that this debate took second place to the more tangible necessities of the day, namely trading agreements and political expansion. As a result, each of the five cities now had an influential subculture of priests, temples and holy treasuries that in turn provided plentiful taxes for the royal coffers of Gath, Ekron, Ashdod, Gaza and Ashkelon.

The priests had sacrificed and looked for signs, confident that within their pantheon they would find exactly the right combination of storm, sun, grain, thunder and lightning deities to combat the unknown strengths of the Hebrew god Yahweh. They particularly liked the old Ammonite god Moloch; sacrificing children to the flames stoked in his rapacious hollows was always a guarantee of prosperity, good crops and triumphs over restless enemies. They took Dagon, of course, half man, half fish, the god of a plentiful harvest, not only in food from the sea but from the fertile coastal plain as well. And on this occasion, they took Ekron's god Ba'al Zebub, Lord of the Flies. They believed he was frightening enough to scare the Hebrew god back into the desert wastes whence he had come, and their uncultured king Saul too, and any of those farmer warriors who by some miracle survived the spears and axes of the Invincibles, themselves demigods with awesome power.

These Philistine gods — Dagon, Ba'al Zebub and Moloch — attended by their devoted priests, formed the front line in the advance along the Valley of Elah. Their effigies sat on three vast platforms on huge wooden wheels with iron axles, each hauled by fifty slaves, their shoulders grated raw by the heavy flax ropes, their backs bloodied by the whips of taskmasters. Before these slaves, showing the way the gods had chosen, the chief priests pranced and screamed, naked bodies daubed white and red, eyes blackened with kohl. They shook staves laden with jangling silver and bronze discs, demanding that invisible Yahweh quake and retreat at their coming.

Side by side, the gods encroached on the lands of Yahweh and his consort Ashtoreth. Dagon, the proud, bearded monarch of the seas, sat with his golden fishtail furled. Moloch bore a potbelly furnace, the smoke billowing from the eyeholes of his golden mask, hungry for more sacrifices. And Ba'al Zebub stuck out his beaked snout, seeking out unfortunate Hebrews, his black wings spread like a devouring vulture.

Behind the great gods of Philistia came the dybbuks from Sheol. Golyat led the ten Invincibles, his horned bull helmet swathed in Moloch's steaming breath. He rode in a chariot rimmed with gold, driver and shield-bearer dwarfed by his massive bulk, his bronze scale shirt winking in the golden sunlight. Behind him were nine more behemoths, their iron-shod wheels grinding remorselessly into Judah, leading rank after rank of well-armed men lusting for battle and the spoils of war.

Hidden among the trees, the fighters of The Fist watched the Philistine host advance along the Valley of Elah. They saw the priests and their gods and edged involuntarily deeper into the undergrowth as the Invincibles passed, the jangling beat of each soldier's ankle bracelets becoming louder with every step, marking time for the incessant advance. Every so often trumpets and horns laid an eerie blanket of sound over the hills and woods, prompting the deep, guttural challenge of ten thousand bloodthirsty troops.

The five warlords, curtained within wooden structures carried by noble camels, passed the hidden Hebrews. Each camel was lavishly draped with Tyrian purple, the cloth adorned with silver and gold and studded with precious gems. Before each were the banners of the five cities, held aloft by warriors clothed in wolfskins and bearskins.

'Where can we attack?' Oren asked no one in particular, clearly shaken by such a relentless advance.

No one answered him. They were so few, their stones mere ant bites at the ankles of a plodding ox.

Dawid looked to where the gods and the royal camels were disappearing in a shroud of dust further up the valley, and still the massed ranks marched past.

'Their supply wagons,' he said, thinking aloud. 'Where are they?'

All turned and strained to see what followed out of distant Azekah. Every army needed its grain, salted meat, dried fruits, tents, weapons, tools and the attentions of a host of women who made their fortunes in the wake of a war campaign. The rearguard was in sight, and still they had not seen the expected heavily laden carts and the inevitable numbers of servants, slaves and prettily painted women.

Oren looked at Dawid, smiling. 'Delayed?' He scratched his chin. 'Now that would be an easier target.'

Her face crusted with grime and her clothes unwashed and stiff with dust, Naomi watched through the bars of the enclosure as Melek screamed at the servants. She took only a little satisfaction in the way it had all gone wrong for the cruel dwarf. Being given command of the supply train was a sought-after position, with perks like having the first pick of the women and food, and above all, not having to fight in the heat and horror of battle. But with the pleasures came responsibilities — ensuring the carts were well maintained, feeding the oxen, camels and mules, and motivating the engineers and drivers to do their jobs to the best of their ability.

In most of these respects, Melek had failed miserably. And with every little thing that went wrong for him, Naomi felt better about the way her life had been turned upside down. She had been dragged from her bed by palace guards in the dead of night, bound and gagged, and as dawn came she had found herself in a hot and heaving cage built into a cart that lurched eastwards with the baggage train. By the time her mistress and the palace servants would have realised she had been taken, she was looking up at the burning city of Azekah.

Now Melek stamped and yelled as the iron axle on one of the carts refused to yield its broken wheel. Nearby a team of carpenters laboured over a crudely fashioned replacement — Melek, of course, had not foreseen that the time would come when he would need spare parts. To make matters worse, the oxen had not been corralled properly and he had ordered a dozen of his personal guard to search for them at the brook.

Naomi knew why Melek had taken her. She and Dawid had not been careful enough. After her beloved Hebrew shepherd's departure in the guise of a Philistine noble, she had realised their mistake, understood why she had seen a shadowy figure at every corner. Now she languished among the dregs of Philistia's women, a prisoner expected to perform menial cooking tasks and services of a far more degrading nature.

She was watching Melek preside over the chaos when the dark horsemen rode into the baggage camp. She knew immediately who they were; Melek's slaves had talked enthusiastically about a small group of Hebrew riders who had attacked at dawn, and now they were back. She admired the way they sat proudly on rare horses, all with turbans covering their faces. They were dressed entirely in black, two per horse, arming and wheeling slings. She looked at Melek. Intent on the wheel repair, he did not give the riders a second thought.

The leader waved an arm in a circular motion and most dismounted. Suddenly there were stones flying at Melek's remaining guards, at the engineers, and, Naomi hoped, Melek himself. There were screams and barked orders as Melek dived for cover like a fox cornered by vicious hounds. One or two of the Philistine soldiers fought back, but they had been unprepared. Only two carried bows, and a few more had swords. The raiders unleashed volley after volley, mutilating everyone around the baggage carts, splattering blood and breaking bodies. She saw one black-clothed rider fall, then their leader gave a command to fall back, and a lithe young rider on a pale mare swept through the mayhem and reached for his fallen comrade. As he did so, the cloth of his *pe'er* fell loose and Naomi recognised him.

Her beloved Dawid was a hero after all.

CHAPTER THIRTY-ONE

The two armies faced each other but would not engage because the heavens opened and turned the valley into bogland. The brook soon ran wild, Moloch's fires smoked damply then went out, and thousands of men grumbled, soaked and longing for the warmth of their homes.

King Saul sighed with relief when he saw the huge chariots leaving the battlefield.

Approaching Ephes-Dammim, where his scouts had told him his son Yonatan was preparing hillside defences, he had puffed out his chest and congratulated the prophet who rode beside him on recruiting so many warriors.

'Farmers,' Shemu'el corrected him, 'and farmer's sons.'

Without turning around for fear of destabilising his unpredictable mule, Saul had given what he considered to be the right observation. 'Where Yahweh leads, we will triumph.'

Shemu'el fought the rising sin of doubt. He had heard news of the Philistine chariots. Many times he had believed in his god and strength in numbers, had seen sweet victories over the Ammonites and Amalekites, but they had been disorganised farmers and peasants too. Now Israel faced a real threat. On seeing the enemy forces marching towards them, he silently begged his God for forgiveness and promised that if the victory were Israel's, he would forsake his worldly ways and give all his wealth to the poor of Ramah, his hometown. Saul, too, had second thoughts about his own presumptions and quailed at the sight of an organised, well-equipped army.

The rains saved him. And Israel. With torrents running down his neck and under his leather jerkin, he coaxed his mule away from the flats of Elah and led his rabble of an army onto the slopes overlooking the valley, where Yonatan and Abner had done their best to provide shelter. The three stood together on the sodden earthworks and saw the low cloud sweeping in from the west, bringing the heavy, driving rain that they knew could last for days.

And they watched as the Philistine host melted into the misty woodlands on the slopes opposite, leaving their three huge gods where they were, forlorn on their wooden platforms, slowly sinking into Judah's mud.

Yonatan was a lot brighter than his father.

Saul was tall and broad, balding yet with a beard that grew thick and bushy from a little below his eyes down to his battle-scarred chest, and a voice that rumbled like the thunder on Mount Gerizim. He was a man who expected to be obeyed in all things. Yonatan, though, commanded respect because his orders sounded more like suggestions and were always delivered with a sparkling smile and a hand run through his rebellious mop of hair.

So when Oren reported to Yonatan that the Philistine baggage train was ripe for capture, the Prince of Israel took it upon himself to deliver Yahweh's first important victory of the war. Yonatan knew his father would lead the entire army in a headlong charge down the already treacherous slopes to take captive a handful of sodden and demoralised soldiers and their baggage train, complete with servants and slaves. So he didn't tell him anything about it, instead *suggesting* to Oren and The Fist that they get some food and rest and be ready to ride in search of the bedraggled baggage train the moment there was a break in the weather; and if there was none, they should depart well before dusk.

Saul's army was put to good use at dawn the next day. Yonatan brought his father a prisoner, a venomous dwarf covered in thick, cloying mud, obviously wealthy judging by the jewelled belt and golden dagger sheath, now empty, the exquisite mail vest and the contempt with which he addressed his Hebrew captors. Yonatan also brought around a hundred slaves and servants skilled in the art of erecting tents and preparing vats of porridge, none of them seeming to care whether they did this for Philistines or Hebrews.

'And the supplies?' asked Saul unappreciatively. 'Any weapons? Iron?'

Yonatan explained that if Saul ordered his men in a human chain from the camp at Ephes-Dammim down to the valley below, the Great King would have enough food to keep his army happy while the rains continued. They would also have enough cover to keep many of them reasonably dry while the Philistines drowned. And they could acquire a wagon-load of iron-tipped spears, never mind the rust forming on them, not to mention a good number of bronze swords.

Saul scowled. He was not a well-mannered man and was a worse father.

But Yonatan happily organised the men of Israel for his father and watched as their spirits brightened, especially when the hungry, wet and frightened harlots of Gath were helped lovingly to higher ground, cheered by the brave soldiers of Yahweh.

Dawid carried a tearful Naomi, his battered and bruised Rose of Sharon, in his arms to a secluded place as far from his countrymen as possible, where he built her a shelter just like the ones he used to make in the hill country near Beth Lechem. He hung his leather pouch and his sling from a branch, then wiped away her tears of despair.

And in the bivouacs of the Hebrew host, men listened to the doleful tunes of a shepherd's pipes that pervaded the damp night air and wondered what dawn would bring.

Abner had a lot of fun with Melek.

While his meanest ruffians pinned him, his dagger carved chunks of flesh from the dwarf's chest and the tender parts of his thighs, perilously close to his genitals. Melek screamed, begged for his life, swore that he would devote himself to the Hebrew cause, and even swore that the Philistine *seranim* quaked in their beds at the name of the mighty Saul — anything he thought this cold torturer wanted to hear.

But Abner knew the man was holding something back. Saul had told him about the alliance between the Jebusites and the Philistines, how he had immediately acted on hearing of the planned pincer movement and sent the bloodthirsty men of Manasseh to lay siege to the impregnable city of Jebus and make sure that not one Jebusite warrior so much as peeped through their gates or over the mighty walls. There would be no attack in Israel's rear. But he wanted to hear Melek's confession.

Abner's knife hovered close to Melek's eyes.

'If you kill me, you kill a man who has the trust of Lord Akish himself,' groaned Melek, summoning all of his courage to sound more important than he felt.

'This Akish,' said Abner, wanting to draw out his evening's entertainment. 'Tell me all about him.'

'He is all-powerful,' replied the gaoler of Gath. 'Yet he is a reasonable man.'

Abner teased a drop of blood from the fleshy eyelid.

'Terms,' gasped Melek, trying not to move his head. 'He will give you terms, if you ask it of him.'

'Terms? What need have we of terms? We will destroy you all, and this Akish will beg for mercy when he feels Saul's heel on his throat!'

Melek felt the blood between his legs and offered his captors a piece of information that he hoped would end his torment. 'You are trapped,' he managed, breathlessly. 'The Jebusites are marching from the east…'

'Go on.' Abner feigned surprise, easing the blade's pressure as if the dwarf was winning him over.

'They … they will drive you under the wheels. The chariots. The… the Invincibles. They cannot be defeated.'

Abner leaned back, withdrawing his blade to tap it in the palm of his hand.

Melek sensed his advantage. 'I will take your terms for you,' he said. 'Send me to Akish, and you will have peace.'

Abner gave a hollow laugh. 'Do you really think we are that stupid?'

Melek screamed as Abner squeezed his testicles, and from somewhere he found the dregs of his dignity. 'Yes, you are stupid, Hebrew! Can you not see? We have the Invincibles and they will destroy you…'

Pain shot through Melek's left eye and he screamed. The watching veterans sighed with satisfaction.

And Melek was broken. He sobbed his promises of support for the Hebrews, his devotion to their god, whoever that god may be. He pledged betrayal of his own people, and he swore he would fight in the front line even against the Invincibles.

Abner put an arm around the dwarf's heaving shoulders. 'Tell me all about the Invincibles. How many they are, how big they are and how they fight. Then tell me their weaknesses.'

Melek described how three slaves, one of them an old man, had bested Golyat and Lahmi without a weapon between them.

Then, as Abner stroked his matted hair and soothed his new friend with oily words, he confessed that he had lost his force of mercenaries, and that the remaining men were over-reliant on a handful of giant charioteers and a missing army of Hittites.

Try as Dawid might, he could not stop the night rain piercing his crude acacia shelter like stones from the slings of the storm gods. He held Naomi close as she shivered; his cape spread on the damp ground offered scant comfort in her despair.

When the wind and rain eased to allow the faintest glow of moonlight, Dawid smelled woodsmoke hanging in the dampness. Picking the most brittle sticks from a pile that he had stored in a dry part of the shelter, he went in search of fire. He followed his nose and found some older soldiers who knew how to nurture fire, knew its worth above everything in weather like this. They gladly let him take a flame. Soon his small fire was providing a welcome warmth as he held Naomi and coaxed her story from her, and she his.

'Take me with you when you go to her,' said Naomi softly when he told her of his mother's plight. 'But perhaps I shouldn't meet your father, this Jesse. He will want to marry you to some rich trader's daughter…'

Dawid held her close. 'I decide who I marry, not Jesse. I have lived these eighteen years by fending for myself, so no one tells me what to do. Not now, not ever.'

She smiled at last, and they talked until dawn in the soft glow of the fire, Dawid enthusing about the pleasures of a simple shepherd's life. Naomi suggested pitching their own tent beneath the walls of Beth Lechem, perhaps even building a small homestead with their own goats and chickens, maybe raising a family… Dawid began to protest, but then realised he could come to like the idea of fathering children, especially as Naomi had visibly brightened with the talk of settling down together.

He took the Star of Anak from his pouch, allowing the firelight to dance on the heavy silver.

Naomi reached out and touched it lightly. 'We could buy our own land with that, build ourselves a palace, with kitchens and servants…'

He swatted her playfully and returned the six-pointed star to his pouch. The rain began again.

'You may be right. It would be somewhere dry, at least, and cool in summer…' he mused, and Naomi sighed as a large raindrop squeezed through the shelter and splashed on his head.

Uriah found them in the grey, wet dawn. He watched as they slept in a tender embrace and wondered if he would ever turn from his life as a warrior and find love again.

He coughed apologetically. Dawid was alert in a flash, his knife in his hand, ready to defend himself and his woman. He relaxed when he saw it was Uriah. Behind him, Ishbi and one of the Hittite warriors waited expectantly. All three wore thick fur cloaks.

Naomi stirred but did not wake.

'Come,' said the Hittite commander. 'We have a dry tent and we need to talk.'

'You have joined us?' whispered Dawid, not wanting to wake Naomi. 'You have been well received?'

'Yes. I think the sight of those unfortunates we brought here was very convincing. But come, Habib wants to share his fire and there are old friends asking for you.'

'Old friends? Who?'

'You'll see.' Uriah offered his hand to help Dawid to his feet. Ishbi shrugged off his cloak and gently covered the sleeping Naomi, then added some twigs to the dying embers. Dawid hesitated, looking at the exhausted girl lying on his cape, her dark hair spilling from beneath the fur.

'But I can't leave her alone...'

Uriah smiled. 'Ishbi and my man will stand guard. Knowing Ishbi, he'll probably have a feast ready when she awakes. He's very resourceful.'

Ishbi nodded and waved them away, busying himself with the fire.

Dawid shivered as he strapped on his belt with its leather pouch and hunting knife. The rain was lighter now, but his damp clothes chilled him to the bone, so he didn't object when Uriah ordered a guard to volunteer his fur.

They picked their way between dispirited huddles of Hebrews, most resigned to their misery, though some sought the warmth of exercise by cutting branches for shelters. Dawid caught the envious glances of men who would think nothing of killing them for their furs, but one look at Uriah and the heavy sword at his side told them that here was a battle-hardened warrior who would not be easily overcome.

Uriah led Dawid away from the encamped Hebrew army to a clearing where three of the captured tents had been pitched, between them a lively fire that spluttered in protest at the rain. A hooded figure sat beneath an overhang that did its best to keep the rain off, turning a spitted fallow deer while another stirred a steaming pot held over the flames by a tripod of spears. An aroma of roasting meat and simmering pottage, rich with garlic, reminded Dawid of his aching hunger.

Uriah stopped and pointed. 'Over there, an old friend of yours.'

Another hooded figure sat on a rock beneath a sturdy terebinth, ignoring the large drops that splashed around him and on the cloak pulled tight around his thin body. His face was in shadow but as Dawid stared, he turned and tugged the hood from his face, and Dawid saw bright eyes set in a craggy, bearded face.

Elhanan.

'Barak!' cried Dawid, and ran to him.

CHAPTER THIRTY-TWO

'Welcome to the camp of the prophets,' laughed Elhanan, crushing Dawid to his bony chest. 'So you survived your sojourn in Gath, eh? I knew you would. And now the boy has become a man!'

'Only with your help, Barak,' he said when Elhanan finally freed him from a surprisingly powerful embrace. 'You trained us well.'

'Ah, but did I? You have done well without me. Look at your fine clothes and that beautiful dagger. A little damp, perhaps, but aren't we all?'

'All fairly won from people who didn't need them,' said Dawid with a wink, 'apart from this cloak. That is loaned to me. But tell me, Barak, why are you here in this awful place?'

'Do you not remember what I told you when we parted last?'

Dawid looked at him blankly and shook his head.

Elhanan prompted him. 'When the darkness comes…?'

'Now that you mention it, yes — you said I would find you when the darkness comes, and then you walked away.'

'And now I am here. And you are here — for a purpose.' Elhanan gazed so deeply into Dawid's soul that he involuntarily looked away.

Uriah interrupted their reunion. 'We should seek shelter,' he said, a drip forming on his nose. 'In the tent of the holy ones?'

'Go right ahead. They are expecting you, and Habib awaits you inside,' said Elhanan brightly. 'But they won't let me in. They think I'm a madman. Who needs a crazy fool like me when everyone's about to try to kill each other on the battlefield?'

Dawid saw the mischief in Elhanan's eyes, but there was something deeper there. There always was with Barak, as if he knew more than he was prepared to admit.

Inside the tent of the holy ones, oil lamps flickered and there was fresh straw covering the floor. And the Phoenician was there, squatting with two elderly women kneading dough for flatbread. It baked on hot stones, giving the smoky, damp air a familiar aroma that promised a simple but ample feast to come. Habib looked up, grinning, and was immediately slapped and berated by the nearest woman for neglecting his duties.

'Welcome, Ox Rider,' he laughed into the dough he was working.

'Habib!' Dawid exclaimed. 'What's all this about? Are you a baker to the prophets now?'

'Just showing these old crones how it's done, the Phoenician way.' For that he got another slap, and the two old women burst into fits of giggles.

Uriah ignored the commotion and went to a large earthenware bowl standing near a goatskin tent flap, summoning the others. Lamps flickered near the water bowl, the light dancing in the polished bronze of a small bell mounted on a wooden frame. Dawid and Habib understood and all three washed their hands, more in ritual than cleansing as no one could possibly wash away all the mud that came with incessant rains.

'Ready?' asked Uriah. 'We can put our cloaks on the floor, I suppose.' Uriah shrugged off his fur and dropped it in a heap, and Dawid did the same.

'Ready for what?' Dawid felt as though he was the only one not privy to some obscure ritual.

Habib shrugged as Uriah rang the bell, sounding three notes. There was a rustling sound, like something being dragged through the straw floor covering, and the flap was pulled aside to reveal a gaunt figure on crutches. It took Dawid some moments to recognise Nathan. His hair was longer, touching the blue-tasselled shawl knotted around his shoulders, beneath that a plain, ankle-length robe. His beard was fuller, untrimmed in an attempt to disguise his thin face and hollow eyes. He glanced vacantly at all three one by one, a spark of the old Nathan returning briefly when he looked at Dawid.

'Nathan?'

'Dawid.'

'What … what happened?'

'Crushed by my own horse. I fell when we patrolled Philistine territory near Timnah. I begged Oren and Rimon to leave me, but you know them. The idiots carried me to safety with a broken hip. Agony.'

'And now?'

'Servant and apprentice to the prophet. You?'

'Tormenting the enemy with my sling. What else?'

'Oh, there's more you can do. That's why you're here, all three of you. Come in.'

An array of oil lamps lit up the prophet's tent. On the floor were two beautifully stitched rugs, showing camels and creatures that Dawid knew were meant to be lions, as well as hunters with bows and soldiers with spears. In the middle was a familiar symbol — the six-pointed Star of Anak. Dawid was about to comment when Nathan invited them to sit, propping himself on his crutch so he could indicate with one hand.

'Over there, please.' They sat on one of the rugs expectantly. Then he added, 'Put these on.' He hauled himself to a low table and picked up three woollen shawls like the one he was wearing. He handed them one each.

'To cover up the heathen in you,' he chuckled. 'Especially you, Dawid. Tie them like this.' He showed them the intricate knots in the blue cords of his own *tallit*. 'Now put them over your heads,' Nathan continued, pulling the shawl over his lank hair. 'It's something to do with respect for Yahweh.'

They obeyed, not wishing to do anything to offend the god, whether by intent or omission.

Nathan clapped his hands and Shemu'el, Prophet of all Israel, entered with two rather elderly men, plainly dressed while he wore the colourful robes of his office. All three wore shawls of respect over their heads. Shemu'el's long grey hair was clasped with a silver broach and hung over his right shoulder, his beard coloured with henna but perhaps a little longer than Dawid remembered, his under-tunic surprisingly clean. The dim lighting hid the marks of age, but Shemu'el seemed lively as his stern eyes studied the three guests. He sat on the rug, facing them. The other holy men did the same, one either side of their lord, the champion and mouthpiece of the one true god.

'Where is the wine, Nathan?'

Dawid thought it a debasing command and began to rise, but Uriah stayed him with a hand on his arm, not taking his eyes off the prophet. Nathan shuffled to the edge of the tent and returned with a skin and a fine silver goblet studded with rare gems. He placed the vessel before Shemu'el and poured, spilling a little as he filled it to the brim. Dawid feared for Nathan, but the prophet didn't seem to mind a little wastage. He dismissed Nathan then picked up the goblet and held it to eye level.

'Blessed are you, Adonai,' he chanted in a surprisingly high-pitched singing voice, 'creator of the fruit of the vine.' Then he handed it to Uriah, a token of welcome.

Uriah drank just a sip and passed it back. Shemu'el gave the cup to Habib and the Phoenician's eyes lit up as he tasted the rich Hebrew wine. Shemu'el did the same for Dawid but ignored his fellow prophets.

'You are wondering what the Most High wants with three, uh, *opportunists* like you?'

Dawid stared at Shemu'el open-mouthed, Uriah smiled and Habib fidgeted proudly.

'You have all lived in Gath, or so I am told,' Shemu'el continued with a hint of conspiracy.

All three nodded, Uriah's affirmation a little more guarded than Dawid's and Habib's.

'And you have become like the people there, as much Philistines as wayfarers.' It was a statement without condemnation. The prophet was not expressing distaste; his tone was warm and friendly. Dawid knew that Shemu'el had not summoned them for a rebuke; he just wanted information from them. 'Tell me of your knowledge.'

Uriah began, relating his experiences as a mercenary with a devoted force of scouts and warriors who had long forgotten their homeland. They had offered their swords in an adventure that had gradually turned sour as the Philistines had grown in wealth and prowess, grinding their enemies into the dust in their remorseless expansion through the fertile plains that skirted the Great Sea. Habib interrupted on several occasions, eager to recount his people's development of trade routes, both overland and by sea, and his unfortunate capture by the Philistines as they became ever more suspicious of the wealth and power of their neighbours. Dawid remained silent. He was the only one present who had met the prophet before and he admired the pompous old man, not least for assisting in his break for freedom long ago in Beth Lechem. He decided that the prophet knew more about him than he was letting on.

Eventually, Shemu'el got to the point. 'These Philistines have brought their warriors into our land.' His eyes flashed with indignation. 'They come with weapons of iron and their gods of war. And they come with great chariots and their champions, whom they call Invincibles, I believe. Yet you three have faced them in battle. Is that true?'

Uriah took it upon himself to explain. 'These two have both fought the giants. And they won, not with armour and weapons, but with their skill, their speed and their quick thinking. They achieved this with another man, who I regret is not here to tell you of this great feat in his own words.'

'He was an old man,' put in Dawid. 'He is still alive as far as we know. He is a man of extraordinary bravery; he did not care for his own life — in fact, he often said he hoped to die, and that's why he lived.'

'Ah,' said Shemu'el, leaning back. 'Was that courage or faith?'

'Only courage,' replied Dawid. 'He had no faith, except in us. We were a team, you see. The Ox Riders.'

'Ox Riders?'

'You have seen them. Small birds that peck for insects out of reach of snapping jaws and grinding teeth.'

Shemu'el nodded, understanding such impressive tactics.

'Another thing,' Dawid continued. 'We considered ourselves dead, worthless. We had nothing to lose. And we found strength in each other.'

'Aha,' said the prophet, but Dawid wasn't certain that Shemu'el understood that part. 'Now we face an enemy greater than we have ever faced before. They line the hillsides opposite us, bristling with iron and chariots. What should we do?'

'What would Saul do?' asked Uriah innocently.

'Saul would lead the Hebrews down the slopes of Ephes-Dammim, into the valley, and throw his farmers into the fray against Philistine chariots and spears of iron,' replied Shemu'el, angrily. Both the flanking holy men jumped at the prophet's outburst but said nothing.

'The Philistines will not come down into the valley,' said Uriah. 'The ground would be churned to mud in no time. The chariots cannot enter the fight, and if they did, they would be stuck and become easy targets. Both Hebrews and Philistines will remain where they are, both hoping the other will come to them.'

'So, a waiting game,' said Shemu'el. 'In the rain.'

'Do you want this war?' asked Uriah.

'Only if we can be sure of winning.'

'You cannot be sure. In fact, you will likely lose.'

Shemu'el didn't like that. He bristled visibly. Then he controlled himself, remembering that his guests were experienced in warfare. 'Tell me then,' he began with a frustrated sigh. 'You are a commander of men. What would you do?'

'Nothing,' replied Uriah. 'I'd hope that this rain drives them away. We have their supplies…'

Shemu'el had already considered that. He sat in a tent stolen from the Philistines, and ate Philistine grain, goats and cattle, and the king's men had a few more iron weapons than they had had yesterday. But he knew that every Philistine soldier carried basic supplies, and Yonatan had admitted that some of their supply carts had escaped the surprise attack.

'I think I understand what you are saying,' he said slowly. 'But why should they not attack for this very reason, that we have their food, weapons and women? And if they do not come to us, what is to stop them raiding Socoh and the farms in the valley?'

Uriah sighed. 'They will try, and they may carry off a few sacks of grain or some cattle. But they came to fight your people, to crush you, and now this rain has changed everything. They came too soon.'

'Too soon, because they need hard ground?'

'Precisely,' confirmed Uriah.

'And now we must wait and watch until they leave?' That did not appeal to Shemu'el, who looked like a man used to the comforts of a dry palace. 'Or wait until the land dries? Perhaps it would be best to lure them to us on level ground without their chariots.'

'There is another way,' said Uriah.

'Go on…' Shemu'el leaned forward expectantly.

'There is a tradition among the Philistines that their ancestors avoided bloodshed by naming a champion to fight their battles for them. Their man against their enemy's man. Single combat, to the death.'

Dawid interrupted. 'I think we know who they would suggest as their champion.'

Shemu'el raised a hand to silence him. 'In your time with them, have you seen this challenge made?' he asked Uriah.

'No. Not exactly. I have seen battles where their Invincibles, these giant warriors, do most of the fighting while the rest of their army makes a lot of noise without getting involved. But they might agree to this idea for two reasons. Firstly, they believe beyond doubt that their champion will win. And secondly, because they no longer have their supply wagons, they will soon grow hungry.'

'And we would have to find a champion of our own.' Shemu'el looked worried. 'I have not seen these Invincibles for myself, but they grow taller and mightier with each retelling among our men. I think it would be difficult to find a warrior willing to fight one such as the bull-god they are talking about.'

'But we know their bull-god is not invincible,' interrupted Habib.

Dawid glanced at his friend. 'Would you fight him again?' he asked.

Habib shook his head and his hand went to his chest, where Golyat's skull club had crushed his ribs. 'No. Not me. But I am not a Hebrew. It is for a Hebrew warrior to prove the might of his god.'

'Our god will triumph,' said Shemu'el, looking straight at Dawid. 'But he may need a little help. From a Hebrew who knows how this bull-god fights…'

Uriah broke the ensuing silence. 'Dawid has succeeded before. But he had help then.'

Dawid said nothing and studied the rings on his fingers.

'Yet this time,' added Uriah, 'he will be able to choose a weapon.'

Shemu'el noticed that Dawid had begun to shift uneasily, as if wrestling with a decision. He came to his rescue. 'There is always Abner. He will fight anyone.' He turned to Uriah. 'Should we decide to do this, how do you suggest we *persuade* these Philistines to make such a challenge?'

'That is easy. You hold their dwarf commander prisoner, do you not?'

'We do.'

'Let him go. Tell him that if such a challenge were to be made, we would accept it.'

Dawid felt the crushing weight of Shemu'el's hints and Uriah's expectations. He did not want to fight Golyat. Before, he had not been given a choice. But now he was his own man with his own wealth. He had a family and a name. Why should he get involved? *Leave it to Abner*, he thought.

Suddenly he realised that Shemu'el had been speaking with Uriah about the best type of weapons with which to fight the giant of Gath.

'So he has never faced a shepherd's sling…?'

'No,' said Uriah.

'Not yet,' said Habib, daring to wink at Yahweh's prophet.

Shemu'el ignored the Phoenician's impudence and looked thoughtfully at Uriah. 'There is one more thing I ask of you and your Hittites,' he said solemnly. 'We have no guarantee that this tactic will end the war. Supposing our champion wins? What then? The Philistines may swarm from their camp and seek revenge.'

Uriah agreed. 'But would that not suit your plans? They cannot bring their chariots, so it would be your best chance to defeat them if you are ready.'

'Indeed,' Shemu'el said, 'yet you have already said that even without their chariots, the odds favour the Philistines.'

'You will have to fight with great courage. I have heard your people are fearsome in battle.'

'But,' said Shemu'el, touching his temple with a forefinger, 'sometimes we need something more than courage.'

Uriah grinned. 'I think you have a plan. Tell me.'

And Israel's prophet voiced the thoughts that had begun to form in his mind since he had encouraged Saul to blockade the city of Jebus.

CHAPTER THIRTY-THREE

It rained hard for three days. When it stopped, the destroying angel came to Ephes-Dammim.

There was nowhere dry to put the sick and delirious and nowhere to bury the dead. When the stench of decay overcame the mustiness of damp air and sodden ground, Abner sent a team of his men to dig a vast grave away from the camp, but their crude shovels were no match for the cloying mud. When Abner went to inspect their work, he stared into the vacant eyes of men whose bones were weak from the creeping sickness and discovered for the first time in his thirty years as a bully that no amount of shouting and threatening could inspire them to dig. He would have begun the executions himself, but a wave of dizzying nausea swept over him and he felt as though a tent peg had been driven through the back of his skull.

He stood his men down and went to find Saul.

The king was not in his command tent, and neither was his son. He tried to question a servant but found to his dismay that he could barely summon the strength to speak. He sat down heavily on the king's cushion, shivering uncontrollably. The servant brought him wine, but his hands were shaking so violently that he could not hold the cup. The servant held it to his lips and he drank a little, thinking how good it would be to sleep. He lay down. The servant covered him with one of the king's furs and sat watching the tough, craggy general muttering in his sleep, thrashing weakly, and wondered what Israel had done to so offend its gods.

When he judged that the ground had dried enough to exercise Morning Star, Dawid took Naomi's hand and led her to the animal enclosure. There he found Oren, Rimon and several of The Fist grooming the horses as they nosed happily at roots and barley mash and tugged at the leaves from a pile of olive branches.

Morning Star was pleased to see Dawid and sensed her opportunity to escape the enclosure. He used his knife to clean packed mud from the mare's hooves while Naomi smeared them with the oil from a supply of overripe olives that Rimon had gathered. He lifted Naomi onto Morning Star and led them away from the stench of the latrines and the lingering smell of sickness and death.

They climbed to a ridge above the Hebrew camp where the breeze was fresher. Dawid helped Naomi down and left Morning Star to seek out sweet spring grass. They sat on a fallen tree trunk, where they could gaze across at the cooking fires and makeshift shelters of the Philistine army opposite and, as Dawid had expected, Golyat was there in the valley. He had been there every day since the rains had ceased, since Melek had been set free and sent scurrying across the raging brook and the muddy valley to admit his shame and issue Israel's challenge. Alone apart from his shield-bearer, Golyat stood with the three abandoned gods of the Philistines behind him, the horns of his bull helmet pointing menacingly towards the Hebrew camp. He wore his traditional fish-scale mail and greaves of bronze, and he carried a massive hammer designed to crush skulls. In his other hand he clutched a formidable, curved sword.

Naomi shuddered. 'Why don't Saul's men charge out there and fight him?'

'A fine commander you'd make,' laughed Dawid. 'That's what they want. Their men will be waiting in the woods, and Golyat would draw our forces right onto their spears.'

'You men are so foolish,' she chided. 'Everyone should just go home.'

Dawid didn't answer her. He stood gazing at Golyat, admiring the power and strength he could feel even at this distance. What was he? More than a man, less than a god, whatever a god might look like. Dawid had sensed his emptiness and the despair of being so different, a giant living among cultured Philistines who used him as a source of entertainment.

Everyone should just go home.

Perhaps Naomi was right. They could ride out together on Morning Star and hide in the Caves of Adullam, away from the world of prophets and kings and warrior giants. Or they could build a house in the hills near Beth Lechem, tend their flock and raise dozens of children.

'I'll fight him,' he heard himself saying.

Naomi had closed her eyes and was enjoying the silence. Now she turned to him, alarmed. 'No, please no.' Her eyes pleaded with him.

'I must. Saul is too old and Abner is sick. They all know I've fought Golyat before. I'm the obvious choice.'

'But there are plenty of able young men in Saul's army. I've seen them.'

Dawid shook his head. 'No match for Golyat.'

'The king's son, then. What's his name…?'

'Yonatan. I don't think Saul would allow it.'

Naomi's shoulders sagged as she realised he had made up his mind. She took a deep breath and tried rebuking instead of pleading. 'What makes *you* so special? You're just a shepherd.

You broke your leg and you were sick for many days. You even walk with a limp. Why should Saul even take a second look at you?'

Dawid smiled, relieved that her anger was ineffectual. 'Saul won't. But his prophet already has.'

In the distance, Golyat's shield-bearer beat on a heavy bronze shield with his sword, insignificant compared with Golyat's mighty blade, but still bulky enough to ring out a challenge to the warriors of Israel.

Saul threw his goblet at the brazier, denting the finely worked silver, wine drops hissing in the fire. The prophet remained calm, though he found this increasingly difficult with the king's volatile moods. Saul had always been impetuous, but with age the lion had become an enraged bull.

It wasn't their first disagreement. Saul consistently failed to understand that his role as defender of Yahweh's people did not extend to questioning the authority of the prophet. And now Saul was yelling at Shemu'el that Yahweh's judgement had visited his army, laying half of them low with sickness, because the Lord's host had not obeyed His command to wipe out the heathen Philistines while they had the chance, rain or no rain. After all, would not the Philistine chariots become stuck up to their iron axles in the mud sent by Yahweh to hinder Israel's tormentors?

And Shemu'el had calmly reminded Saul that the Lord worked in mysterious ways and He would take the opportunity to teach His Hebrews an important lesson — not to worry, for He had *another way*. If the king whom the people had chosen, and whom he, Shemu'el, had anointed to lead Israel to victory after victory, could not calm down and behave like *the anointed one*, then El Shaddai would raise up someone else to do it *properly*.

That was when Saul hurled his favourite wine goblet at the royal brazier.

'I'm telling you, we should attack now,' he shouted, 'before the valley dries out and their chariots move again!'

'And I'm telling you, Saul, they'll wait on their hillside so our men have to fight uphill. And in their front line will be their biggest warriors, especially those colossal killing machines.'

'You're afraid.' Saul visibly calmed with the revelation. 'That's it, the fearless prophet is afraid...'

Shemu'el controlled himself, showing no emotion. It was always the best tactic when dispensing the will of Yahweh. He hated hearing the truth, though he preferred to call his reasoning pragmatism. No, he was not a coward, but a foot placed wrongly now and his dreams of Israel as a powerful nation would be dashed as swiftly as an axe splits a log.

'Well, well, my dear Saul,' he said slowly, 'it seems you have forgotten just who it is who poured the anointing oil on your brow, how Yahweh's blessing flowed upon your hair and beard, like a flock gracing the slopes of Mount Gilead?' Shemu'el knew that poetry, even as extravagant as this, had a calming effect on the puppet king.

Saul looked bemused for a moment, then walked to the brazier and picked up his goblet. He stared into the cup as if wondering where the wine had gone, and in that moment Shemu'el decided to take a risk to get his way.

'To show you that I am not afraid, I am putting myself forward as the champion of Israel to fight the heathen who stands in the valley and taunts the righteous people of El Shaddai.'

Saul looked up, shocked. Shemu'el was an old man and had not held a sword since the day he had taken it upon himself to butcher the Amalekite warlord Agog. He wouldn't stand a chance. And now Saul felt trapped by Shemu'el's manoeuvring, and he, the true champion of Israel, would be seen as a coward if he did not match the prophet's unexpected offer. He puffed out his chest.

'No, Shemu'el… It is I who has the strength of El Shaddai in my right arm. I will go.'

Shemu'el struck with the speed of a viper. 'And risk the life of the Lord's anointed? No, you will not fight this Golyat. You must remain with the men of Israel ready to lead them to victory when their champion falls. Now, name your man who will be put to the test of *Urim and Thummim*.'

Saul was relieved. He did not want to fight the giant, and he knew that the *Urim* and *Thummim* selection ritual had worked well for him before. The name was on his lips without a second thought.

'Abner.'

'But he is sick,' Shemu'el reminded Saul.

'A sick Abner can defeat Abaddon himself. He will recover at my command. Now, whom do you put forth before the Lord? Surely there is one who can defeat the enemy of El Shaddai?'

Shemu'el didn't hesitate. 'Dawid ben Jesse the Judahite of Beth Lechem.'

Saul looked at his prophet askance. 'Who?'

CHAPTER THIRTY-FOUR

The dark figure watched from the dawn shadows as the twenty riders of The Fist checked their weapons, tightening their black riding turbans across their faces. Elhanan was pleased that the young leader, Oren, had heeded Dawid's plea to ride out at sunrise to give the Philistines something to think about. While the king had huffed and puffed, then yelled at his captains for not having the courage to face the heathen enemy, even offering his daughter to any man who would fight the giant when Abner clearly could not, Dawid had quietly explained to Oren, Rimon and the other riders that he had been charged with the responsibility of taking up the challenge himself, by none other than Israel's prophet, Shemu'el.

Elhanan watched The Fist's armed riders lead their horses between the dark tents, low voices answered by the grunting coughs of men heavy with sleep and sickness. He smiled grimly as the first fingers of sunlight warmed his weathered face, then he pulled his fur closer around his shoulders, and followed on foot as the youths mounted to gingerly wind their way down the muddy track between the earth trenches towards the brook.

He sensed the prophet's presence even before Shemu'el spoke.

'Elhanan.' His voice was soft and surprisingly respectful.

Elhanan turned to face Shemu'el as the older man emerged from the shadows of Saul's command tent. There was enough light now to see the deep lines on the prophet's face, his eyes rimmed red from lack of sleep. Both men stared after the last of the riders as they picked their way to Israel's valley of destiny.

'Tell me about him,' said Shemu'el.

Elhanan gazed at the spot where the last horseman had disappeared from view like a ghost rider in the swirling mists. 'He's just a boy,' he said. 'Just a boy who became a man too soon.'

'Is he aware of this moment, or is he just an adventurer seeking the king's riches?' Shemu'el saw strength and wisdom in the hermit's wild eyes.

'Does it matter?' Elhanan smiled at Shemu'el. 'It wouldn't be the first time the weak have been chosen to confound the mighty.'

Shemu'el snorted. 'Are you so sure?'

'Yes.'

The prophet looked into Elhanan's eyes, saw passion there and understood his faith.

'I think perhaps you *are* mad,' he smirked, 'just as our God is mad, and it is the sane who will be brought low.'

Elhanan raised an eyebrow. 'Strange talk, from God's own mouthpiece!' There was no hint of scorn.

'These are strange days.'

'These are *new* days,' replied Elhanan quickly. 'We have a king now, and we *navi* cannot be heard in all the din of silver piled upon gold, of armies and weapons. Our place is in the wilderness.'

Shemu'el nodded. 'Go with him. Watch over him. Be the angel at his shoulder.'

Elhanan put a strong hand on the prophet's shoulder and looked into his eyes, glimpsing the war in Shemu'el's soul yet sensing his strong desire for … for what? Peace, yes, and prosperity. But something more than that. A people, a nation perhaps, who knew who they were and *why* they were.

'He doesn't understand this moment,' said Elhanan, 'but he believes in himself. Yet I doubt he is truly aware of the power he faces, and I doubt he is able to kill a child of Abaddon, so yes, I will watch for him.'

A look of relief crossed Shemu'el's face. No one could accuse Israel's chief prophet of cowardice, but he would rather remain in the Hebrew camp to keep an eye on the volatile Saul.

Elhanan took a few steps along the track that had been churned afresh by The Fist's horses, then turned back to Shemu'el. 'You will not see me again after this day.' Shemu'el was about to protest, but Elhanan held up a hand. 'It is best. You don't need a madman like me muddying your crystal-clear waters!'

Shemu'el mouthed a blessing and stood watching as the crazed hermit went to oversee Yahweh's mysterious work. When Elhanan had disappeared from sight, he shivered at the sharpness of the air around him, the crackle of anticipation as the gods postured.

How strange of Yahweh to choose this hermit and a shepherd chancer to shape Israel's destiny, he thought.

Oren led The Fist to the edge of the raging brook and signalled his riders to fan out in line abreast to face the empty fields that lay before them, rising towards the wooded hillside where numerous columns of smoke marked the enemy's morning fires. The lifeless Philistine gods silently protested their boredom, staring across at the small cavalry force arrayed against them. From the hillside behind came the sounds of a dispirited, hungry army as it stirred itself for another day of pointless watching and waiting.

Oren watched through narrowed eyes, Dawid still and tense beside him on Morning Star.

'I still think we should attack together,' said Oren without taking his eyes off the woods opposite. 'We could have twenty arrows in his neck and pound him with as many slingstones before he knows it.'

'Too slow in this mud.' Dawid's voice was unsteady and his words clipped.

'So what now?'

'When he comes, then...'

Dawid was interrupted by a single note sounded by a horn high on the hillside. A warning, or a call to arms. They had been spotted. The woods seemed to suddenly pulse with life, thousands of men shaking away sleep, hurriedly dressing for battle, strapping on sword belts and shields. Behind The Fist, the Hebrews, too, stirred into action, wondering what this new Philistine signal could mean.

'There,' breathed Oren, but Dawid had already seen the Philistine archers and spearmen emerging from the treeline to stand ready beside their huge gods. At least a hundred men, more joining them as they belatedly found weapons and armour, were looking down with undisguised contempt at twenty horsemen, but remaining close to the woods with the advantage of a steep slope. An impetuous archer shot an arrow towards The Fist but it fell comically short, not even covering half of the distance between the opposing forces, eliciting a sharp rebuke from a Philistine officer.

The riders of The Fist watched impassively.

For an age, the only movement was the occasional restless shifting of the horses, all eager for action after the long days of rain. The sun climbed patiently into a clear blue sky. Oren began to fidget; beyond him Habib was humming tunelessly and Rimon muttered curses at the Philistine defensive line. But all were silenced when there was fresh movement at the treeline, and to a man the Philistines crashed sword and spear on their shields, just once, and in unison gave a drawn-out challenge: '*Golll...eee...yat*!' Weapons crashed on shields a second time and from the darker undergrowth the ten Invincibles emerged, massive and fully armed, enfeebling the oaks beside which they stood and the soldiers that massed before them. Next to Dawid, Oren gave an involuntary gasp.

'Which is Golyat?' he asked, awed by the sight.

'The biggest one,' said Dawid, nudging Morning Star forward to tentatively negotiate the boisterous stream. 'The one dressed up as a golden bull.'

'Dawid, wait.' Oren sounded panicky. 'Take this...' The leader of The Fist unsheathed his bronze sword, flipped it skilfully and held the hilt towards Dawid. 'It might be long enough to penetrate that monster's thick skin.'

Dawid twisted and reached for the sword, and as he took it, movement on the Hebrew slopes caught his eye. Standing tall among the hundreds of watching Israelites, his feet planted apart on the earthworks, was the unmistakable figure of Yonatan. His bronze scale armour, taken from a fallen enemy in some long-forgotten campaign, glinted arrogantly in the strengthening sun. He held a thrusting spear high and called, '*Dawid ben Jesse! Dawid ben Jesse!*'

The shout was taken up by farmers and mercenaries to whom the name meant nothing, but hope surged through their veins as they stood and cheered. The sound echoed back from the slopes opposite, and Dawid raised his sword to Yonatan as he nudged Morning Star across the raging brook. She tossed her head proudly. He thrust the sword through his belt and, without thinking beyond making a brave challenge, felt for the pouch at his waist. He eased his hand inside, checking for the comforting presence of his sling and running his fingers over the flat stones within, and touched the Star of Anak. As Morning Star climbed out of the chilly waters of Elah's brook, he felt the sharpness of its six points and recalled how Golyat himself had given it as a gift. Time to return it.

Dawid reined in Morning Star while they were still well out of range of Philistine arrows. Only his eyes showed beneath the *pe'er*. He watched and waited as Philistine eyes bored into him across the patchy, flattened barley.

The line of soldiers parted to allow Golyat and his shield-bearer through. He advanced with huge strides, his immense iron-studded sandals sinking into the mud with each step. His movements were slow and deliberate under the weight of his armour, his bronze greaves dulled with filth, the horns of his golden bull helmet tossing from side to side in a swaying rhythm. In one huge fist he clutched a curved blade, in the other a new and terrifying weapon — a heavy iron chain the length of three spears to which was attached a clump of ugly spikes, dragging behind him in the slimy mud. Dawid imagined the devastating effect of such a weapon among the massed ranks of Golyat's enemies. In the slippery mud, he wouldn't be able to get near enough to his quarry to use Oren's sword.

Morning Star whinnied her protest and took a step back, even though the terrifying beast was yet some distance away. Dawid reassured her with soft words and dismounted, sending her back towards her family at the brook with a hefty slap to the rump, but after only a few paces she stopped and turned to face him, refusing to leave him alone.

'Go,' he pleaded, but she fixed him with a defiant stare and would not move. Dawid shrugged and turned back to Golyat, who was advancing steadily, watching Dawid with demonic eyes that glowed red beneath the golden helmet. He stopped suddenly, his shield-bearer almost sliding into him, such was his effort to keep up. Dawid fought against overwhelming fear and nausea.

'Who?' Golyat demanded.

Dawid did not reply from behind the tightly wrapped *pe'er* that hid his face. He pulled the sword free and edged towards higher ground, hoping to give himself a small advantage even if it did put him between the Philistines and their champion. Golyat tugged on the chain and with incredible power swung it in a circular motion, the ball of spikes hissing so close that Dawid could feel the air ripple. He stepped back, no longer able to seek higher ground. Golyat let the ball of spikes fall to the ground, his point made.

'Who?' he grunted again, pointing at Dawid with his sword.

Dawid did not reply, deciding to let Golyat guess. He held his sword at arm's length, pointing at those terrible eyes and, with what he hoped looked like a fighter's crouch, stepped towards Golyat. The spike ball sang again, leaving him no choice but to step back.

'Fight me!' thundered Golyat.

Dawid suddenly rushed forward, trying to get within the circle of Golyat's deadly cluster of spikes. The giant heaved on the chain as Dawid struggled to find purchase. He realised with a rising sense of panic that the slimy ground had robbed him of his speed.

Golyat swung the spike ball. It gathered momentum and hurtled in a wide arc towards him. Dawid fell but still clutched his sword. He looked up and saw to his relief that the spikes would pass behind him, but the chain was coming towards him at head height. He pressed his body into the mud and felt a rush of wind as the chain passed just above him. Then he was on his feet again with time to take two more steps as the chain swung full circle and was upon him. He didn't have time to consider the conditions under his feet. He jumped, just clearing the groaning chain, then threw himself at Golyat with his sword outstretched.

He aimed for a point in his neck just above the scale vest.

But the ground gave way again and he knew as he made his attack that he would not be able to reach that vulnerable place. The point of his sword struck Golyat's armour just below the ribs and slid harmlessly to the side. Dawid crashed into the immovable giant and fell untidily at his feet.

Golyat dropped the chain and kicked Dawid hard in the ribs. The blow lifted him off the ground. The air burst from his lungs and as he landed, he felt pain like a knife between the ribs. He realised that though he was far enough away to avoid another kick, he was within range of that huge sword. He sensed rather than saw the blade as Golyat heaved a killing blow and he rolled away, over and over, as the curved blade slashed into the mud beside him.

It was the cheering of the watching Philistines that saved him. Golyat turned to acknowledge the crowds, raising his sword to them, prolonging the moment. Dawid got to his feet and retreated, realising the folly of hand-to-hand combat with an opponent like Golyat.

As the giant revelled in the praise of his audience, Dawid stabbed his sword into the ground and reached into his pouch. He slipped one of the stones into the cradle of his slingshot, and as Philistia's champion turned back to him, the stone was flying straight and true.

It hit Golyat on the shoulder, left a sizeable dent in the giant's armour and flew high into the air with a bright ringing sound. Golyat stopped, twisting his muscled neck to look at the spot where this unexpected missile had hit him. The Philistine onlookers fell silent. Then Golyat threw back his horned head and laughed. His supporters laughed with him, and his shield-bearer began to hurry to his master's side. Golyat waved him away and was turning back to Dawid when a second stone crunched into his golden helmet with such force that it lodged firmly in the soft metal just above Golyat's eyes. He dropped his weapons as he staggered backwards and lifted the helmet to inspect the effects of this surprising weapon, realising his mistake too late.

Dawid looked at the Star of Anak as he placed it, visualising its metal points stabbing in exactly the same place as he loosed his third missile. It sank into Golyat's forehead with such force that even the immense strength of the giant's neck was defied as his head snapped back, forcing him to drop his helmet as he staggered.

With enormous effort, Golyat looked at Dawid, trying to focus. His head swam and he felt his legs buckle. His greaves sank into the soft earth and he sat back heavily on his heels. He watched his enemy walk towards him and wondered why it was becoming dark so early in the day. The small warrior was unwrapping his headcloth as he limped through the mud. Then Golyat recognised his assailant.

Dawid, too, wondered why darkness was falling before the noon hour, but he brushed the thought aside and squatted before Golyat, looking into his startled eyes. The silver amulet had pierced the giant's forehead so deeply that only three of its points remained visible. Thick blood oozed, gathering at his eyes, giving the impression that he wept black tears.

'*Shalom*, old friend,' said Dawid.

Golyat tried to move, but he couldn't. He wanted to talk to Dawid, to congratulate him on another great victory, but he felt as though he had swallowed his tongue. Instead he looked with wonder at the youth who had bettered him twice. If he could have summoned the strength, he would have embraced him and, in doing so, this time welcomed death. But try as he might, he could not move his arms, his legs, his head or his slackened jaw.

Dawid watched Golyat dribble and wasn't sure what to do, but he sensed the darkness and looked around. The shield-bearer was backing away, quaking with fear. The Philistines were murmuring, their voices like a swarm of bees. Dawid looked towards the Hebrew camp, expecting to see rejoicing and hear the cheers of his people, but they were silent. Even the faithful line of his brother riders was motionless. Then he looked up.

The gods, or perhaps just one very big god, had bitten away half of the sun.

CHAPTER THIRTY-FIVE

Out of the gathering darkness, as the mighty men of Israel and Philistia cowered in terror at the power of Yahweh, the avenger came. Elhanan was not afraid. He knew his god was capable of anything, be it a wondrous sign from the heavens or choosing an unlikely youth to confound the dreaded Nephilim. He had waited for this day ever since the voice in his head had guided him eighteen years ago to a filthy, sweaty room in Beth Lechem where the boy was born in blood and tears. Dawid — born to change the world, to bring a new order. A carefree, courageous adventurer who was unaware of what he had just begun and would now have to finish, if he could. And if he couldn't…?

An eerie silence pervaded the Valley of Elah as chilling darkness descended. Golyat was no more than a shadowy shape before Dawid, the light fading in his eyes, Abaddon's strength draining from tired limbs.

Dawid shivered. He could think of nothing to say to the dying giant. He reached for the Star of Anak where it lay embedded in Golyat's skin and tugged at it. Buried in bone, it would not give. He pulled harder and it came free with a hideous squelching sound, and more of the viscous blood flowed. Golyat did not flinch. He held the star before the giant, whose eyes momentarily glowed brighter, like embers that had found a draught. Dawid thought he sensed acquiescence, perhaps even approval, but the flames dulled as swiftly as they had flared with the sound of someone approaching through the boggy field.

'Dawid.'

'Barak?' Dawid lowered the Star of Anak and held it in his lap.

'Yes,' confirmed Elhanan. 'Can you finish this?'

Dawid peered into the gloom and made out the shadowy form of the hermit standing a few paces behind Golyat.

'Finish what, Barak?'

'Kill him.'

'He is dying,' Dawid said to the shadow.

Elhanan appeared to stoop and pick up something heavy. Dawid realised it was Golyat's curved sword, three times the size of the weapon that Oren had given him by the brook. He knew what must happen, and he knew that he could not obey. He peered at Golyat, realising that the gods were allowing the light to slowly return because he could see that the giant's eyes were closed.

'He is not dying.' Elhanan's voice was tinged with uncharacteristic cruelty. 'There is only one way and it must be done now.'

'You kill him then, if you must.'

Elhanan did not reply and, for a moment, he did not move. Then there was a rush of air and Dawid felt a sticky wetness splash across his face and neck. He heard the heavy thud of Golyat's head as it landed nearby, followed by a shriek of wind as his opponent's body slowly toppled to the ground, one arm flung carelessly into Dawid's lap. The six fingers of Golyat's huge hand twitched as they touched the Star of Anak that lay there. Dawid vomited bile and his head swam as the wind seemed to pass through him, snatching his heaving breath away as it surged through his throat. He collapsed beside the massive, headless corpse, fighting for breath, his head pounding, his fingers clutching at gory mud.

Almost imperceptibly, the light was returning, a golden glow racing across the valley to shine upon the Hebrew camp. Elhanan hung his head and shuddered as he took a deep breath of cool air. He looked at Dawid and saw the dark stains of mud and gore on his clothes. He watched as the youth heaved himself out of the filth to sit, all the time gazing blankly at the severed head.

Golyat's lifeless eyes stared back.

'His end is your beginning,' said Elhanan. Cradling the giant's sword, he crouched before Dawid. 'The light returns,' he went on calmly, despite the horror of his deed. 'And you are about to find yourself in the midst of a bloody battle.'

Dawid tried to focus on the hermit. He didn't care any longer about wars between nations.

In the distance a horn sounded, its baleful wail taken up by a hundred more. Elhanan gripped Dawid's shoulders and shook him hard.

'Dawid, look!'

Wearily, the blood-spattered shepherd turned to peer into the gloomy valley that led east towards Judah's hill country. His eyes widened as the strengthening sunlight revealed perhaps three hundred soldiers marching in tight ranks, crashing sword upon shield as the horns announced their coming. And held aloft by a warrior on a black stallion was the wolf banner of the Jebusites.

'A fallen champion won't stop Akish now,' said Elhanan. 'The Philistines will attack your people the moment they see that banner, which is just about now. And their thousands will sweep right down this hillside where we sit contemplating your skills as a warrior and the power of our God.'

Elhanan shook him again, so hard that Dawid began to protest, before he realised that the hermit was right. He took in the sight of the approaching force then put his fingers to his mouth and whistled. As Morning Star trotted out of the gloom, he managed a smile for Elhanan.

'It's not as bad as it looks, Barak,' he said. 'You taught me that.'

He pulled Oren's sword from the mud and returned it to his belt. Grasping Morning Star's mane, he heaved himself upon her then offered Elhanan his hand.

'Come, Barak,' he said as the Philistine horns replied to those in the valley, 'ride with me.'

Elhanan passed Golyat's sword to Dawid and, taking his hand, swung onto Morning Star with surprising agility.

As Dawid nudged Morning Star back towards the brook and the gods released the sun from their dark grip, the long-awaited clash of arms between Philistia and Israel erupted. The entire Philistine army swarmed from the woods in a sliding mass. They careened down the slope towards the Hebrew ranks which, spurred by the sight of Philistia's champion lying headless in the mud, had surged out of the safety of their hilltop bunkers. The war cries from both sides, each believing the gods favoured them for different reasons, grew in intensity as the light returned.

Morning Star was as strong and sure-footed in the mud as Dawid had expected, even carrying two men, yet he kept her to a steady walk, even though it seemed the Philistines would surely catch them.

But the enemy had not accounted for The Fist. Oren led his twenty horsemen across the brook and onto the Elah fields, where they closed ranks to a tight arrowhead formation. Their cry of *El Shaddai, El Shaddai* was clear above the din of three converging armies as they rode past Dawid and Elhanan straight into the disorganised ranks of Philistine warriors.

Dawid wanted to watch the mayhem and shock of their charge, but he concentrated on crossing the brook as the Hebrew host streamed around them to engage an enemy on equal terms, without its feared chariot force. He held the sword of Golyat high in both hands as Yonatan and Saul led their ragtag army across the brook with renewed hope, their men screaming blood-curdling war cries as they saw the symbol of Philistia's fallen power glinting in the day's second dawn.

Elhanan dismounted, laid a hand on Dawid's knee and squeezed. 'Be careful how you handle your fame and glory,' he said with a frown. 'If you can take one more word of advice, you might seek a little humility.'

Dawid continued to hold the sword high and did not answer. His arms were tired and his whole body ached. He wanted to join the battle, imagining the damage Golyat's kin might be doing to his friends of The Fist and the rabble of Saul's army. Humility could wait for another day.

Elhanan smiled and walked away as Israel's farmers surged towards the battlefield, a holy man striding against the tide of war, turning his back on the affairs of men. As the last of Saul's host passed him, Dawid lowered the sword and placed it across Morning Star's shoulders.

'One more effort,' he told her as he slapped the muscle of her neck and wheeled her towards the onrushing banners of Jebus. Behind him was the clash of weapons, the awful sound of men dying, both Philistines and Hebrews.

He urged Morning Star into a canter.

Mounted on his black stallion, Uriah the Hittite felt a familiar surge in his veins as he led his foot soldiers towards the bloody battlefield. He held his banner as high as he could so that the Philistines could see the wolf device of Jebus and believe that their allies would close in on the Hebrew hordes from the rear.

The ingenious plan of the crafty old prophet seemed to be working. The Philistines believed their eyes and thought the Hebrews were trapped in a pincer movement. From where he strained to keep his stallion trotting at the same pace as his loping warriors, he could see several of the Invincibles closing in on the advancing Hebrews. Even on foot in this mud, he knew their clubs and swords would cause havoc among the poorly armed men of Israel.

He filled his lungs and screamed the Hittite war cry: '*Hattihattu, Hattihattu!*' Three hundred faithful warriors responded, running with fresh energy at the Philistine giants. As they closed in, the nine huge warriors saw the threat that hurtled towards them from the side and tried to change direction. Several slid on the muddy ground and fell heavily just as Uriah's stallion closed in, the animal's hooves crashing down on first one, then another. The felled giants were not fatally wounded, but their plight gave the men of Israel renewed hope where moments before they had wavered in their charge at such unnatural beasts. Their weapons of bronze knives, pitchforks and spears were driven beneath scale armour to wound, if not kill, the fallen.

Three hundred Hittite mercenaries threw themselves at the panicking Philistine masses, halting their charge in a sickening clash of iron and bronze. Uriah urged his stallion through the remaining giants, slashing right and left with his sword, hoping the scale armour on his mount's chest would preserve the noble animal's life. His blade threw bright droplets of blood high into the air with every sweep, and he knew without turning that his men followed with shield and spear in his wake.

The stallion did not falter despite the treachery of the sodden ground, and suddenly he was in the clear as the rearmost Philistines turned and ran. Uriah could not see the point of pursuing them. He reined in and turned to see his men now shoulder to shoulder with the Hebrews, hewing and hacking at a defeated enemy. He allowed several Philistines to escape past him as he scoured the field to evaluate their losses and decide what to do next, but it was impossible to tell whether enemy or friend lay screaming in the mess of slime and gore.

Dawid saw Uriah's distinctive plait flying freely from beneath his helmet as the Hittite slashed at the enemy, his stallion proud and strong in the mayhem of battle. He saw the warrior heave at the reins to look around and knew in that moment that the battle was won.

He did not have the strength to lift Golyat's sword, so he clutched it where it lay across Morning Star's striving neck, barely noticing the blood on his hands where the blade cut deep, even through his leather riding breeches. He searched the field for Yonatan and Saul, and above all Oren and The Fist. His head pounded and he wanted to throw up, yet he forced himself to straighten his back and look for the most likely Philistine to ride down. But he was too far to the rear, and Morning Star was tiring. All around him men lay dying, and he did not know whether his mare trampled Philistine or Hebrew.

Morning Star sensed her master's despair and stopped. She, too, was exhausted.

Dawid looked around at the broken bodies, all sacrifices to one god or another. Absently he thought that it would take many days to burn or bury the dead — probably without knowing which king they followed or which god they worshipped. War was brutal and ugly, bereft of glory or celebration.

A powerful voice commanded his attention.

'You. Shepherd. I see you have a sword.'

Yonatan was covered in blood, whether his own or that of Israel's enemies, Dawid couldn't tell. His jerkin was torn, his helm long gone in the battlefield, his only weapon a puny knife. His hair and beard were matted with sweat and his chest heaved as he struggled for breath. But the Prince of Israel was standing beside Morning Star with his hand outstretched, asking Dawid for a weapon.

'I have two,' said Dawid, 'and one is somewhat heavy.'

Yonatan eyed the sword of Golyat. 'That one you have won for yourself.'

'It is yours, my lord, if you can wield it.'

Yonatan declined. 'Can you spare the other...?'

'Gladly,' said Dawid, handing Oren's sword to Israel's heir. 'The enemy flees, and if you will forgive me, my day is done.'

'They flee because you defeated their champion,' replied Yonatan.

'I am honoured to have been of service. But the men of Israel have earned their rewards this day.'

Yonatan beamed. 'Indeed. As has everyone who trod the mud of Elah today, including those Hittites, may El Shaddai shower them with blessings.' He looked towards the fleeing Philistines. 'You will eat at my hearth tonight,' he added, stepping away from Dawid and Morning Star. 'And I think my father will give you my sister as your reward.'

Dawid blinked. That sort of pledge was the last thing he wanted.

Yonatan clearly wanted to be with his men as they hunted down fleeing Philistines, but he had the manners to bow to Dawid first. 'My thanks, brother.'

Dawid shook his head in disbelief and made one more demand of Morning Star, asking her to take him back to Naomi.

EPILOGUE

Oren the Tall was summoned to Ramah a few months after the defeat of the Philistines. There he found the old prophet Shemu'el enjoying peaceful times with his wives, sons, daughters and grandchildren, a scene far removed from the memories of filth and blood in the Valley of Elah. Shemu'el himself welcomed The Fist's commander but wasted no time in sending him to a solid stone house that stood next to the prophet's palace. When his stallion had been stabled and he had washed away his journey's grime, he was pleasantly surprised to find Nathan hunched over a table spread with cured skins and an array of scribe's reeds. A pair of crutches were propped next to him, his hair unoiled and his beard dragging over a parchment that demanded his meticulous scrutiny.

Oren coughed to attract his old friend's attention.

'Ah, Oren, welcome to Ramah. I've been expecting you.' Nathan heaved himself to his feet and knocked over his crutches but, using the table to steady himself, he beamed at his visitor.

Oren bowed, as was customary in the presence of a prophet, however young, then cast aside formalities and ran to embrace and kiss his former chieftain. The show of affection overwhelmed Nathan, who held Oren close for several heartbeats.

'Now return me to my chair before the pain comes back,' he said. 'Tell me how you fare, and the others — have you seen Ari and Rimon? Our family at Adullam?'

'All is well, old friend, though we miss Dookhi,' replied Oren when he had settled Nathan in his seat. 'There are twenty of us now, all horsed and armed. Adullam's temptations are many, as you know, and The Fist has sired not a few children to fill the caves with much wailing and laughter!'

'And Rachael? What of the priestess?'

'She sends greetings, and more, of course. I think she should be the new wife of this prophet, if the priests would allow it! And she would ease your pain and help you in your labours —' Oren pointed to the skins and an untidy pile of wax tablets stacked on the floor — 'and ensure Israel's line of prophets does not end with you.'

Nathan laughed. 'You may be right. A marriage between Yahweh and Ashtoreth, I think. My father would make a show of being enraged, for the priests.'

'Your father?'

'Don't pretend you didn't know. This is my home, and yes, Shemu'el is my father. And he has indulged Ashtoreth more than once in his long life, but don't tell the priests. As a man is, so should his son be, do you not think?'

'What the priests don't know, the priests cannot destroy, that's my view.'

'Indeed.' Nathan winked, then became thoughtful. 'Have you heard anything of Dawid? Shemu'el seeks him, probably to make him king as he did with Saul.'

'Nothing,' replied Oren. 'He is the ghost of Elah, a shadow like the valley when Golyat fell. Though everyone looks for him, he cannot be found.'

'As I thought.' Nathan indicated the skins and wax tablets around him. 'Everyone seeks him. I have copies of letters of praise and complaint, of warnings and reward, but no one knows where he is. Come, be seated, and let me show you.'

Nathan clapped his hands and called for refreshments, but no servant came, so Oren was sent to the kitchens to ask for food and wine. When he returned, Nathan was studying the neat script in his own hand.

'I have made copies of many letters brought to me by my father's men, who range across the land seeking Dawid.' He read aloud:

'Yonatan, Prince of Israel, to my father Saul, the king.

You ask me about Dawid ben Jesse. He is a Beth Lechemite and skilled with sling, harp and shepherd's pipes. I can tell you no more, but I will commend him to you as your armour-bearer when I find him. I sought him all through the Valley of Elah beyond Socoh and pursued him to Beth Lechem, but I am told he has taken to the hills and cannot be found. I have told his father, a rich man by the name of Jesse, of your proposal to give my sister in marriage to this comely youth, and I can tell you that the old man was so overcome by this offer that he fell at my feet, weeping with joy. When I find Dawid ben Jesse, I will bring him to you.'

Oren whistled. 'Saul wants to give his daughter's hand to Dawid? That would place him at the king's right hand, and perhaps in line for the throne after Yonatan. No wonder he flees!'

'Indeed. But it appears our young hero is, I fear, no friend of the priests of Yahweh.' Nathan rummaged through his copies, finding a parchment. 'This was sent to my father, and with it is his reply.'

Nathan made space on the table as two servants placed food and wine before them, and when they had gone, he indicated to Oren that he should read aloud:

'*Jesse of Beth Lechem, to Shemu'el, Prophet of Yahweh.*

May the Lord bless your coming in and your going out. My people yearn for your return to our unworthy house, and to hasten your coming I send you this small gift of new wine from my vineyards. My Lord, we have need of priests in Beth Lechem; be pleased to send us holy men well versed in the Law. We also seek the judgement of my lord in the matter of the death of our priests this Shavuoth just passed. They did not die of old age, as is customary for priests, but by the sword. By my own life I swear I had nothing to do with this crime and know not by whose bloody hand they died. May you live long and see the prosperity of your children's children.'

'*Shemu'el, voice of El Shaddai, to Jesse of Beth Lechem.*

Your wine is camel's piss, an offence I will overlook if you tell me where Dawid is. Better still, have your worthless sons find him and bring him to me at Ramah. They can also bring that vintage you promised me when last I visited Beth Lechem.'

Oren raised an eyebrow. 'It is said that these priests incited the stoning of Dawid's mother. Not the act of the righteous, whatever the accusation. So we can assume this is why Dawid remains in hiding?'

'Just one of his reasons. But there is more: Dawid has friends and allies. Not least Uriah and Yonatan, who now seem to be brothers when a short time ago they were enemies! Let me read this to you, and then I can tell you why you have been summoned here.' He cleared his throat and began:

'*Uriah the Hittite to Yonatan, Prince of Israel.*

Lord Yonatan, my small force of seasoned warriors is at your disposal should you have need of us. I commend to you the young man who bears this tablet. He is a Phoenician who once fought the giants of Gath. Ask him what he knows about shepherding goats.'

Nathan reached for another parchment and continued to read aloud:

'*Yonatan, heir to Saul, to Uriah the Hittite.*

First Hittites, then a Phoenician. How many foreigners must we employ to fight for the Lord of Hosts? I trust you have enjoyed our silver and the spoils brought to you by Abner. Should you have need of food or wine, your man Habib of Tyre carries my seal, which is all the authority you might need. Also, I find I have an urgent need to learn about goats. Fear not, I will keep this vital information to myself. You can trust me.'

Nathan looked up and indicated that he had one more letter to share.

'*Uriah the Hittite to Yonatan, Prince of Israel.*

There is barely enough clay here to make the tablets that Habib now brings to you, for there is much to tell about the shepherd. He is young and will heal in time. I do not mean that he was injured, but rather that a darkness has come upon him in much the same way that, for a short time, the gods blocked the sun at Ephes-Dammim. The light will return. He is well cared for by his woman, Naomi. He is a most fortunate shepherd!

He returned to his home city to seek his father and care for his sick mother, but she had been sorely treated and in his anguish, he sought revenge against those who had harmed her, but I will say no more of this until we speak face to face, when you come to see the shepherd for yourself. He has heard that all Israel seeks him, but for now, he must find strength within himself and overcome this darkness. His songs are all sad, not fitting for the court of the mighty. Now I must find a cart and a mule for these tablets and the gift that the shepherd has asked me to send to you. It is a very large sword, sharp and heavy. I think you will agree it is beautifully fashioned and knows how to remove a head. As for the shepherd, he says he would rather use a sling. Selah.'

'Selah?' Oren seemed bemused. 'That is not a word you would expect a Hittite to use! I hear it only in the songs of our people, and yet even I do not know what it means! But that sword…'

'Yes, that sword. I would venture that it has great power and is a symbol, an emblem of authority in the right hands, if they can wield it. And now it is Yonatan's, who will be king after Saul. But my father believes otherwise. He no longer thinks Saul or his progeny should rule Israel.'

'Then who?'

'I will tell you what he has said, but not until you have performed a small task for me. For Israel and the tribe of Judah.'

Ever obedient to his former leader, Oren bowed. 'Name it.'

'When you have rested and taken wine with me, I want you to seek Dawid. Take writing implements and be thorough, reporting all that you find, then bring him to me here. If he will not come, bring parchments with words that describe him best. Begin at Beth Lechem; talk to his mother Nitzevet if you can find her. Seek his brothers and this Uriah, as well as those who follow him. I do not think we have heard the last of this Dawid ben Jesse…'

Spidery blue veins crossed Jesse's flushed face and his vacant eyes looked at Oren in confusion. Eliab and Kerith organised food and wine for him while Jesse shuffled around, bumping into furniture and calling for absent sons, though five of them were there. Oren was relieved when Kerith gently led Jesse to a shaded terrace, settled him on a plump cushion, and sang to him as he fell asleep.

'Now we can talk,' she said.

'That would please me,' Oren said with a bow, 'especially if you can tell me where Dawid is.'

'Come,' said Kerith, beckoning. 'You should talk to those who know him best.'

She led him away from Jesse's house, through a grove of newly planted olive trees and away from the sights and smells of Jesse's livestock. The ground still hard after the summer's strong sun, the path easy and shaded. Nestling beside a low hillock was a small patch of green, where Jesse's servants laboured over a network of irrigation channels carved into the rocky earth. A small mudbrick house stood near a well over which was built a crude wooden pulley, the water lifted to the surface by an ass. An old man, his skin dark and leathery, then poured it into wooden channels aimed towards the field. There barley and wheat grew, as well as onions and lentils, and in one corner, in the shade of a huge acacia, lilies and poppies.

'This is Nitzevet's house,' said Kerith with a hint of pride. 'Jesse gave it to her after … when she…'

'When she was wrongfully accused,' Oren helped her.

'Yes. Dawid came here not long before news arrived of Israel's great victory. He brought Naomi.'

'And then?'

'He wanted to care for Nitzevet. Naomi helped him. Did you know she is with child?'

Oren shook his head. He wasn't surprised. Dawid seemed to be a young man in a hurry to do what older men must.

'But now he's gone,' Kerith went on. 'There were soldiers in Beth Lechem asking questions. He left within a few days.'

'Did he say where he was going?'

Kerith tugged at his sleeve again. 'Come, there's someone you should meet.'

The house was small, built of clay and straw bricks with stone steps outside leading to a flat roof, where the women cooked each evening as the sun dropped behind Beth Lechem's western hills. Oren followed Kerith, ducking awkwardly through the low door, immediately refreshed by the cool air within the darkened room.

'Welcome, Kerith,' said the voice of an older woman with kindness in her heart. 'And welcome, traveller.'

'*Shalom*,' said Oren, straining to see who spoke. He hesitated while his eyes grew accustomed to the shadows, slowly making out the scarred and broken features of Dawid's mother. He waited for permission to squat opposite her in the time-honoured fashion of gentle interrogation, while Kerith went to draw water and find nourishment.

They talked about the weather, about life in Beth Lechem, about whether the Philistines would stay behind their city walls and whether King Saul would throw Israel's young men into battle again. Eventually, Oren asked why Nitzevet had been treated so harshly.

'I was the wife of Jesse, son of Obed, descendant of Boaz who married the Moabitess, Ruth.' Nitzevet settled into telling the full story, her voice ragged with emotion. 'My husband's grandmother was not even a Judahite, and yet it is I who was put aside according to the law to make Jesse seem noble in his own eyes, and perhaps those of the Lord? Ha! What do men know? They tug their beards and deliver hot air when they meet at the gates, and the priests murmur and the women bear children. For me, eight. Seven that Jesse knew were his and one born afterwards, when the holy man hopped and spat and prophesied that this little bundle of noise was set apart for the Lord and would be great.' She paused as if suddenly realising that she was ranting, then added, 'But I was to remain silent.

Kerith knew because she was there — my husband's new wife, his handmaiden and my friend. She knew me, knew how I yearned for one more, and how I prayed to Yahweh that this time I might be delivered of a little baby girl. Jesse was drunk again and knew not that it was I who spread my legs and praised his manhood, who said how wonderful it was to feel the gentleness of his lips upon mine. I said this in the accent of Kerith's people, the Amorites, for neither is she of Judah. He grunted and farted and left his seed, and I was delivered of another boy — the one that God has seemingly chosen to be his instrument of judgement upon the Edomites, the Ammonites, the Philistines. Yes, I am the unfortunate Judahite woman who dared to raise seven sons for the fat pig who owns the pastures around Beth Lechem. It is I who was put away because *he* decided … well, never mind. I was hated by the priests and the women who wash their clothes by the brook. I was scorned by my own sons, who treated me like a piece of goat's dung. Will they treat me thus now that my son has killed the Philistine giant? Do I even care?'

Oren looked at the broken woman and despaired of Judah's religion. He could barely guess at the savagery with which the mob had abused Nitzevet. He realised that only her head had moved since he had entered, despite the passion in her voice, and one arm was bent at a peculiar angle. How she must have suffered.

'And now you seek my son?' Nitzevet changed the subject.

'Yes. I want to write his story.'

'Write? You have the gift of letters?'

'Yes, and you have told me enough to begin.'

'We will break bread, eat, drink and talk. Then you can write. For as long as you want to stay here with us.'

When Kerith returned with food, she whispered that Naomi was outside with the horses and goats. Oren found her, round and radiant at the animal enclosure, talking gentle nonsense to Morning Star as the mare nosed in a pail of grain mash. As he watched, he suddenly realised why Dawid had left Morning Star at Beth Lechem in Naomi's care — it wasn't just his woman who was pregnant.

'How soon? For both of you?' he asked.

'For me, one more moon, I think,' said Naomi softly.

He saw the sadness in her eyes and guessed. 'Tell me, Naomi.'

'We can be sure that Morning Star's foal is not made by a Philistine stallion,' she replied with a hollow laugh.

Word came to Beth Lechem of a warrior tribe camped at the springs of Ein Gedi on the shores of the Salt Sea. The merchant who sought Jesse's fleeces and the first of his olives seemed unconcerned and reported how he had given the encampment a wide berth, not knowing their intentions, but was convinced his camel train had been watched from the rocky crags that overlooked the trade route.

Starved of news or gossip since the days of war with Philistia, the old men aired tales of marauding tribes from the high plains of Moab who seldom ventured into Judah's hill country. Their women embellished the stories until the whole of Beth Lechem believed the city was about to be besieged by a huge army of terrible warriors.

They were disappointed to the point of indifference when only three came. The riders approached like turbaned ghosts from the desert, but they weren't heavily armed. They rode past the city gates, ignoring the old men who watched with narrowed eyes as they dismounted outside Jesse's house. Two held back while a third loosened his *pe'er* to show his face and demanded to see the patriarch or his eldest son. Eliab, now used to deputising for his father since returning from the war, thought he recognised the lively youth who wore a splendid silver torc around his neck, and whose cloak seemed to be of a richer weave than those of his companions.

'If I'm not mistaken, you are the Phoenician?' he asked.

Habib was disappointed that Eliab's memory of him seemed vague. 'I am. I come from your brother, Dawid ben Jesse.'

'Ah. The fugitive. How is he?'

'He is well. He commands a hundred men. Reubenites and Moabites, mostly. And many goats.'

Eliab laughed. 'Goats he could always command. But wild men from beyond the Salt Sea…?'

'All have gathered to his banner. But I am the only one from Phoenicia.'

'His banner? You make him sound like a king. What is his mark?'

'A silver star,' replied Habib proudly. 'The emblem of Anak, now called the Star of Dawid. But he is no king, nor an enemy of Israel. He seeks only to provide for outcasts and the downtrodden.'

'How very noble. And will he come to Beth Lechem?'

'Only if there are none of Saul's men here.'

'There are none. Why does he hide from Saul?'

Habib laughed. 'Because he has heard that the king would have him marry his daughter!'

HISTORICAL NOTES

WHAT'S IN A NAME?

I've used what I hope are accurate transliterations of the key characters' names in this novel. It won't have taken you long to work out who's who!

'David' is such a common western name based on an ancient Hebrew name that might have been 'Dawid', probably pronounced 'Dahveed' (with a soft 'd'). 'Shemu'el' is the Old Testament prophet 'Samuel'. 'Yonatan' is King Saul's son, 'Jonathan'. 'Golyat'? You guessed. And so on.

Most of the characters are real people in the sense that they are recorded in ancient literature. For example, Uriah the Hittite makes an appearance later in the Biblical story of King David in a rather unfortunate episode involving Uriah's wife, Bathsheba (Bat-Sheva).

The prophet Nathan wrote a book that is sadly lost to us. How I would love to write it for him as a sequel to *Line in the Sand*! May the gods grant me inspiration…

QUESTIONS AND ANSWERS

Anyone who has read the Biblical accounts of David and Goliath will be aware of the various facts woven into this story and the questions that surround the tale, such as:

Who killed Goliath — David or Elhanan? (Some translations of 2 Samuel 21:19 indicate that Elhanan slew Goliath.)

Why were the Caves of Adullam so important to David later in his life?

Why was David able to forge an alliance with the Philistines when he was later fleeing from the Israelite king who wanted to kill him?

What kind of friends were David and Jonathan?

Could the Prophet Nathan have inherited the role of Chief Prophet from Samuel?

Was Samuel Nathan's father?

How long had David known Uriah the Hittite before he had him murdered and stole his wife, Bathsheba?

And, of course, who or what were the Nephilim?

The Bible reports that giants such as Goliath had six fingers and six toes (2 Samuel 21:20). This is thought to be some kind of supernatural mark of differentiation. It seems to me that the story of David, like so many biblical chronicles of Israel and Judah, is stitched together from different sources. This means that editors writing long after these events took the liberty of choosing which facts to include to suit their particular beliefs and the expectations of the Jewish people. As the story of King David is reported in several different books of the Old Testament and referred to in the Qur'an, thus leading to several anomalies, please forgive this author for taking liberties with the tale and its telling!

DAVID'S PARENTS

I was deeply moved by the story of Nitzevet, David's mother, as told by Chana Weisberg of the Chabad-Lubavitch organisation (www.chabad.org). In *The Bold Voice of Silence* she describes the Talmudic tradition that Jesse divorced Nitzevet after struggling with his interpretation of Torah traditions, though she paints a far more respectful portrait of David's father than I have.

POLYTHEISM

These were the main gods at the time of David and Saul:

El or El Elyon — the original Canaanite god.

Ba'al — son of El, known as Ba'al-Zebub ('Lord of the Flies') in Philistia.

Dagon — Philistine deity.

Moloch — Ammonite god to whom children were sacrificed, worshipped in Canaan.

Ashtoreth — Canaanite goddess, also known as Astarte and Ishtar in other ancient cultures.

Yahweh — Israelite deity.

El Shaddai, Elohim, Adonai — other names for Yahweh.

Which one was biggest, best and most powerful, I cannot say. The argument rages today, with different names.

FURTHER READING

At the outset of writing this book, I listened to a very convincing lecture by Professor Jeffrey R. Zorn of Cornell University, entitled *Who Was Goliath?*, in which he suggests that the Philistine giant was an elite chariot warrior. I am also indebted to the British Egyptologist and author David Rohl, not least for succinct explanations of his New Chronology theories, specifically his interpretation of the Amarna letters and probable references to King Saul. I would also like to express my gratitude to Professor Aren Maier, director of the Tell es-Safi excavations that have uncovered so much about ancient Gath, including an inscription thought to include the name Goliath.

Books that have helped me include the Bible, of course, though the account of David and Goliath was written many years after the event; *The King David Report* by Stefan Heym; *The Source* by James A. Michener; *David's Secret Demons* by Baruch Halpern, and various books published by Osprey about warfare in the ancient Middle East. I have read many books about ancient Israel both online and in my studies, too numerous to mention, and all were influential in their way.

But somehow I feel as though I know nothing when compared with the likes of Maier, Zorn and Rohl. I hope that the little I know, when tipped into a mind blessed with imagination, has proved to be a winning formula.

A NOTE TO THE READER

Thank you for reading *Line in the Sand*. Reviews by knowledgeable readers are an essential part of a modern author's success, so if you enjoyed this novel I would be grateful if you could spare the short time required to post a review on **Amazon** and **Goodreads**. You can also connect with me on **my website** and **sign up to my newsletter on Substack**.

Alistair Forrest

alistairforrest.com

Sapere Books is an exciting new publisher of brilliant fiction and popular history.

To find out more about our latest releases and our monthly bargain books visit our website:
saperebooks.com